PROFILES IN AMERICAN HISTORY

Significant Events and the People Who Shaped Them

D1212281

(Continued on inside back cover)

PROFILES IN
AMERICAN HISTORY

Reconstruction to the Spanish-American War

1865
▼
Thirteenth Amendment abolishes slavery.

1866
▼
Opposing "black codes" in the South, Congress enacts the Civil Rights Bill and the Fourteenth Amendment.

1877
▼
Carl Schurz begins reform of the Civil Service and the Bureau of Indian Affairs.

1877
▼
Chief Joseph surrenders after Nez Percé trek to Canada fails.

1876
▼
Sioux defeat the forces of General George Armstrong Custer at Little Big Horn.

1874
▼
Frances Willard begins Women's Christian Temperance Union.

1881
▼
Booker T. Washington founds Tuskegee Institute.

1884
▼
Helen Hunt Jackson portrays mistreatment of Indians in *Ramona.*

1885
▼
Mark Twain publishes *The Adventures of Huckleberry Finn.*

1886
▼
Samuel Gompers founds American Federation of Labor.

1910
▼
W. E. B. Du Bois founds National Association for the Advancement of Colored People.

1898
▼
William McKinley asks Congress to approve military intervention in Cuba; Theodore Roosevelt leads the "Rough Riders" in capturing San Juan Hill.

1896
▼
Stephen Crane publishes *The Red Badge of Courage.*

1894
▼
American Railway Union strikes the Pullman Car Company.

1890
▼
Elizabeth Cady Stanton founds the National American Woman's Suffrage Association.

PROFILES IN AMERICAN HISTORY

Significant Events and the People

Who Shaped Them

Reconstruction to the Spanish-American War

JOYCE MOSS
and
GEORGE WILSON

AN IMPRINT OF GALE RESEARCH INC.

PROFILES IN AMERICAN HISTORY:

Significant Events and the People Who Shaped Them

VOLUME 5: RECONSTRUCTION TO THE SPANISH-AMERICAN WAR

Joyce Moss and George Wilson

Staff

Carol DeKane Nagel, *U•X•L Developmental Editor*
Thomas L. Romig, *U•X•L Publisher*

Christine Nasso, *Acquisitions Editor*

Shanna P. Heilveil, *Production Assistant*
Evi Seoud, *Assistant Production Manager*
Mary Beth Trimper, *Production Director*

Mary Krzewinski, *Cover and Page Designer*
Cynthia Baldwin, *Art Director*
Arthur Chartow, *Technical Design Services Manager*

The Graphix Group, *Typesetting*

∞™ This book is printed on acid-free paper that meets the minimum requirements of American National Standard for Information Sciences—Permanence Paper for Printed Library Materials, ANSI Z39.48-1984.

ISBN 0-8103-9207-0 (Set)
ISBN 0-8103-9212-7 (Volume 5)

Printed in the United States of America

Published simultaneously in the United Kingdom by Gale Research International Limited
(An affiliated company of Gale Research Inc.)

I(T)P™
The trademark ITP is used under license.

Contents

Reader's Guide

The many noteworthy individuals who shaped U.S. history from the exploration of the continent to the present day cannot all be profiled in one eight-volume work. But those whose stories are told in *Profiles in American History* meet one or more of the following criteria. The individuals:

- Directly affected the outcome of a major event in U.S. history
- Represent viewpoints or groups involved in that event
- Exemplify a role played by common citizens in that event
- Highlight an aspect of that event not covered in other entries

Format

Volumes of *Profiles in American History* are arranged by chapter. Each chapter focuses on one particular event and opens with an overview and detailed time line of the event that places it in historical context. Following are biographical profiles of two to seven diverse individuals who played active roles in the event.

Each biographical profile is divided into four sections:

- **Personal Background** provides details that predate and anticipate the individual's involvement in the event
- **Participation** describes the role played by the individual in the event and its impact on his or her life
- **Aftermath** discusses effects of the individual's actions and subsequent relevant events in his or her life
- **For More Information** provides sources for further reading on the individual

Additionally, sidebars containing interesting details about the events and individuals profiled, ranging from numbers of war casualties to famous quotes to family trees, are sprinkled throughout the text.

Additional Features

Maps are provided to assist readers in traveling back through time to an America arranged differently from today. Portraits and illustrations of individuals and events as well as excerpts from primary source materials are also included to help bring history to life. Sources of all quoted material are cited parenthetically within the text, and complete bibliographic information is listed at the end of the entry. A full bibliography of scholarly sources consulted in preparing the volume appears in the book's back matter.

Cross references are made in the entries, directing readers to other entries in the volume that elaborate on individuals connected in some way to the person under scrutiny. In addition, a comprehensive subject index provides easy access to people and events mentioned throughout the volume.

Comments and Suggestions

We welcome your comments on this work as well as your suggestions for individuals to be featured in future editions of *Profiles in American History.* Please write: Editors, *Profiles in American History,* U·X·L, 835 Penobscot Bldg., Detroit, Michigan 48226-4094; call toll-free: 1-800-877-4253; or fax: 313-961-6348.

Preface

"There is properly no History; only Biography," wrote great American poet and scholar Ralph Waldo Emerson. *Profiles in American History* explores U.S. history through biography. Beginning with the first contact between Native Americans and Vikings and continuing to the present day, this series offers a unique alternative to traditional texts by emphasizing the roles played by individuals, including many women and minorities, in historical events.

Profiles in American History presents the human story of American events, not the exclusively European or African or Indian or Asian story. The guiding principle in compiling this series has been to achieve balance not only in gender and ethnic background but in viewpoint. Thus the circumstances surrounding an historical event are told from individuals holding opposing views, and even opposing positions. Slaves and slave owners, business tycoons and workers, advocates of peace and proponents of war all are heard. American authors whose works reflect the times—from Walt Whitman to John Steinbeck—are also featured.

The biographical profiles are arranged in groups, clustered around one major event in American history. Yet each individual profile is complete in itself. It is the interplay of these profiles—the juxtaposition of alternative views and experiences within a grouping—that broadens the readers' perspective on the event as a whole and on the participants' roles in particular. It is what makes it possible for *Profiles in American History* to impart a larger, human understanding of events in American history.

Acknowledgments

For their guidance on the choice of events and personalities, the editors are grateful to:

Jonathan Betz-Zall, Children's Librarian, Sno-Isle Regional Library System, Washington

Janet Sarratt, Library Media Specialist, John E. Ewing Junior High School, Gaffney, South Carolina

Michael Salman, Assistant Professor of American History, University of California at Los Angeles

Appreciation is extended to Professor Salman for his careful review of chapter overviews and his guidance on key sources of information about the personalities and events.

For insights into specific personalities, the editors are grateful to Robert Sumpter, History Department Chairman at Mira Costa High School, Manhattan Beach, California.

Deep appreciation is extended to the writers who compiled data and contributed the biographies for this volume of *Profiles in American History:*

Diane Ahrens
Erika Heet
Dana Huebler
Lawrence K. Orr
Colin Wells

The editors also thank artist Robert Bates for his research and rendering of the maps and Paulette Petrimoulx for her careful copy editing.

Introduction

The Civil War introduced changes in the United States that only escalated once the fighting ended. The nation, both North and South, was in turmoil. In the South fields lay devastated and state governments needed rebuilding. War and its consequences—the abolition of slavery and destruction of the planter class—dislocated Southerners from old positions in society and the economy. Meanwhile, the North saw rapid growth in industries that drew people away from small towns into developing cities. Railroad building, which had proceeded apace during the war, progressed even more furiously afterward. For the first time the distant regions of the nation became linked to one another.

Reconstruction, bringing the defeated states back into the Union and rebuilding society, began during the war. The peacetime Reconstruction that followed led to conflict between branches of the federal government. The president sponsored one Reconstruction plan from 1865 to 1866 that Congress replaced with a more radical plan from 1867 to 1877. State politics meanwhile saw Republicans elected to office in the South for a brief period, followed by the return of Democrats to power. Using politics to further their ends, these Democrats were quick to deny civil and political rights to the newly freed blacks. Race riots erupted and lynchings mounted. Meanwhile, Southern labor was transformed. White planters, at a loss without slave labor, and ex-slaves, anxious to farm for themselves, fell into new work patterns. As African Americans struggled for survival, economic gain, and civil rights, individual blacks surfaced as leaders to direct the group's progress.

Industry polarized society as a few businessmen amassed great fortunes, starting companies that experienced stunning successes. These companies employed hundreds of immigrants, who worked under dismal, uncontrolled conditions. The post-Civil War era became known as the Gilded Age, but the glitter cloaked the suffering of thousands. Mindful of profits and investors, business tycoons paid little heed to their laborers. There were some attempts to provide decent living conditions, but working conditions were generally grim. Individual workers—men and women—struggled for power to improve their situations by organizing labor unions. Outside the labor movement, women in particular felt driven to participate in organizations for social reform.

Meanwhile, authors of the era turned to realism, a type of writing that uncloaked the glitter and portrayed past and present society as they perceived it. Their writings captured the dialects, humor, cruelties, and inner struggles of Americans. At the same time, nonfiction writing of the period began to examine government actions in relation to the Indian populations.

Involved in Reconstruction, Indian affairs, and the growth of industry, the federal government gained power during the post-Civil War years. This power increased at the end of the nineteenth century as the government stepped into a new position by involving itself in international affairs. Business interests, human sympathy, and other motives prompted the nation to engage in the Spanish-American War. Victory pointed America in the direction of empire building, which led to debate in the nation about its own destiny and the principles on which it had been founded. From Reconstruction to the Spanish-American War, the United States had undergone internal changes. The war transformed it into a world power.

Picture Credits

The photographs and illustrations appearing in *Profiles in American History: Significant Events and the People Who Shaped Them,* Volume 5: *Reconstruction to the Spanish-American War* were received from the following sources:

On the cover: **Courtesy of the Library of Congress:** Frances Willard, W. E. B. Du Bois, George Armstrong Custer.

Courtesy of the Library of Congress: pages 9, 19, 32, 37, 43, 51, 61, 79, 84, 91, 106, 108, 129, 135, 141, 163, 168, 173, 182, 198, 200, 203, 219, 223, 237, 245, 249, 257, 263, 269; **courtesy of the Smithsonian Institution:** pages 46, 48; **courtesy of University Research Library, Department of Special Collections, University of California at Los Angeles:** pages 57, 96, 159; **courtesy of National Park Service, U.S. Department of the Interior:** page 67; **Nebraska State Historical Society:** page 69; **courtesy of University of Chicago Library:** page 119; **National Association for the Advancement of Colored People:** page 146; **Stephen Crane Collection, #555, courtesy of the Clifton Waller Barrett Library, Manuscripts Division, University of Virginia Library:** page 178.

Reconstruction

1863
Abraham Lincoln experiments with Reconstruction in Louisiana.

1865
Civil War ends. Thirteenth Amendment is ratified. Lincoln is assassinated.

1866
Congress introduces its own plan for Reconstruction, readmits Tennessee to Union, and passes a Civil Rights Act.

1865-1866
Southern states enact black codes.

1865
Congress forms the Freedmen's Bureau. **Thaddeus Stevens** proposes to divide up plantations for freedmen.

1865
Andrew Johnson becomes president, outlines his plan for Reconstruction.

1866
Ku Klux Klan forms. Race riots erupt in Memphis, Tennessee, and New Orleans, Louisiana.

1867
Congress passes its own Reconstruction Act, which organizes the South into military districts.

1868
Fourteenth Amendment is ratified. Congress readmits Alabama, Arkansas, Florida, Louisiana, North Carolina, and South Carolina to the Union.

1868
Johnson is impeached and acquitted. Ulysses S. Grant becomes president.

1877
Military rule ceases in the South.

1876
Democratic Party resumes control in the South, governing in nine states.

1873
Panic of 1873 ushers in six years of depression.

1870
Fifteenth Amendment is ratified. Congress readmits Georgia, Virginia, Mississippi, and Texas to the Union.

RECONSTRUCTION

Eleven Southern states—South Carolina, Georgia, Florida, Alabama, Mississippi, Louisiana, Texas, Virginia, Tennessee, North Carolina, and Arkansas—seceded from the Union in the rebellion that prompted the Civil War. President Abraham Lincoln began the process of reconstruction—bringing these states back into the Union—before the war was over. He developed a generous policy, calculated to attract Southerners away from the Confederacy and shorten the war. On December 8, 1863, Lincoln promised pardons to all who would swear to support the U.S. Constitution and federal laws on slavery. Speaking for the presidency but not for Congress, Lincoln promised to recognize a state when its oath-takers amounted to one-tenth of its voters in the 1860 election.

After Lincoln was assassinated and **Andrew Johnson** stepped into the presidency, peacetime Reconstruction began. There were basic questions to answer: Should the rebels be punished? What rights should the newly freed blacks have? And under what conditions would states be readmitted to the Union with the right to vote in national elections and send senators and representatives to Congress? Post-war Reconstruction called for more than readmitting some states; it demanded the reshaping of society and government.

1

Concerning the conditions that would have to be met, Johnson came up with a mild plan: Property would be restored to all Confederates who took an oath to support the U.S. Constitution and Union except for rebel government leaders and those who owned over $20,000 in property. These leading rebels could apply for individual pardons, and then they too might be forgiven. For a state to reenter the Union, it had to adopt the Thirteenth Amendment, repeal secession, and cancel any debts it had amounted as a Confederate state.

Congress was outraged at Johnson's plan and demanded harsher conditions. The fear was that the same Southerners who had governed the war effort would be elected to Congress, and there would be twelve more of them since freeing the slaves entitled the South to more representatives in the House. With so much power, Southerners might even recreate the plantation system. Already their states were passing black codes to limit the freedom of the former slaves.

These codes named a few black rights—to make contracts, sue in court, and hold property—but also restricted the behavior of the black population in a state. They commonly forbid blacks from carrying guns or assembling after dark. In South Carolina, the codes made it unlawful for blacks to own shops or work as artisans in the state; they were allowed only to become farmers or servants.

Reconstruction Amendments

Thirteenth Amendment Prohibits slavery in the United States

Fourteenth Amendment Defines who is a citizen and what rights citizens have

Fifteenth Amendment Prohibits discrimination in voting because of race, color, or past condition of slavery

---

Congressmen, given such evidence, distrusted that the South would institute reforms without supervision. They therefore favored a period of federal rule in the rebel states, after which they could return as equals to the Union. While Congress subscribed to the idea that the states, not the federal government, had the authority over the social and economic life in their areas, it moved to guarantee certain basic rights through amendments to the U.S. Constitution.

Suspicious of how unwilling Southern states might be to change, a few congressmen advocated sweeping reforms. **Thaddeus Stevens** planned to confiscate all Southern farms larger than 200 acres and divide them into 40-acre tracts among the freedmen. However, most congressmen were less demanding. They did not call for redistributing Confederate lands to the freedmen. In fact, some abandoned lands on the Sea Islands off the coast of South Carolina had already been divided into 40-acre plots for freed blacks. But after the war, the property was restored to its former white owners. General William Tecumseh Sherman had earlier declared that the islands would be reserved for blacks, yet Congress did not try to stop the state from restoring them to whites. It did, however, insist on citizenship and the vote for blacks.

Rejecting the president's plan for Reconstruction, Congress developed its own plan. States would have to approve the Fourteenth Amendment, which declares that all people born or naturalized in the United States are full citizens. The amendment canceled both the three-fifths clause, which stated that a black was equal to three-fifths of a person, in the U.S. Constitution and the Dred Scott decision, which stated that blacks were not citizens. Tennessee ratified the amendment and was readmitted by Congress, but the ten other states remained out of the Union.

Most Democrats favored Johnson's plan, while Republicans supported Congress's hard-line approach. In the election of 1866, the nation voted into office a majority of Republican senators and representatives. The country had spoken, rejecting the president's Reconstruction plan by electing congressmen who would develop a harsher plan.

Congress began in 1867 to pass three Reconstruction Acts, dividing the South into five military districts. For a while, the U.S. Army would have the authority to maintain order in the South. Congress also outlined its procedure for readmitting the ten states to the Union. Southern voters, blacks included, would elect delegates to state conventions that were responsible for writing new state constitutions that

▲ **Military divisions of the South following the Civil War**

guaranteed the black population the right to vote. Then each state would elect new officials, ratify the Fourteenth Amendment, and be allowed back into Congress.

The Fourteenth Amendment, probably the most far-reaching act of Reconstruction, was a response to violence. Race riots had erupted in Memphis, Tennessee, and New Orleans, Louisiana, in 1866. That same year, the Ku Klux Klan appeared. One of several secret organizations, it forced Republican blacks and whites out of power. Armed Klansmen scared citizens away from the polls or forced them to vote for Democrats. They feared black control of their local governments, although blacks did not in fact gain control in any state. Fourteen were elected to the House, and two talented black statesmen, Hiram R. Revels and Blanche K. Bruce, won seats in the Senate. But there were no black elected governors (P.B.S. Pinchback was Louisiana acting governer once the elected governor resigned), and whites filled most of the key positions.

Meanwhile, the struggle raged on between Johnson and Congress. Congress passed the Tenure of Office Act, which required the president to get Senate approval before dismissing an official. Johnson ignored the law, and Congress tried to remove him from office. They impeached or brought charges against him for the misconduct of dismissing officials illegally. In the end, Johnson was not convicted, but his power was broken.

In fact, the main post-war struggle concerned not politics but land and labor. Republican state governments took on the job of rebuilding harbors, roads, and bridges in the war-torn region. But issues related to land and jobs were mostly left to the people to work out for themselves. There was an exception. The federal government formed an agency, the Freedmen's Bureau (Bureau of Freedmen, Refugees, and Abandoned Lands). The Bureau issued food and clothing to blacks, helped them reunite with their families, provided medical care, and most of all acted as a job agency.

Though congressmen such as Stevens wanted to redistribute old landholdings, the reverse occurred. Southern land was collected into fewer and larger holdings than before the war, and the farmers concentrated more exclusively on one crop, usually cotton. No one had money, so a system of credit developed in the region. Local merchants lent out tools, seed, and animals to be repaid with interest at a later date.

At first, landowners tried to force blacks to sign work contracts and labor in gangs. Filled with desire to own their own parcels, however, the former slaves soon abandoned contract labor for sharecropping or tenant farming. Sharecroppers received a plot of land, seed, tools, and food and clothing. In return, they promised the landowner as much as fifty percent of the harvest, using their own half to pay for the goods purchased earlier on credit. The system made it nearly impossible to climb out of debt and get ahead. In tenant farming, tenants promised to sell their entire crop to a merchant for the use of land, tools, and other items. They too were forced into debt, required by the merchant to buy goods on credit at his store. Poor whites as well as blacks fell victim to both systems, which tied the farmers to the same landlord year after year in a slavelike manner.

Meanwhile, there were some new developments in Southern society. While the Republicans were in control of

▲ **Thomas Nast illustration of Klansmen terrorizing Southern blacks**

state governments, they sponsored some of the first public schools in the region. Blacks demonstrated a keen interest in education, founding Howard, Atlanta, and Fisk universities, as well as primary and secondary schools. Such activity met with militant resistance in Tennessee, for example, where whites burned down thirty-seven black schools in 1869 alone.

In the end, Democrats drove the Republicans out of power, becoming once again the dominant political party in the South. Local Democratic clubs organized themselves into armed bands and broke up Republican meetings, starting riots that killed hundreds of blacks. Congress passed the Ku Klux Act, one of three so-called Force Acts that gave the president the power to use federal agents to make sure citizens were not prevented from voting. Then the Fifteenth Amendment was passed to guarantee black men the right to vote.

Congress would do little more to force change in the South. By 1876 Democratic governments with old attitudes were back in control of nine Southern states. They had thrown out the carpetbaggers, Northern-born white Republicans who came South after the war supposedly with no more than a carpetbag, or small suitcase, ready to live off Southern pickings. There was equally low regard for Southern-born white Republicans, called scalawags, a term used also for dirty, feeble cattle. Blacks were lumped with carpetbaggers and scalawags and unfairly accused of behaving corruptly in government.

As the 1870s wore on, the North was distracted by a depression, and conflicts broke out over other matters in the nation, such as factory working conditions. Events in the South faded into the background. In 1876 Rutherford B. Hayes won the presidency in a close election that led to the total withdrawal of federal troops from the South. When the troops left in 1877, Reconstruction was officially over.

Andrew Johnson

1808-1875

Personal Background

Early life. Andrew Johnson was born December 25, 1808, in Raleigh, North Carolina, the third child of Jacob and Mary (McDonough) Johnson. His parents were poor working people. Unable to read or write, his father earned a living by performing various odd jobs. Jacob, however, gained some respect as a hard worker and as a fearless helper in times of need. He had risked his own life to rescue one of the more prosperous men of the community from a boat accident. Andrew's mother meanwhile worked as a seamstress and laundress, so effectively that she was known as "Polly the Weaver." Still, the family was among those known in the area as poor white trash. More prosperous citizens looked down on them, even whipping the children if they strayed into a neighborhood where they were not wanted.

Unfortunately for Andrew, his father died when he was just three years old. His mother soon remarried, again to a poor man. She and her new husband could barely afford to raise the children. For a time, Andrew may have boarded with an uncle, Jesse, who lived in a small house on a great estate. Certainly, Andrew was part of the gang of cousins called Jesse Johnson's boys. The gang played ball, swam, and fished in the mill pond as did other boys their age. They also got themselves into trouble, such as trespassing, or by

▲ Andrew Johnson

Event: The post–Civil War reconstruction of the South.

Role: Andrew Johnson attempted to reunite the South with the Union in the manner initiated by his predecessor, Abraham Lincoln. His intent was to reestablish Southern states as full partners in the Union as fully, painlessly, and quickly as possible. However, some members of the Congress, who came to be called radicals, disagreed with his approach. The resulting disputes between Congress and the president led to a slow and painful rebuilding of the United States.

some accounts, trespassing in the nude on a nearby estate. The misdeed earned the boys a whipping.

Apprentice tailor. Because his family was poor, Andrew did not attend a day of school. At the age of ten, he was apprenticed to a tailor, James Selby. In return for his training, Andrew agreed to work for Selby until he was twenty-one. Meanwhile, the apprenticeship gave Andrew an education, which greatly excited him. Selby was obligated to teach his apprentices the alphabet and basics of reading. He also allowed townspeople such as Dr. William Hill to come to the shop and read to the workmen, which Andrew greatly enjoyed. He particularly liked the times when Hill read famous speeches from the book *United States Speaker,* so much so that Hill finally gave the book to the boy.

Runaway. When he was fifteen years old, Johnson and some other boys ran into trouble when they threw sticks of wood at a neighbor's house. The neighbor, Mrs. Wells, threatened to sue for damages. To escape a possible court order to pay Mrs. Wells a sum they could not afford, Andrew and his older brother, William, decided to run away from Raleigh. The two boys walked fifty miles to Carthage, where Andrew found work as a tailor. A few months later, he moved out of state to Laurens, South Carolina, and again found a job in tailoring.

Andrew had broken the law when he ran away from his apprenticeship, and he was anxious to clear his name in Raleigh. He returned there as soon as possible and tried to buy his own apprenticeship from Selby. The old man had since retired to the country and would not agree to free Andrew unless a substantial sum was paid in cash. Andrew did not have the money, so he left Raleigh again, traveling this time to Tennessee.

He was just getting established in the town of Columbia when he was called back to Raleigh because of family problems. In 1826 he packed up his mother and stepfather, put their belongings in a two-wheel cart, and again headed for Tennessee. Legend has it that the cart, driven by his mother, was pulled by a blind pony, while Andrew, leading the family cow, walked beside with his stepfather. They settled in Greeneville, Tennessee, where eighteen-year-old Andrew found work in George Boyle's tailor shop.

Marriage. Soon after, Andrew met a young and attractive six-teen-year-old quiltmaker named Eliza McCardle. The two were opposites in many ways. Johnson was rough and barely educated, and Eliza, a modest, retiring, attractive brunette, had a better than average education. They fell deeply in love and in 1827, they married. The couple would remain happily wed for nearly fifty years and raise five children.

Politics. Johnson went into partnership with Hentle Adkin-son, and the two set up their own tailor shop. As the business grew, Johnson worked to educate himself. He read every book he could obtain, while Eliza coached him in writing and arithmetic. He also followed state politics and freely spoke his mind about them. After participating in a debate about criminals' rights, he discovered that he was an able speaker and enjoyed debating. He joined debating societies to improve his ability. As he rose in the community, friends nominated him for a position as town alderman. Running as a candidate for the working man, Johnson won the election; his career as a politician had begun. He steadily rose to other positions, in 1843 becoming a congressman from Tennessee; in 1853, governor of the state; and in 1857, United States senator.

While in Congress, Johnson voted against any measures that would add to the taxes of the common workers. Also, he proposed a Homestead Act, which would allow families to claim up to 160 acres of government-held territory if they worked the land. (The act finally passed in Congress three years later in 1860.) The proposed act angered many Southerners, who worried about the loss of western territory to homesteaders who were antislavery. Angry Tennessee lawmakers decided to cut Johnson from Congress by eliminating his district. Enraged, he ran for governor of the state and won.

Johnson was a popular governor who championed the average people of the state over the wealthy landowners. His concern for the underdog, however, was restricted to whites. He did not consider blacks as equals and owned ten slaves himself. As a member of the Senate in 1860, when Southern states began to secede from the Union, he supported slavery but refused to support the Southern states, declaring, "I am opposed to secession" (Hoyt, p. 59). In a speech before the Senate, he called secession wrong and hinted that those who wanted it were angry only because their candidate had lost to a Northerner in the presidential election. The speech was so powerful that Alexander Stephens, vice president of the Confederate States, blamed it for causing the war. Without Johnson, Stephens claimed, the South could have seceded without being questioned. Still, Johnson was considered an advocate for slavery and, therefore, somewhat friendly to the South.

Vice president. With the war dragging on in 1864, a new presidential election in the offing, and his own popularity waning, President Abraham Lincoln needed a running mate who would be popular with pro-Southern Northerners, known as Copperheads. Johnson was ideal. Although most of his state sided with the Confederacy, he had remained pro-Union. When a stuffed likeness of him was burned in his state, he became for Northerners a symbol of the reformed slave owner. Doubtful about his chances in the 1864 election, Lincoln needed to strengthen the ticket. Johnson became the candidate for vice president, and the team of Lincoln and Johnson won.

The Lincoln Reconstruction. Lincoln believed that the Southern states should be readmitted to the Union as gently and quickly as possible. His policy called for ten percent of the voters of a state to take an oath to support the U.S. Constitution and the Union and for the state to abide by federal laws concerning slaves. Thereafter it would be readmitted with full representation in Congress.

Louisiana had been the first Southern state to rejoin the Union under Lincoln's plan. However, as soon as the war was over, Louisiana, followed by other rebellious states, started passing laws to keep blacks from voting and "black codes" to curb the ex-slaves' freedom of movement and to restrict their behavior in other ways. Race riots erupted, but Lincoln stuck to his Reconstruction policy.

Just prior to Lincoln's assassination, Thaddeus Stevens and other members of Congress who were angered by the passage of black codes began to push for harsher readmittance policies (see **Thaddeus Stevens**). When Johnson took over as president, he continued Lincoln's policies and became involved in a bitter tug-of-war with Congress over who would engineer the course of Reconstruction.

Two views of Johnson. When he entered the office of vice president, Andrew Johnson was ill. His doctor had prescribed whiskey as a treatment, and Johnson had heeded this advice on the way to taking the oath of office. He was, therefore, somewhat drunk when sworn into office. Johnson was a very able speaker when he had time to prepare, but he was also known to lose his temper and speak crudely when riled. After taking the oath, he made a speech that was sometimes not understandable and sometimes angered the congressmen who had gathered to witness the event. He would recover from the illness and the prescription, but the accusation that he was a drunk would plague him from then on. In fact, though Johnson did drink, he was not an alcoholic.

Now with the oath of office as president facing him, Johnson showed a different side of himself. Though he had also been targeted for assassination, he risked personal danger and visited Lincoln as he lay dying. Johnson then gathered with a few leaders to take the oath of office, asking for their support and clearly defining the tasks ahead for the country. The senators who witnessed this were impressed with Johnson's sincerity and humility. The public read the positive news reports of the event, and President Johnson took office on a high note.

A changing attitude toward the South. Many people of the United States believed that Southern leaders had a hand in Lincoln's assassination. Suddenly the newspapers and Congress began calling for harsher treatment of the South. Stevens argued that Southern states no longer had rights under the Constitution but were conquered territories that should be readmitted only after proof of loyalty. Furthermore, no leaders of the Southern secession should be allowed to hold public office. And since the owners of the large plantations had supported and even instigated the war, their lands should be broken up for the benefit of the freed blacks and poor whites.

Johnson and Reconstruction. Johnson seemed to ignore this new call for a harsher policy toward the South. At the same time, he opened his office doors to most anyone with a plea or a plan. Many of his visitors were Southerners who impressed him with their sincerity. The president decided to carry on the Reconstruction, or readmission, in much the same manner as Lincoln had. He added some mild requirements. States had to ratify the Thirteenth Amendment, which abolished slavery, elect new officials, and forget about paying Confederate debts.

Andrew Johnson on Blacks

Johnson's view of black people was typical of many whites of his day: "Everyone would and must admit that the white race is superior to the black, and that while we ought to do our best to bring them up to our present level, that, in doing so, we should at the same time raise our own intellectual status so that the relative position of the two races would be the same." (Trefousse, p. 236)

Still, a majority of congressmen, led by Stevens, did not agree with Johnson's approach. Stevens feared that the same Southern leaders who had directed the war would soon be back in authority. He also believed that readmitting the states was the responsibility of Congress rather than the president. Beginning on March 2, 1867, and continuing for a year, Congress passed a series of Reconstruction Acts. The Southern states were dissolved and replaced by five military districts ruled by five Union generals. As the former states proved their earnestness to repent and rejoin the Union, provisional governments would be set up, constitutional conventions held, and votes taken to assure that state's commitment to the Union. Each potential state was required to accept the Thirteenth Amendment and prepare a state constitution banning slavery. It also had to accept the Fourteenth Amendment, which made former slaves full citizens. No previous Confederate official, military officer above the rank of colonel, or landowner with a holding valued at more than $20,000 could serve in public office. In the end, Congress's plan was the one adopted. The process of readmission to the Union started over with each state having to meet the new requirements.

Congress or the president? The real issue in Washington was a contest over who had authority to direct the reuniting of the South into the Union. Opposed to any more harsh measures than were absolutely necessary to control crime and establish sound government, Johnson tended to ignore the black codes that were springing up and to accept the need to place some of the old officials back in power. After all, as some of his temporary governors pointed out, there were not many good leaders in the South who had been loyal to the Union throughout the war. Johnson replaced many of the officials in the five military districts with people more in sympathy with his plans. Congress responded by passing a Tenure of Office Act, which required the president to get the Senate's consent before dismissing any official who had been appointed with congressional approval. The battle between Congress and the president raged on.

Feeling that the Tenure of Office Act was unconstitutional, Johnson continued to replace government officials without Senate approval. The tenure issue came to a climax when Johnson sought to remove Secretary of War Edwin Stanton. In favor of a harsher policy toward the South, Stanton was certainly not in agreement with Johnson's plans. Congress quickly amended the Tenure of Office Act to include members of the president's cabinet. To avoid conflict with the Tenure of Office Act, Johnson merely suspended Stanton and gave a temporary appointment to Grant.

These disputes angered Johnson because they delayed real reconstruction of the South. He decided to try to strengthen his influence by taking a speaking tour of the major cities. Unfortunately, the president was hot-tempered and, when prodded, spoke his mind without much careful thought. Aware of his weakness, his foes in Congress stationed hecklers at the major speeches to rile the president. Their strategy worked. Johnson responded angrily, and the tour was a disaster.

When he appeared before a large crowd gathered to celebrate George Washington's birthday, Johnson complained that some congressmen were trying to destroy the Union. A voice from the crowd goaded Johnson to name names, whereupon he mentioned three of the most powerful Congress members: Stevens, Charles Sumner, and Wendell Phillips.

Johnson's earlier act of replacing Stanton with Grant gave these men ammunition. They moved for impeachment of the president. The House of Representatives voted in favor of it, and the trial was set before the Senate. The charges—the Stanton issue, abusive language, opposition to congressional acts—were so vague that even the Stevens-controlled Senate could not make them stick. Johnson was acquitted and continued in office for two more years. However, the trial had nearly destroyed his effectiveness. Reconstruction, already in shambles because of the bickering between Congress and the president, fell into an even harsher military rule. After two years, Johnson was replaced as president by Ulysses S. Grant.

Aftermath

Return home. In 1869 Johnson returned home to Tennessee to banners welcoming the former president. He retired but continued to have ambitions of returning to Washington and to government. He still hoped to have a voice in the Reconstruction of the South. Johnson made several bids for reelection to the House or Senate. They all failed until 1875, when he was elected to the Senate.

Senator Johnson. Grant's presidency had been filled with underhanded deals, and his administration was accused of accepting bribes and of selling government offices. On his first day back in the Senate, Johnson rose to speak. He criticized Grant's poor management of the country.

Johnson also pleaded for justice for the South, which had now suffered ten years of military rule. One part of his speech said much about the man whose crude manners had often caused misunderstanding but whose concern for the people and the Constitution was unwavering:

> Let us come up to this work [reconstruction] forgetting what we have been heretofore. Let us lay aside our party feelings; let us lay aside our personalities and come up to the Constitution of our country and lay it upon an altar and all stand around, resolved that the Constitution shall be preserved. (Hoyt, p. 136)

Death. The Senate meeting had been a specially called session. Johnson returned home weary from the effort and from damage due to cholera he had contracted two years earlier. On a visit with Eliza to see their daughter Mary, he suffered a stroke. He was bedridden and then suffered another massive stroke. Johnson died on July 31, 1875. He was buried with a copy of the Constitution pillowing his head, just as he had requested.

Hoyt, Edwin P. *Andrew Johnson*. Chicago: Reilly and Lee, 1965.

McKitrick, Eric L. *Andrew Johnson and Reconstruction*. Chicago: University of Chicago Press, 1960.

Trefousse, Hans L. *Andrew Johnson: A Biography*. New York: W. W. Norton, 1989.

Thaddeus Stevens

1792-1868

Personal Background

Early life. As newlyweds in 1786, Thaddeus Stevens' parents, Joshua and Sarah, traveled by covered wagon from Essex County, Massachusetts, to Caledonia County, Vermont. They purchased a farm, which along with Joshua's occasional outside employment gave the couple a comfortable life. Soon the family grew with the addition of four sons: Joshua, Jr., in 1790; Thaddeus on April 4, 1792; Abner in 1794; and Alanson in 1797.

Apparently the family held little interest for Joshua, who began to spend more and more time away from home. Sarah finally refused to allow him into the home at all, so the chores of the farm fell to her and the boys. She added to the family income by nursing the sick of nearby Danville, sometimes for pay and sometimes as a volunteer. Thaddeus was of little help with the farm labor since he had been born with a club foot. He proved, however, an able assistant in his mother's nursing work, which exposed the young boy to suffering and poverty. It was an experience that he would remember throughout his life.

Schooling. Around 1807 Sarah sold the farm to move to the next town, Peacham. This town had a school, and Sarah was determined that her boys be educated. Caledonia County Academy, a one-teacher school with about 100 students, charged twenty-five cents a month tuition.

▲ **Thaddeus Stevens**

Event: The military reconstruction of the South.

Role: By the sheer force of his will, his understanding of the workings of Congress, and his commitment to principle, Thaddeus Stevens controlled both houses of Congress toward the end of the Civil War. In this role, he greatly affected the speed with which the rebel Southern states, or "conquered provinces" as he viewed them, were readmitted to the Union. Stevens helped set harsher conditions for their reinstatement than originally planned.

Thaddeus was unable to play at childhood games because of his club foot, and other children often made fun of him. He escaped such cruelty by reading. Although he remained at the academy for only four years, his own reading took him far beyond the average student.

In 1811 Thaddeus was admitted to Dartmouth College but was later expelled. He attended the University of Vermont for awhile before later returning to Dartmouth, where he graduated in 1814.

Pennsylvania. By the time he graduated, Stevens had decided to become a lawyer. He chose to set up his practice in the small town of Gettysburg, Pennsylvania. There Stevens taught school while he studied for the bar, and he began to take an interest in politics. A new political party, the Anti-Masons, was just gaining strength in the East. The new party was formed to stop the growing power of the Masons, a powerful and secret society. Stevens had grown to be a champion of the downtrodden, and thus was naturally opposed to any secret organizations, or, for that matter, anything that might possibly foster inequality among people. He joined the Anti-Masons and attended their convention in Baltimore in 1831.

Within two years, Stevens was a member of the Pennsylvania legislature. There he served six terms, although his outspoken manner and harsh language resulted in occasional defeats at the polls. In 1842 he moved his home and law office to Lancaster, another small Pennsylvania town.

View on slaves. Stevens had long spoken for complete citizenship for slaves. As a successful lawyer, he was very busy but never too busy to take up the cause of an escaped slave or any victim of poverty. One time, for example, he decided to travel north to buy some law books. On the way, he encountered a black woman who feared that the local tavern owner was about to sell her husband, John, into slavery. Stevens took up her cause. He tried to buy John's freedom for $150, but to no avail. When he learned that John was the tavern owner's own son, Stevens tried to appeal to the man's sense of kindred. The tavern owner needed money, however, and thought that his son would bring a good price. Stevens thereupon bought John for $350, set him free, and returned to Lancaster. He had spent the money intended for law books.

Personal life. It has been suggested that Stevens remained a bachelor all his life because of his club foot. Certainly he was bothered by the superstition of his time that such a handicap made him a devil's child. In addition to his club foot, another physical trait may have interfered with Steven's pursuit of female companionship. At thirty-nine an attack of brain fever left him bald, a condition he hid under a red-brown wig that others ridiculed.

Stevens, nevertheless, did have a few noteworthy relationships with women. Perhaps foremost among them was his mother, who taught him to survive and overcome failures in life. She had worked tirelessly so that he and his brothers would have an education, and he remembered her always as the most extraordinary of women. As a rich young lawyer in Pennsylvania, he courted Sarah Sergeant for a time, but the relationship ended abruptly when she suggested he buy her a diamond ring.

In 1848 Stevens hired a thirty-five-year-old housekeeper, Lydia Smith, an attractive woman whose ancestry was part black. He developed an intense affection for her and the relationship lasted until the end of his life. In his will, Stevens would leave Smith $5,000, and to his nephew, his entire estate if he gave up alcohol. If not, the money was to fund an orphanage that would be open to children of all colors. Stevens attained wealth rapidly, acquiring property and also suffering some business reverses. Above all, though, he was a politician whose main ambition was to exercise the powers of public office.

Freshman congressman. After six terms in the Pennsylvania legislature, Stevens was prepared to run for Congress. An excellent speaker and organizer, he won a seat in the House of Representatives in 1849. It had long been a habit for the House to begin each session with a series of pro-slavery speeches by Southern representatives. The Southern representatives, fearful of the growing Northern sentiment against slavery, berated Northern representatives and often threatened destruction of the Union through secession. Timid Northerners, afraid that secession might harm their businesses, were easily led by the South. Stevens, however, did not scare easily. In his first speech to the House, on February 29, 1850, he served notice on the Southern representatives that he would not yield to their demands and threats. As was his habit, he clearly stated his position without regard to other people's sensitivities. Bits of this speech reveal his own commitments and his earnestness:

> While I announce my hostility to slavery in every form and every place, I also avow my determination to stand by all the compromises of the Constitution....
>
> I am opposed to the diffusion [spread] of slavery, because confining it within its present limits will bring the [Southern] states themselves to its gradual abolition....
>
> You [Southern Congressmen] have too often intimidated Congress. You have more than once frightened the tame North from its propriety and found dough-faces [Northerners who sided with the South] enough to be your tools. (Korngold, pp. 85-87)

The speech was so strong that several Southern representatives rose to object and even his fellow representative from Pennsylvania, Thomas Ross, felt it necessary to apologize to the South. Stevens responded to Ross and the others with the acid language for which he would become well known. He rebuked fellow congressmen who had taunted Northern representatives who were against slavery. He, himself, Stevens claimed, chose not to stoop to such behavior. If he cared to use such language he could find the words any day by entering the fishmarket. However, he said, "I beg these respectable fish ladies to understand that I do not include my colleague from Pennsylvania (Ross) among those whom I deem fit to be their associates. I would not so degrade them" (Korngold, p. 88).

Stevens was a dedicated congressman who worked tirelessly for causes he believed in. He opposed the enactment of the Fugitive Slave Laws, which encouraged bounty hunters to search for escaped slaves and return them to the South. In his view, if a slave escaped to a free state, that slave became free. He also opposed all bills in the House that seemed to favor the South. And he continued to campaign for a cause he had championed before entering federal politics—the financing of public education. While in the state legislature, he had proposed a tax to support the schools, which was unpopular with the wealthy. He continued to press for public education and any other issues that would help remove class differences. He became known as the "Great Leveler."

After two terms in Congress, Stevens had few friends in or out of government. In addition, his political organization was fading. When his Anti-Mason party lost power, he hesitated to join another party and was defeated in his quest for a third term. He returned to private law practice but would later become a member of the new Republican party of Abraham Lincoln.

Successful attorney. For six years, Stevens remained out of politics. A prosperous law business and involvement in other ventures, such as an iron foundry, occupied much of his attention. However, there was always time to keep up with local, state, and national politics. At the age of sixty-seven, Stevens returned to politics and was again elected a U.S. representative.

Control of Congress. Now all his past experience in government came to the fore. Stevens knew the procedures of government perhaps as thoroughly as anyone then in government. He knew legal practices as well, and he had earned a reputation for always being straightforward and honest, if not blunt and sometimes impolite. Re-entering the House of Representatives in 1859, he used his skills to become the master of both houses of Congress. Never the clerk of the House, nor its Speaker—although his choices were appointed—he was content to control the flow of legislation as chairman of important committees, such as the House Ways and Means Committee. He was in this position when the Civil War began two years later.

Financing the war. One of the few in the North who anticipated that the budding Civil War would be a long and bloody one, Stevens immediately began to ensure that the government provide proper financing for its growing army. He knew that the North had the greater numbers but doubted that it could muster more fighting men and worried that the South had at least as good military leadership. After all, without slaves to do the work, only one in five Northern men could be spared to actually fight the war. On the other hand, the South could leave a few white men to direct the slaves at producing food and weapons. The rest of the Southern men would be free to fight. Also, the leaders of the Southern troops had graduated with high honors from West Point. Under Stevens' direction, Congress passed bills to finance the soldiers, provide for weapons, and pay pensions when the soldiers had served long enough to deserve them.

Two years into the war (1863), it was time to think about restoring the nation if the North put down the rebellion. Stevens began to consider the conditions under which the South would be readmitted to the Union. In his view, the South, by beginning the rebellion and forming a different government, had officially broken with the North and had no rights under the Constitution. Under what he called the "laws of war," these ex-states would be considered conquered territories and should meet conditions of good citizenship in order to be readmitted. At first, Stevens had thought these conditions would be met if a state stopped fighting and if its citizens signed an oath of allegiance to the Constitution.

Lincoln's readmission plan. Lincoln agreed, but he acted as if readmitting the Southern states were the president's privilege. As early as 1863, his actions suggested that he planned to take a soft approach to readmitting the states. In New Orleans, which had been won by the North, Lincoln appointed a military governor. The president also directed the oath-taking and the meeting of a convention to write a state constitution. That done, Lincoln readmitted Louisiana to the Union and approved its sending representatives to Congress. It would later have to requalify under stricter requirements drawn up by Congress.

At first, Stevens and Lincoln shared a common goal—to reunite the Union as quickly and painlessly as possible. They differed, however, on whether the president or Congress should control readmitting the Southern states. When Lincoln began in Louisiana to act independently of Congress, Stevens objected and began to initiate his own plan for the South—one of Reconstruction, not ready readmission.

Participation: Reconstruction of the South

Post-Civil War South. Soon Stevens began to see the postwar scene differently from the president. When the 3.5 million slaves were freed, each slave counted as one person in the census rather than three-fifths of a person as before the war. The extra population gave the South twelve more seats in Congress, which threatened again to upset the balance of power between the North and South. Furthermore, the Union, already $2 billion in debt from the war, would have to assume the debt from the Southern states, too.

Meanwhile, Southern soldiers, proud and angry in their defeat, felt a mounting hatred for the North. They had not been beaten on the field of action but rather starved into submission. Stevens feared that, with more influence in Congress, Southerners and their friends among the antiwar Northerners (called Copperheads) would soon rule the country and slavery would resume. He set about correcting the potential problem by insisting that the new representatives from Louisiana not be seated in Congress. Though Stevens, like Lincoln, wanted a quick and peaceful rebinding of the Union, he distrusted the willingness of the South to change and favored much harsher treatment of the rebel states.

Plan for the South. Just prior to Lincoln's assassination, Stevens had been pressing for stricter readmission standards for Southern states. Stevens' policy called for a majority—not the ten percent Lincoln wanted—of a state's citizens to vote for readmission and to swear an oath of allegiance to the Union. Furthermore, the new state would have to agree to accept the Thirteenth Amendment, which abolished slavery. It would also have to renounce any responsibility for the debt of the Confederate States of America, which would place added pressure on states still in the Confederacy to join the Union. And a large number of former Southern leaders would be excluded from holding public office: officials of the Confederacy, Confederate officers above the rank of lieutenant colonel or navy lieutenant, and businessmen who had supported the war effort of the South.

The president or Congress? Like Lincoln, Stevens was willing to compromise, and a sound policy might have been adopted if the president had not been killed. But in 1865, into the office of president stepped Andrew Johnson of Tennessee (see **Andrew Johnson**).

Johnson, like Lincoln, believed that the president should oversee the readmission of Southern states into the Union. He ignored Stevens' calls for a harsher policy and, one by one, began to readmit each state according to his own mild plan. Besides having ten percent of its voters sign an oath, a state had to ratify the Thirteenth Amendment, which abolished slavery. After meeting this and a few more conditions, the state was allowed to rejoin the Union and send representatives to Congress. Under Johnson's plan, leaders in the new state governments included high-ranking officials of the former Confederacy, Confederate generals, and wealthy landowners. Even Alexander Stephens, who had been vice president of the Confederate States and was in prison on charges of treason, was nominated for a Senate seat. Stevens' earlier fears of a return to pre-Civil War struggles appeared to be real, and once more he battled the president.

Stevens used his power over Congress to turn the tide. Under his guidance, Congress refused to accept the representatives from states readmitted to the Union by Johnson. In addition, the "ironclad oath" was to be enforced as a condition of admission to the Union. The oath held that anyone elected or appointed to federal office from the former rebel states had to be someone who never plotted to secede.

The Ironclad Oath of Loyalty of July 2, 1862

Be it enacted ... That hereafter every person elected or appointed to any office of honor or profit under the government of the United States ... shall, before entering upon the duties of such office ... take and subscribe the following oath or affirmation: "I, A.B., do solemnly swear (or affirm) that I have never voluntarily borne arms against the United States since I have been a citizen thereof; that I have voluntarily given no aid, countenance, counsel or encouragement to persons engaged in armed hostilities thereto; that I have neither sought nor accepted nor attempted to exercise the functions of any office whatever, under any authority or pretended authority [inhospitable] to the United States.... And I do further swear (or affirm) that, to the best of my knowledge and ability, I will support and defend the Constitution of the United States.... (Hyman, p. 158)

Stevens and Reconstruction. Stevens was determined that Congress, not the president, would direct Reconstruction. Convinced that Johnson's approach was too weak, he pushed for his own Reconstruction plan. To accomplish this, he had the House of Representatives create a Committee on Reconstruction. Naturally, Stevens was the chairman of the committee. In his plan, he intended to restore order in the Southern states without restoring their power. In addition, he wanted the South to pay its share of the enormous war debt facing the nation. He believed that the wealthy plantation owners of the South had been doubly guilty: they had held most of the slaves in the South, and they had been responsible for the move to secession. The Great Leveler planned to take care of these problems in a single move against the 70,000 Southerners who each owned more than 200 acres of land. He proposed to take the large plantations, break them up so that each freed man could have forty acres, and sell the rest to restore the national finances. He then proposed to use public lands in the South to support the freed men.

The whole South had been put under military control just after the war. Stevens thought military control meant dictatorship and the South should be relieved of it as soon as possible. However, the turmoil in the South would make that a slow process. Soldiers were returning home to find their farms and towns destroyed, and local governments had broken down. Into this mess had come a number of scoundrels ready to take advantage of the disorder. As a short-term solution, Stevens proposed to create territories in the South and establish territorial governments. This was one of several proposals Stevens made to Congress at the time.

Under the Stevens plan, all national and state laws would apply equally to all citizens regardless of race or color. To avoid stacking the government with Southerners because of the greater numbers to be counted by freeing of slaves, Stevens proposed that representation in Congress be determined on the number of legal voters in each state. It would be some time before all the freed blacks could be registered to vote. Furthermore, he demanded that Congress establish firm conditions for readmission before any Southern senators or representatives were seated in Congress.

Congress, however, did not accept Stevens' proposals. Even his supporters in Congress did not approve of the harshness of some of his plans. In addition to this, conflicting reports of events in the South were clouding the issue. Johnson had sent General Ulysses S. Grant on a hasty trip to parts of the South. Grant had reported that the people of the South were ready to accept readmission. At the same time Major General Carl Schurz had spent some months in the South and reported that the old hostile leaders were rapidly resuming leadership there and that the South seemed to have no intention of freeing the slaves. Blacks were being forced to stay on their old jobs by armed bands of white men.

By the time all of Stevens' proposals were made to Congress, the war had been over for two years and conditions in the South were not improving. Although a Freedmen's Bureau had been created just after the war to help freed slaves and poor Southern whites, it had been able to help only about 200,000 ex-slaves. One slave owner estimated that nearly 1 million ex-slaves had died of starvation and disease.

Johnson and Reconstruction. All the while, Johnson continued his soft Reconstruction plan, operating as if Congress had nothing to do with readmitting the Southern states. Stevens decided it was time for Congress to act. In 1865 the Committee on Reconstruction recommended a bill declaring that no senator or representative could be admitted to Congress from any of the Southern states until Congress decided that the state was entitled to representation. Congress passed the bill. Johnson vetoed it, and an attempt to override the veto lost by two votes. It was the first of many vetoes. The president planned to veto every bill that would have any effect on the South until Congress admitted that it had no right to interfere with his plan for Reconstruction. He even vetoed a Civil Rights Bill that simply declared that all persons born in the country were citizens. In this case, Congress overrode the veto.

Meanwhile, bills that would later take effect as the Fourteenth and Fifteenth Amendments to the Constitution were being proposed by Congress and rejected by the president. The contest between president and Congress continued. When Johnson declared himself to be totally for the Union and named Stevens and two other congressmen as his chief enemies, Stevens responded, "I can have no hostility to the President.... I have very grave objections to the course he is pursuing" (Korngold, p. 322).

Fourteenth Amendment. By autumn of 1866, the Fourteenth Amendment declaring that blacks were citizens of the United States had been passed by Congress and vetoed by the president. Congressional elections were coming up and these would test whether the people of the United States approved the president's plan or the authority of Congress. The people voted for Congress. A main reason for this decision was evidence from the South that Johnson's plan was not working. More than a thousand blacks had been killed since the war with no one held accountable.

The Tenure of Office Act. Now with the voters backing Congress, Johnson decided on another plan of attack. He would replace anyone appointed to political office who had been backed by Congress. If he could not control Reconstruction, he could at least slow the speed with which congressional bills were enforced. Congress countered in 1867 with a Tenure of Office Act that required congressional approval to remove a government worker whose appointment had needed congressional approval.

Meanwhile, the leaders of the South refused to accept congressional regulations. The result was that military rule was formalized. The South was divided into five regions, each governed by a military governor.

Impeaching the president. In violation of Congress's Tenure of Office Act, Johnson continued to fire people in government positions, most of whom were Republicans. He even fired Secretary of War Edwin M. Stanton, who had been appointed by Lincoln. Angered by Johnson's tactics, Stevens took action. On February 22, 1868, Stevens, now seventy-five, took the floor of the House of Representatives to move that the president be impeached.

Aftermath

The impeachment. The House of Representatives voted to impeach Johnson. He was called to trial before the Senate, where the impeachment was narrowly defeated. Although he remained in office, Johnson was never again an effective leader.

Death. The strain of chairing the House Committee on Impeachment, along with his efforts toward Reconstruction, eroded Stevens' already failing strength. While still a member of Congress, Stevens fell seriously ill and died on August 11, 1868. In his lifetime, his main achievement was the passage of the Fourteenth Amendment. His personality was a mix of traits that would continue to befuddle others after his death. Although he could be a spiteful opponent, he fought hard for the rights of those less fortunate than he.

Military rule of the South continued for nine years after Stevens' death. It was 1877 before the Southern states had settled back into place and were taking an active part in the Union. Had Stevens lived, he probably would have had a strong influence on the rest of the Reconstruction process.

For More Information

Brodie, Fawn M. *Thaddeus Stevens: Scourge of the South.* New York: W. W. Norton, 1959.

Hyman, Harold Melvin. *Era of the Oath.* Philadelphia: University of Pennsylvania Press, 1954.

Korngold, Ralph. *Thaddeus Stevens.* New York: Harcourt, Brace, 1955.

Indians and Government Policy

1840s
▼
Westward movement brings white settlers to the Great Plains, the Southwest, and the Pacific Northwest.

1850s
▼
U.S. Army skirmishes with Sioux and Cheyenne on the Plains and Kiowa, Comanche, and Apache in the Southwest.

1875
▼
Gold rush to the Black Hills results in Black Hills War.

1868
▼
Fort Laramie treaties require Sioux and other Plains tribes to settle on reservations.

1865-1867
▼
Plains Indians attack emigrants on the Bozeman Trail to the Montana goldfields.

1864
▼
Colorado militia massacre Cheyenne at Sand Creek.

1862
▼
Sioux warriors massacre settlers in southwest Minnesota.

1876
▼
U.S. general **George Armstrong Custer** fights Sioux at Little Bighorn.

1877
▼
Chief Joseph of the Nez Percé surrenders.

1877-1881
▼
Carl Schurz controls the U.S. Bureau of Indian Affairs, which encourages Indians to adopt white ways.

1879
▼
First off-reservation school for American Indians, the Carlisle School, opens in Pennsylvania.

1890
▼
Murder of Chief Sitting Bull results in flight of Sioux, which leads to their massacre at Wounded Knee, South Dakota.

1887
▼
Dawes Severalty Act attempts to break up tribes.

1886
▼
Apache leader Geronimo surrenders.

1883
▼
Lake Mohonk Conference is held to discuss reforms in Indian affairs.

INDIANS AND GOVERNMENT POLICY

The United States repeatedly changed its policy toward native American peoples during the 1800s. It first viewed the tribes as separate nations, entitled to treaties that would document and confirm any deals made with the U.S. government. Toward the end of the century, however, Congress abandoned the practice of making treaties with Indian tribes. Congressmen seemed to entertain only two options with regard to the Indians—they could either be killed off or persuaded to settle on individual farms and adopt other white ways.

Pushed westward in the beginning of the century were the Cherokee and other tribes of the East, who were forcibly removed to Indian territory (Oklahoma). As the century wore on, the westward movement escalated and endangered the Indians of the Plains, the Southwest, and the Far West. There was bloodshed, but in the end war did less harm to tribes of the Plains, for example, than the coming of the railroads.

Nineteenth-Century U.S. Indian Policies	
1800–1871	Acquire lands from Indian nations through treaties.
1812–50	Remove all tribes to land west of the Mississippi River.
1861–65	Get Indians to fight for the Union in the Civil War.
1868	Restrict tribes to reservations; kill uncooperative Indians.
1871	Do not enter into any more treaties with Indian peoples.
1880s–1900	Break up tribal units; force Indians to adopt white ways.

▲ **An Apache encampment in 1873**

Train travelers slaughtered thousands of buffalo on which the Indians depended for food and clothing, and some settled in tribal territory. Their territory shrinking, the tribes then violated the territorial boundaries among them. Competition among the tribes grew as they struggled to survive on the dwindling supply of land and buffalo. While some agreed to move to reservations, land set aside for their use, others refused to be confined to a limited land area.

Fighting was one of several options used by Indian nations. They attended conferences and signed treaties with whites, but in the end fighting seemed the only way to hold onto tribal lands. White soldiers first clashed with the Sioux in Wyoming in 1854. During the Civil War, white settlers were murdered in a Sioux uprising in Minnesota in 1862. Two years later, Cheyenne women and children were massacred at Sand Creek, Colorado. The war meanwhile raged on, drawing Indian soldiers into action on both sides. Some fought for the Union while others, including Indian slave owners, sided with the Confederacy. After the war, the government penalized all Indians because some had sided with the South. Changing old treaties, it made tribes give up more land and grant railroads the right of way through Indian territories. One plan called for the U.S. government to build forts along the Bozeman Trail in Montana. Red Cloud's War, fought in 1865 by Sioux warriors, changed these plans. The Indian victory prompted the U.S. government to abandon the trail and the idea of building forts along it, whereupon Red Cloud agreed to sign a treaty at Fort Laramie in 1868. The treaty promised that the Black Hills would be reserved as Sioux territory.

The 1870s and 1880s saw a continuous stream of white-Indian clashes. At first, the federal government's goal was to drive all the tribes onto reservations. While Red Cloud and others signed treaties agreeing to the reservations, Sitting Bull is an example of a Sioux chief who refused. William Tecumseh Sherman, head of the army of the West at the time, insisted that *all* Indians cooperate or be killed off.

The Black Hills had been reserved for the Sioux in the Fort Laramie Treaty, but more and more white prospectors rushed to the area after gold was discovered there in 1874. Fighting broke out between U.S. soldiers and Sioux warriors for control of the Black Hills. In the Battle of Little Bighorn, a Sioux-Cheyenne force wiped out General **George Armstrong Custer** and his army of 250. Like Red Cloud's victory, this one proved only temporary; in the end, the well-equipped government forces outnumbered and overpowered the Sioux. Crazy Horse, a leading warrior, finally surrendered in 1877.

That same year, **Chief Joseph** of the peaceful Nez Percé was forced to fight white soldiers. With only 300 warriors, Joseph defeated a force of several thousand before leading his band on a lengthy journey to safety in Canada. The U.S. Army caught up with Joseph's band thirty miles from the border and the chief had to surrender. Afterward, Indian-white relations in the Plains and Northwest quieted for a time. But disharmony continued in the Southwest. The Apache Wars broke out in the 1870s after a massacre of Indians by troops in Arizona. Warriors conducted raids under leaders such as Geronimo, who surrendered in 1886. Then all three frontiers, the Plains, the Northwest, and the Southwest, grew quiet.

An Indian reform movement meanwhile surfaced among whites in and out of government. Directed by R. H. Pratt, the first Indian boarding school opened in 1879. The Carlisle School enrolled as many as 1,000 students, training them in English, farming, cooking, and twenty different trades. Supported by **Carl Schurz,** head of the Bureau of Indian Affairs, the school intended to blend Indians into mainstream America. Other reformers, with the same goal, began in 1883 to hold annual conferences to discuss reforms in Indian affairs at Lake Mohonk, New York. Their recommendations influenced the government, leading to an attempt to break up reservations.

Passed by Congress in 1887, the Dawes Act (Dawes Severalty Act) proposed to divide Indian reservations into private 160-acre parcels for Indian families. Orphans would get smaller shares, and any tribal lands left over after the division would be sold to whites. Indians, it was believed, would then settle down to farm in the style of mainstream America, and tribal bonds would be destroyed. Described by Theodore Roosevelt as a mighty engine designed to break up America's tribal mass, the Dawes Act certainly reduced Indian territory. Within two decades, America's native nations had lost 60 percent of the territory they held in 1887.

Some of the Indians tried to resist the whites by performing the Ghost Dance. Started in Nevada by Paiute Indians, it began to spread in 1889 when the prophet Wovoka predicted the white race would be stamped out by natural disasters. Indians could avoid these disasters, he counseled, by performing a dance, which would bring back their dead friends and renew their strength. The movement spread to Sioux, Cheyenne, Arapaho, Comanche and other Plains tribes, with hundreds of Indians dancing feverishly and fearful whites trying to stop them. In the process, Chief Sitting Bull of the Hunkpapa Sioux was murdered (1890), after which some of his followers fled their reservation. Pursued by the U.S. Army, they tried to surrender at Wounded Knee Creek, but fighting broke out and nearly 300 men, women, and children were massacred in the last bloody conflict of the century.

George Armstrong Custer

1839-1876

Personal Background

George Armstrong Custer was born on December 5, 1839, in New Rumley, Ohio. Called Armstrong or "Autie" (as he pronounced it as a child), he was the first child of his parents' marriage, though both had other children by spouses who had died. Emanuel Custer worked as a blacksmith before buying a small farm, where he and his wife Mary raised their family. Autie was followed by three younger brothers and a sister: Nevin, Thomas, Boston, and Margaret. The Custer boys were a high-spirited bunch, working hard on the farm and playing hard when finished. They ran, wrestled, rode horses, hunted, and loved to play practical jokes on one another.

Reluctant student. Though Mary Custer ran the household, her daughter from her previous marriage, Lydia Ann Kirkpatrick, looked after the younger children most of the time. Older than Autie by fourteen years, Ann grew especially close to the active, blond youngster. He visited her a few times after she married and moved to Michigan. At fourteen, he moved to live with her and her husband, David Reed, in Monroe, on the western shore of Lake Erie. There he attended Stebbins Academy, returning home in the summers to help with farmwork. He did not care for school and only studied when he was interested, which was not often. His grades were unremarkable. At sixteen he moved back home and went to school in nearby Hopeville.

▲ **George Armstrong Custer**

Event: Indian wars; Battle of the Little Bighorn.

Role: For a decade, from 1866 to 1876, General Custer and his famous Seventh Cavalry pursued and fought the Sioux Indians in the Dakota Territory. At the Little Bighorn River in 1876, the Sioux and their allies met Custer and his attacking force and wiped them out completely.

Leader. When the Custer boys went on their adventures, Autie was the leader, not only because of his age, but also because of his personality and athletic ability. He was slim but wiry and muscular, and his endurance amazed his friends, as it later would his fellow soldiers. He never seemed to get tired. When he was not getting into scrapes with his brothers or friends, he often could be found chasing after local girls.

West Point. In 1857, by writing to his congressman, Autie won a prized appointment to the U.S. Military Academy at West Point, New York. There he quickly became well-known, though not for academic achievement. Caring even less for regulations than for schoolwork, he began piling up school warnings, called "skins." Cadets were allowed 100 skins in a six-month period before being dismissed. Custer came within ten skins of dismissal over and over again, but he always managed to mend his ways in the nick of time. His close calls with disciplinary problems gave rise to talk of "Custer's Luck." Already an excellent horseman, he excelled at riding drills, outstripping others at jumps and hurdles and learning to use a sword on stuffed dummies while racing by on horseback. He continued to play hard, but after a night of drinking while home for vacation, he promised his sister that he would never drink again. He kept his promise.

Staff officer. In 1861, just as the Civil War was breaking out, Custer graduated from West Point as a second lieutenant in the U.S. Cavalry's Second Regiment. He served on the staff of several generals, including that of General George McClellan, commander of the Union forces, who made Custer a captain. His job was to gather information for the general during battle. Still a boy barely out of his teens, Custer threw himself into the job without regard for his own safety. He roamed tirelessly along the battle line, encouraging the troops, fighting alongside them, and sometimes leading them in charges himself. All the while, he kept up close observation of battle conditions. McClellan later gave this account of Custer's performance:

> In these days Custer was simply a reckless, gallant boy, undeterred by fatigue, unconscious of fear; but his head was always clear in danger and he always brought me clear and intelligible

reports of what he saw under the heaviest fire. I became much attached to him. (Utley, p. 19)

Judge's daughter. McClellan, himself too cautious in attacking, was replaced as overall commander in 1862, and Custer went to spend the winter at Ann's in Monroe. There Elizabeth Bacon, a lively girl two years younger than he, caught the young man's eye. Slender and stylish, with shiny brown hair and a beautiful face, "Libbie" also possessed charm and intelligence. Custer began paying her frequent visits. However, her father, who was a judge and one of the town's leading citizens, did not look kindly on Custer's courting his daughter. Not only was the young man from a lower social class, but he was a soldier. Custer continued his visits to Libbie and found time to see other girls as well.

Brigade. In the spring of 1863, Custer was assigned to the staff of General Alfred Pleasanton, commander of the cavalry corps of the Army of the Potomac. He soon proved once again his talent for gathering dangerous intelligence on the enemy, as well as his ability to lead other men in combat. He also began thinking about his next promotion, which seemed slow in coming. He knew that, like McClellan, Pleasanton valued and liked him. Yet other West Point graduates his age were already colonels. On June 28, Custer was amazed to receive a letter addressed to Brigadier General George A. Custer. At Pleasanton's order, the twenty-three-year-old had jumped four ranks to become the youngest general in the Union army. He was to command his own cavalry brigade.

Gettysburg. A week later, the new general was tested in one of the war's bloodiest battles, as the Confederates attacked the Union army at Gettysburg, Pennsylvania. Custer's brigade, made up of the four regiments of the Michigan cavalry serving in the Union forces, was one of three at Gettysburg that faced the feared "Invincibles," the Confederate cavalry of General "Jeb" Stuart. Since the beginning of the war, Stuart's expert horsemen had defeated their Union opponents at every turn.

Wolverines. The cavalry battle took place well to the east of the main battle between the foot soldiers. Stuart wished to break through the Union cavalry and swing around to attack the main Union lines from the rear as the Confederate foot soldiers hit from the front. Time and again the gray horsemen charged, and each time Custer's blue-clad Michigan forces held them off. Twice, leading the countercharge, Custer rallied his troops, shouting, "Come on, you Wolverines!" (Utley, p. 23). (Wolverines are small but fierce forest animals common in Michigan.) For the first time, Stuart was stopped in his tracks, and much of the credit went to the fearless young man who had been general less than a week. If Stuart had broken through, Gettysburg might have been a major loss for the North, rather than an important victory.

With his long, curly blond hair, a wide red sash tied around his neck, a broad-collared sailor's shirt with general's stars on the collar and shoulder, and the personal red and blue flag with crossed white swords that followed him everywhere, Custer was easy to spot in the confused fighting. As he led them to further victories, many of his "Wolverines" began sporting red sashes of their own, proud to belong to the cavalry's best brigade.

Boy general. For the rest of the war, Custer kept up an unbroken series of brilliant victories, showing both energetic courage in battle and a flawless grasp of combat tactics. After Gettysburg, the "Boy General" was the favorite of the newspapers, which closely followed his exploits. His successes helped win over Libbie and her hesitant father, and in the spring of 1864, the two were married in Monroe. Libby returned with her new husband to the brigade's headquarters, setting a pattern for the future in which she would accompany Custer wherever possible.

Later that spring, Pleasanton was replaced as cavalry commander by General Philip Sheridan. Again, Custer's energy, talent, and reliability won the trust and affection of his superior. Sheridan soon promoted him to major general, in command of a full division (several brigades). Sheridan's friendship would be important to Custer in the years to come, because after the war it was Sheridan who was put in charge of U.S. Army operations in the West.

Participation: Indian Wars

Soldier in peacetime. The war ended in 1865, and Custer led his division in the celebratory parade past the White House. It was a festive occasion, with President Abraham Lincoln and other leaders reviewing the troops. When a little girl in the crowd threw a bunch of flowers in front of Custer's horse, the horse suddenly bolted and ran out of control past the president. On its back sat Custer in his dress uniform, his red sash and long blond hair blowing in the wind. People wondered whether Custer—an expert rider—really lost control of the horse or whether he merely seized the chance to show off.

If he was only putting on a show, it was his last shot at glory for a while, because events during peacetime proved far different from the excitement of wartime. Custer was given command of a new cavalry division in eastern Texas to establish federal control of the former Confederate state and keep an eye on Mexico at the same time. But by now most soldiers—largely volunteers rather than career soldiers—wanted to go home. They lacked the enthusiasm of earlier times, resisting orders, deserting in large numbers, and treating the local population badly. Custer, trying to establish discipline, punished offenders harshly, threatening them with the firing squad for desertion or disobedience. He became unpopular for the first time and felt as distant from his men as they did from him.

Command of the Seventh. With the end of the war, settlers had begun moving west in huge numbers. Gold and silver mines, railroads, cattle ranches, farms, and towns appeared, as the nation's postwar prosperity brought an age of expansion. In the way of this push westward stood the Indians, some 300,000 of whom lived west of the Mississippi River. Most of those not killed by white diseases had already been conquered and moved onto reservations. They fell under the control of the Department of the Interior's Bureau of Indian Affairs. A few tribes, though, held out against the whites in a last attempt to retain their land. Numbering about 100,000, tribes included the Apache in the Southwest, the Paiute in the Northwest, and the Nez Percé and Ute in the Rockies. In the Great Plains, where the Seventh Calvary was stationed, fierce resistance came from the Sioux, the Cheyenne, the Arapaho, the Kiowa, and the Comanche.

In early 1867, Custer took command of the Seventh Cavalry Regiment, headquartered in Fort Riley, Kansas. His new assignment was to control these tribes and to protect the white settlers.

Court-martial. Custer got into trouble with the army on his very first campaign in the West. Desertion remained a problem, and one group of men rode off in plain sight of their commanding officers. Enraged, Custer ordered some soldiers to catch them and "bring none back alive" (Utley, p. 52). Wisely, the soldiers did not follow the order, but they did fire on the deserters, killing one and wounding two others. Custer also took his men with him on an exhausting and dangerous journey to meet Libbie and escort her to their headquarters, when she could easily have gone most of the way by train. One man was killed by Indians and another wounded when Custer sent them back to look for a lost horse, but he did not stop to find and help the soldiers.

The army did not take kindly to such behavior. At a court-martial (military trial), Custer was convicted of unauthorized absence from his command and mistreatment of the captured deserters. The court suspended him without pay for a year. His friends offered their support, declaring that Custer had been persecuted by those jealous of him. Further softening the blow, Sheridan offered the Custers his personal house at Fort Leavenworth, Kansas, for the winter of 1867-68. Sheridan himself took a long leave and would assume command of the army's western operations in 1868.

Reinventing a legend. Custer's first western campaign had ended not only with trouble from the army, but also with complete failure against the Indians. Throughout the West, soldiers had to get used to a new way of fighting. Tactics designed to work against other soldiers in eastern fields and woods were useless against a new enemy in a new landscape. Yet Custer's self-confidence allowed him to adapt. As he learned the ways of the West, he would also replace the image of Custer the Boy General with Custer the Frontier Indian Fighter, adding another colorful dimension to his own legend.

Total war. A telegram reached Custer on September 24, 1868, two months before his year-long suspension was due to end. It was signed by Sheridan.

> Generals Sherman, Sully and myself, and nearly all the officers of your regiment, have asked for you.... Can you come at once? Eleven companies of your regiment will move about the 1st of October against hostile Indians. (Utley, p. 57)

Campaigns against the Indians over the summer had bogged down completely, as small scouting parties under Sully failed to stop the

▲ A Sioux encampment

Indian raids on white settlers. Sheridan and Sherman now wanted
to try a new strategy. They would copy Sherman's policy of total
war, which had been used to defeat the South in the Civil War. They
would make war on the whole population, not just the fighting men.
They would burn the Indians' villages and crops, kill their horses,
and interrupt their hunting, pursuing them through the winter until
hunger and cold forced their surrender. Sheridan chose Custer as
the man to carry out this plan.

Washita. There was no time to waste, for the plan relied on taking advantage of harsh winter conditions. Custer joined the Seventh Regiment at Fort Dodge, Kansas, in mid-October. Five weeks later, in late November, the first snows had fallen as the regiment rode out of Dodge in search of Indian villages. The villages they sought lay clustered together about 100 miles south, in the Washita River Valley. There some 6,000 Cheyenne, Arapaho, Kiowa, and Comanche had set up their winter *tipis* or shelters. One group of Cheyenne was led by Black Kettle, a chief who struggled to keep peace between his people and the invading whites. While younger warriors constantly pressed for war, Black Kettle had just returned from nearby Fort Cobb, where he had talked the situation over with the colonel in charge.

Custer and his men, following tracks in the snow, came upon Black Kettle's village late in the evening of November 26, at the end of a hard day's march. They attacked early the next morning, striking from four directions at once. Caught sleeping, the Cheyenne could organize no defense. Some managed to get away, but many others were captured or killed, including women and children. Black Kettle and his wife lay among the dead. One group of twenty soldiers, under a Major Elliott, was wiped out by warriors from the larger villages downstream. Under the threat from this stronger force, Custer withdrew his 800 men.

Indian fighter and author. The Battle of the Washita River and the following campaign that winter cleared the Kansas area of Indians the army called "hostile." It also established Custer as the foremost Indian fighter in the public's mind, a reputation he would maintain until his death. Over the next several years, there were no major campaigns. Instead, the Custers enjoyed an active social life at army outposts such as Fort Leavenworth, Kansas.

Custer also began publishing magazine articles about his exploits. The articles were enormously successful and were collected in book form in 1874 under the title *My Life on the Plains.* (His enemies accused him of stretching the truth to make himself look better; one called the book *My Lie on the Plains.)* Custer began wearing fringed buckskin jackets and taking well-publicized hunting trips on the Plains. At the same time, on trips east he dabbled in Washington politics and New York business, experiencing little success at either. His instincts, so well suited to battle, failed him when faced with wily, experienced senators or financial wizards from Wall Street.

Railroad. By the early 1870s, Sherman and Sheridan had decided that the army had one crucial ally in its struggle for control of the Plains: the railroad. The tracks of the "iron horse" split the great herds of buffalo on which the Indians relied for food and clothing. The trains also brought settlers to populate the vast western lands and made it easier to move troops rapidly. The Indians, too, realized the railroad's importance. As the Northern Pacific Railroad began laying tracks through the Dakota Territory in the early 1870s, the Sioux and others who occupied the lands resisted fiercely. The army's primary task in the West, therefore, became the protection of the railroad's builders. In 1873 Custer's Seventh Calvary was assigned to Fort Abraham Lincoln, near Bismarck in present-day North Dakota.

Yellowstone and the Black Hills. That summer, the Seventh accompanied railroad workers west past the Yellowstone River in present-day Montana. The expedition was attacked twice, on August 4 and again on August 11. Both times, Custer's cool and resourceful leadership kept his force from being overcome by superior numbers of well-armed Sioux. The following year, Custer led an expedition to the Black Hills in the western Dakota Territory to check on reports of gold there. He enjoyed the expeditions hugely, hunting and collecting numerous samples of wildlife. Some animals he sent to zoos back east; others he carefully stuffed and added to his own growing collection.

Sioux dissatisfaction. The Black Hills fell within the area promised to the Sioux by an 1868 treaty with the government. When Custer's expedition confirmed the rumors of gold in the area, would-be prospectors rushed to the hills and the government began pushing the Sioux to sell. Many Sioux were angered, especially young warriors who followed the intelligent, powerful, and very independent Sioux chief Sitting Bull. Yet the Sioux remained peaceful; they did not attack the whites who, despite government promises, flooded their land looking for gold.

Looking for an excuse to seize the land, the government gave up any attempts to stop the invading whites. When that failed to pro-

▲ Sitting Bull

voke the Sioux, government officials demanded that Sitting Bull and his numerous followers report to the Bureau of Indian Affairs by January 31, 1876, or face the army. The government knew that the Indians would not report. However, officials needed an excuse to drive the Indians off land that had been promised to them but which public opinion now demanded be opened to whites.

Little Bighorn campaign. Failing to provoke the Sioux or round them up, the government planned a major campaign against them for 1876. Custer and the Seventh were sent to locate the large Sioux bands led by Sitting Bull and the Sioux war leader Crazy Horse. The Sioux, with Cheyenne allies, were thought to be camped somewhere near the Little Bighorn River, south of the Yellowstone River in Montana. On May 17, 1876, against a background of band music and newspaper reporters taking notes on Custer's "dashing suit of buckskin," the Seventh set off from Fort Lincoln (Utley, p. 165).

Last Stand. Unknown to Custer, large numbers of Sioux from the Dakota Reservation were also heading west to find Sitting Bull and his followers. Over a single week in mid-June, Sitting Bull's village grew from 3,000 to 7,000 people, including about 2,000 warriors. Custer's Seventh Regiment, by contrast, numbered about 650. Custer and his men came upon the village on June 25, along the Little Bighorn River.

As in earlier campaigns, Custer believed speed was essential. He was more concerned that the Sioux would get away than that they would fight. Accordingly, he divided the regiment into three groups, one under himself, another under Major Marcus Reno, and the third under Captain Frederick Benteen. Benteen and Reno would push in from the east, preventing escape, while Custer made a direct strike on the village itself. Reno attacked first, but the Indians forced him to retreat across the Little Bighorn River, where he was joined by Benteen.

Meanwhile, with around 200 men, Custer hit the village, but Benteen and Reno were unable to fight through to support him. The Indians reacted quickly, forcing Reno to retreat. Custer's group was overwhelmed and every man killed, including Custer and his younger brothers Tom and Boston. Only twenty-two Sioux perished in the fighting.

▲ A Sioux depiction of the Battle of Little Big Horn

Aftermath

Controversy. Although Custer became a legendary figure in American history, there are many different interpretations of both his life and his death. In the past, he has been seen as a frontier hero. More recently, as the crimes committed against the American Indians have been recognized, he has appeared as the perfect example of the Indian-hating white man bent on wiping out the Indians. Similarly, some blame him for recklessness and poor judgment at Little Bighorn, while others point to the failure of Benteen and Reno to come to his aid.

As often is the case, the truth probably lies between the extremes. There is evidence that Custer admired much about the Indians, but he shared the anti-Indian attitudes common among whites of his time, particularly among military men. And there is no reason to suppose that his military judgment deserted him for the

48

first time at Little Bighorn, though he might have considered the possibility that there would be many more Sioux than he knew about. Perhaps he simply came to the end of Custer's Luck.

Army Losses at Battle of Little Bighorn

	Officers	Enlisted Men	Scouts and Civilians	Total
Killed on the Custer field	13	193	4	210
Killed on the Reno field	3	44	6	53
Total	16	237	10	263

(Adapted from Gray, pp. 406-407)

Fruitless victory. Though the Sioux won an inspiring victory at Little Bighorn, most had been driven out of the Black Hills by the end of 1876. Sitting Bull fled to Canada, and upon his return in 1881, he was imprisoned for two years. Crazy Horse, persuaded to give himself up, was imprisoned with his men; he was killed while trying to escape. The Sioux surrendered after Sitting Bull's return in 1881, and in 1890 U.S. troops killed more than 200 Sioux at Wounded Knee, South Dakota. Just before the massacre, Sitting Bull was killed as he led his people in protest against the government. Today, some 30,000 Sioux live on reservations in the Dakotas.

For More Information

Connell, Evan S. *Son of the Morning Star.* San Francisco: North Point Press, 1984.

Gray, John S. *Custer's Last Campaign.* Lincoln: University of Nebraska Press, 1991.

Utley, Robert M. *Cavalier in Buckskin: George Armstrong Custer and the Western Military Frontier.* Norman: University of Oklahoma Press, 1988.

Carl Schurz

1829-1906

Personal Background

The Schurz family. Schurz humorously begins his autobiography by saying he was "born in a castle" (Schurz, p. 3). Though he was indeed born in a castle on the Rhine River in Germany on March 2, 1829, his parents were poor. Peasants worked the land of the castle owner and lived in small homes on the castle grounds. In time, these homes gathered into villages with their own leader, or *burghalfen*. Schurz's grandfather worked the castle lands and was the *burghalfen* of the peasants living there. Schurz's father, Christian, was a teacher in the nearby town of Liblar but did not earn much money, so he, his wife, Marianne (Jüssen), and the children lived with Christian's parents at the castle.

Early life. When Carl was four years old, the family moved into a very small two-story house in Liblar, a town of about 800 people with just one main cobblestone road. There is no record that Schurz lived and played differently from the other peasant boys, but his father did recognize very early that his son was a good student and was interested in music. He converted part of the home into a hardware store to supplement his teacher's pay of ninety dollars a month so that he could follow his dream of sending Carl to the "gymnasium," the German high school.

Carl's sixth year was a memorable one because the family

▲ Carl Schurz

Event: Establishing government policy regarding the Indians in the West.

Role: Carl Schurz, a German exile, escaped to America, where he became an editor, then a United States senator and a Civil War general. Appointed secretary of the interior in 1877, he was responsible for the Bureau of Indian Affairs and made far-reaching decisions about movements of Indian tribes from their lands.

acquired a small piano, and he was placed in the Liblar village school. Because he had already been taught to read and write by his father, he attended for only three years before he was sent to a more challenging school in nearby Brühl. There he studied reading, writing, Latin, and music. One year later, he was ready to move on to secondary school in Cologne, then a major city of 90,000 people. His father arranged for him to board with a local locksmith.

Meanwhile, Christian's hardware business failed to grow as he had hoped and, at the same time, Carl's grandfather retired. To ensure income for the family, Christian decided to construct another building near the hardware business, a place to rent out for meetings and parties that had a grain store above it. This venture fared so poorly that brothers and brothers-in-law pooled their resources to rescue the family fortunes. Christian sold all the property in Liblar and moved to Bonn.

Bonn was a university town, and Christian decided to build a restaurant where students could eat. He borrowed money from a friend to build the restaurant and a nice home for the family, but then the buyer of his Liblar property failed to meet the contract. Without that money, Christian went bankrupt, and he was sent to debtor's prison.

The family businessman. Carl was then seventeen years old and preparing to take the very difficult entrance exams for the university. But the family's bankruptcy brought that dream to an end, and he left school to help rescue his father. By making business arrangements with family friends and acquaintances, Carl soon satisfied the creditors and secured his father's release from prison.

University student. The family circumstances, however, did not recover enough for Schurz to live again in Cologne and attend the gymnasium. Still he was determined. He studied for the university entrance exams on his own. While he studied for the gymnasium final exam he began to attend classes at the University of Bonn as an "irregular" student. Eventually he passed the exams and was admitted as a regular student.

Schurz planned to become a professor of history. In the winter of 1847, he attended the class of a young professor, Gottfried

Kinkel, who was to greatly influence his life. The two became life-long friends.

Rebellion and democracy. By early 1848, the rebellion that would establish democracy in France had begun and was spreading over the assortment of small states that now make up Germany but were then governed by Prussia. The news ended Schurz's university career and his ambitions to become a history professor. He joined a growing student movement that was fighting for a democratic government to replace the autocratic Prussian rule. Kinkel was a leader of the student rebellion, and he and Schurz became very active in the new Democratic party. Together they published a newspaper, *Bonner Zeitung,* in which they encouraged university students to rebel.

The move for democracy was partly successful. University students pressed for an American-style constitution and were promised one. The German states held elections, and Frederick Williams IV, the king of Prussia, was elected to be Emperor of a German National Empire with the promise of reforming the government. Frederick, however, changed his mind and refused the honor, and riots spread across Germany. Many Germans fled from this anarchy to America, where a new discovery of gold was offering great opportunities. In this turmoil, Frederick withdrew his promise for democracy and began an armed effort to subdue the rebels. Kinkel and Schurz fought courageously in the small German states along the Rhine River, but in vain. Within a year, students throughout the region were defeated, and the leaders, including Schurz, were imprisoned and sentenced to death.

Schurz was held in Rastatt, a walled and heavily guarded town-sized prison. Knowing his ultimate fate, he decided to escape. The prison's sewage system emptied into the river, so Schurz lowered himself into the sewer and crawled under the prison wall to re-emerge through a manhole near the river. From there, French officials boated him to French soil. He fled to Paris and then to London.

Schurz rescues Kinkel. In London, Schurz learned that Kinkel was still in prison. He immediately left for Germany intent on rescuing his friend. He planned to disguise himself, a challenge considering his distinctive appearance: Schurz was blond, heavily bearded, and at five feet eleven inches tall, considerably taller than the average man of his day. (At the same time, he was so thin that cartoonists would later make fun of his stature.) Nevertheless, he risked capture and returned to Germany. He safely reached the prison and bribed a prison guard to help in the escape on November 6, 1850. In the dark of night, the guard lowered Kinkel by rope through the window of his upstairs prison room. Schurz was waiting below to join his friend, and the two made a frantic flight across Germany to Zürich and freedom.

Once on free soil, Kinkel decided to test his fortunes in Scotland, while Schurz went to Paris. However, the two rebels were now internationally famous, and the Paris police asked Schurz—considered an undesirable troublemaker—to leave France. He moved to London, where he taught German for two years before deciding to leave Europe to try his fortune in America. Before he left, he married a young woman he had met in England, Margarethe Meyer, who also was a displaced German. They married on July 6, 1852, and left for America in August. During their marriage, which ended with Margarethe's death in 1876, they lived sometimes together and sometimes apart because of Margarethe's ill health and her preference for recovery in Europe. The Schurz family would grow to include two daughters and two sons.

American citizen. Arriving in New York in September 1852, the Schurzes almost immediately became involved in American politics. They visited Washington, D.C., where Schurz became acquainted with some of the congressmen, and settled for nearly three years in Philadelphia. Schurz decided to become an American citizen and studied English intensely. He mastered the language in three years while working as an editor of German-language newspapers.

After a brief return to Europe because of his wife's ill health, the Schurz family moved to Waterton, Wisconsin, which was heavily populated with new German immigrants. Schurz's ability to speak in both English and German made him popular with politicians, and Schurz became active in the Republican party. While studying law, he campaigned for a variety of political causes. For example, he spoke among the German Americans in favor of Abraham Lincoln during the famous Lincoln-Douglas debates. He began to practice law and to spend much of his time traveling the country speaking out about the issues of the day. He was quick to attack the new Fugitive Slave Law and became a spokesman for emancipation. At the 1860 Republican National Convention, at which Lincoln was selected as the party's presidential candidate, Schurz headed the team of delegates from Wisconsin. He then campaigned for Lincoln, particularly among new German Americans.

Civil War general. When Lincoln was elected president, he made Schurz minister to France. However, the Civil War was beginning, and events were not going well for the North. On assignment in France, Schurz decided in the early months of 1862 he could no longer stand being so far from combat. He returned to America and was commissioned brigadier general of a volunteer group. His division became part of the troops commanded by General John C. Frémont, who had become a major general. Schurz had once been in awe of the western explorer Frémont and had campaigned for his presidential nomination in 1856. But he was soon disillusioned:

> I heard him spoken of in Washington as one of the coming heroes of the conflict, in almost extravagant terms.... [He] was, indeed, promptly made a major general in the regular army, and entrusted with the command of the Department of the West.... But he sorely disappointed the sanguine expectations of his friends. He displayed no genius for organization. Frémont's headquarters seemed to have a marked attraction for rascally speculators of all sorts, and there was much scandal caused by the awarding of profitable contracts to persons of bad repute. (Schurz, p. 198)

Carl Schurz on Freedom of Speech

Just before the Civil War, many Northerners tried to suppress any speeches that might anger the South. A group of abolitionists had just been driven out of Boston when Schurz spoke there about free speech: "If there is a light that may guide us in the storm, it is the protection of liberty extended to all, the rights of individuals mutually respected.... Then the freedom of thought, and the freedom of utterance, may issue from this crisis ... not only as the great agency of progress, but as the firmest bulwark of peace and order ... as the great safety-valve of the social machinery." (Schurz, p. 239)

Schurz proved to be an effective, if not glamorous, war leader. He led troops in the second Battle of Bull Run and at Chancellorsville, Chattanooga, and Gettysburg. As the war drew to a close, his troops joined those of General William Tecumseh Sherman in

North Carolina. As soon as peace was restored, Schurz resigned his commission and returned to his work as an editor. After a brief tour of the South to survey its readiness to rejoin the Union, he became editor of the *Denver Post* and then the *Westliche Post,* a German-language newspaper in St. Louis. Schurz meanwhile remained involved in politics. In 1869 he became U.S. senator from Missouri.

U.S. senator. As senator, Schurz was an outspoken opponent of the policies of President Ulysses S. Grant. Schurz opposed American involvement in Santo Domingo, the president's military approach to rebuilding the South, and Grant's decision to sell arms to France. In 1875 Schurz actively campaigned for Rutherford Hayes in his bids for governorship of Ohio and then, the following year, for the presidency of the United States. When Hayes was elected president, he appointed Schurz secretary of the interior. Schurz thus served as senator and cabinet member, the two highest political offices that could be held by a naturalized citizen. As secretary of the interior, he became involved in Indian affairs.

Participation:
The Settlement of Displaced Indian Groups

Bureau of Indian Affairs. In 1876 the Department of the Interior included the Bureau of Indian Affairs. It was a sometimes corrupt, often disorganized bureau that had, until 1849, been supervised by the War Department and still frequently followed a strategy of extermination of the Indians. Schurz took over a bureau that often had to turn to the War Department for help, though it was supposedly run by a commissioner of Indian Affairs who was advised by a civilian board appointed by the secretary of the interior. The commissioner oversaw agents responsible for nearly every Indian tribe. Communication between the commissioner and the Indian agents was frequently not as direct as between the agents and the local representatives of the army. Using this awkward arrangement, the bureau oversaw a policy of relocating Indian groups onto reservations, most frequently on parcels of land in Indian Territory, now present-day Oklahoma.

Schurz's view. With little previous knowledge of native Americans, Schurz at first favored their relocation. He allowed, and even supported, moving the Nez Percé tribe under Chief Joseph to new land. When the northern Cheyenne rebelled and tried to return to their former land, he allowed the army to round them up and return them to the reservation. He supported similar treatment for the Apache. However, Schurz had a history as a humanitarian; he was, for example, an early champion of total emancipation for black slaves. As he grew more familiar with the plight of the Indians, he began to listen to civilian leaders such as William Welsh of Philadelphia and General John Pope, both of whom had much experience with the Indians. They supported treating the Indians with dignity and trying to integrate them into American society. (This approach would, of course, deny Indians the right to continue their own life-styles, a fact humanitarians of the day failed to appreciate.) Schurz soon adopted this idea. He ordered Indian schools to be built at Hampton Institute (Virginia), Carlisle Barracks (Pennsylvania), and Forest Grove (Oregon) for training Indian peoples in English and in white life-styles and land ownership policies. To begin Indian reorganization, Schurz created an Indian police force.

House cleaning. However, no attempt to help the Indians would ever be effective unless the Bureau of Indian Affairs was turned into a trustworthy organization. Schurz told Commissioner John Q. Smith to investigate rumors of corruption among the agents. Smith, however, was a holdover from a previous department and was quick to defend the Indian agents. Nothing came of his investigation. Still convinced that changes needed to be made, Schurz created in 1877 a new board of inquiry to investigate the bureau. This board found that corruption was indeed widespread in the bureau. Indian agents were growing rich by appropriating food and other materials intended for Indian tribes and selling these goods for profit. Chief Clerk S. A. Galpin turned a deaf ear to the Indian accusations against these agents, and Smith supported Galpin.

General of the Army William Tecumseh Sherman saw this friction as an opportunity to restore the Bureau of Indian Affairs to the War Department. He sided with Smith and Galpin. However, Sherman had not counted on Schurz's ability to organize a strong argument and to speak in public. In a speech to Congress on December 6, 1878, Schurz thoroughly convinced members that it would be

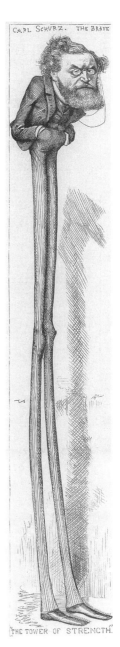

CARL SCHURZ. THE BRAVE

'THE TOWER OF STRENGTH'.

▲ Schurz was lampooned in the press because of his beliefs and physique folly to turn Indian affairs over to a War Department that preferred to kill off the native Americans. Preventing a takeover of Indian affairs by the War Department may have been Schurz's greatest contribution to the Indians.

Career setback. That same year, Schurz was given an insoluble problem by a small group of Indians, the Ponca, who earlier had been moved from South Dakota to a reservation in Oklahoma. Some of them wanted to return to their original homeland while most were satisfied to remain in Oklahoma. Meanwhile, white Americans were pressing for land in Indian Territory. Any loss of Indian population there, Schurz thought, would open the door for these whites to seize Indian land. He opposed the return of a few Ponca under Chief Standing Bear to their original land. Although most of the Ponca agreed with Schurz, the decision drew wide criticism from the few eastern white people who were beginning to press for better treatment of the Indians. They criticized Schurz so severely that he never recovered his earlier reputation.

Schurz could not regain his status even when he successfully resolved a Ute incident that threatened an uprising by the civilians and army in Colorado. A few Ute there had killed the Indian agent Nathan C. Maky and kidnaped his wife and daughters. The white population in Colorado, along with the military, demanded that the Ute be punished, or better yet, exterminated. Schurz personally took charge of the affair. Through negotiations with Chief Willie Ouray, he arranged for the return of the women and the surrender of some of the Ute involved in the kidnaping. In return, the Ute people were left alone, although some of them were relocated to Utah. Ouray was so grateful for the way Schurz handled the affair that he willed Schurz his deerskin jacket and pants, powder horn, and tobacco pouch. Schurz treasured these gifts for the rest of his life.

Schurz's treatment of Indian peoples, however humanitarian his intent, did not always satisfy either whites or Indians. Some whites admired his readiness to examine the wrongs done to Indian peoples, but many Indians opposed his early defense of the reservation system, just as many opposed his later attempts to integrate Indians into white society and teach them white practices of land ownership. On learning of Schurz's death, one Indian leader reportedly said, "Good!"

Schurz resigned as secretary of the interior in 1881 but continued to be active in politics at home and abroad. He discussed reform with Germany's leader, Otto von Bismarck, advising him as he instituted health, accident, disability, and old age insurance in Germany. Schurz also pressed for the building of the Panama Canal. Meanwhile, his successors in the cabinet continued to pursue his reservation policy toward the country's Indian peoples.

> **Other Activities of Carl Schurz**
>
> **1881-1883** Editor-in-chief of the *New York Evening Post.*
>
> **1884** Leader of the "mugwump" movement demanding reform within the Republican party.
>
> **1892-1901** President of the National Civil Service Reform League.

By 1884 Schurz had returned to writing and editing. He began a history of the United States by publishing a pamphlet titled *The New South.* Schurz also published a biography of statesman Henry Clay. For four years, he traveled in Europe as an agent for the Hamburg-American Steamship Company. In 1892 he became editor of *Harper's Weekly.* For the next six years he would use this position to press for the civil service reform for which he had seen a need as he battled corruption in the Bureau of Indian Affairs. He also used the *Weekly* to oppose what he saw as the trend in America toward empire building.

Retiring from *Harper's* in 1898, Schurz devoted his last years to speaking and writing. He began his autobiography, *Reminiscences.* Carl Schurz, having attained the two highest political offices attainable by a naturalized citizen and having championed reform throughout his life, died in New York City on May 14, 1906.

For More Information

Schurz, Carl. *The Speeches of Carl Schurz.* Philadelphia: J. B. Lippencott and Co., 1865.

Trefousse, Hans L. *Carl Schurz, A Biography.* Knoxville: University of Tennessee Press, 1982.

Wershch, Rüdiger, editor. *Carl Schurz.* München, Germany: Heinz Moos Verlag München, 1979.

Chief Joseph

1840-1904

Personal Background

Chief Joseph was born on the plains of what is now Oregon in the summer of 1840. He was a tall, statuesque boy with black eyes and smooth, copper-toned skin. Joseph's younger brother, Ollokot, looked like him, and when they stood together dressed in their tribal clothing, they were often mistaken for identical twins. Young Joseph and Ollokot were sons of the great Chief Tu-eka-kas, or Old Joseph, a Cayuse Indian, and one of his Nez Percé wives. Aside from Ollokot, Joseph had another brother, Shugun, and two sisters, Celia and Elawmonmi.

Physical and spiritual training. Under the guidance of his parents, Joseph learned at an early age to hunt, fish, and gather medicinal herbs and roots. He skillfully made spears from the wood of red fir trees and carved knives and arrows from stone. He quickly mastered the art of riding horses bareback and imitating animal calls.

Joseph's father taught respect for the land, the animals, his elders, and, most important, the Great Spirit who watched and guided the Nez Percé tribe. When Joseph was nine or ten years old, he was sent, like all other Nez Percé children, on a spiritual journey to communicate with the Spirit Chief. Stripped of all clothing and without food, Young Joseph climbed high atop a mountain over-

▲ Chief Joseph

Event: Indian resistance to white influence.

Role: Chief Joseph of the Nez Percé Indians devoted his life to the protection of his people's land in northeast Oregon and to peaceful resistance to the influence of the U.S. government.

looking his village and began praying to the Spirit Chief. According to another member of the Nez Percé tribe, Young Joseph fell asleep and, in a dream, saw what appeared to be "a man wrapped in a yellow blanket" coming to him (Howard, p. 41). The image of a man wrapped in a yellow blanket was the Nez Percé symbol for thunder. When Young Joseph came down the mountain and rejoined his family, a ceremony was held to give him his spiritual name, Hin-mah-too-yah-lat-kekt, meaning Thunder-rolling-in-the-mountains.

Joseph later told of spiritual teachings he received from other members of his tribe:

> Our fathers ... told us ... that we should never be the first to break a bargain; that it was a disgrace to tell a lie ... that it was a shame for one man to take from another ... his property without paying him for it. (Howard, p. 38)

Nez Percé history. The Nez Percé (meaning Pierced Nose) tribe was so named by French fur traders who noticed that some of the members wore dentalium shells in their pierced noses. Although this was not a tribal custom, it became an identifying factor for anyone outside the tribe. The Nez Percé preferred to call themselves by their original name, Numipu, or We People.

Physically, the people were strikingly tall and strong-boned, with copper-toned skin and dark eyes. The men and women traditionally wore their hair long and in two braids, with one side adorned with feathers. Jewelry fashioned out of dentalium shells, bear claws, and elk teeth was worn over robes of buckskin, otter-skin, and colorful beaded cloth.

The Nez Percé lived in bands in the Northwestern Territory, covering what is now parts of Idaho, Washington, and Oregon. Chief Joseph's band often resided in the Valley of Winding Waters, or Wallowa Valley, in northeast Oregon. In the spring and fall, the tribe migrated to Montana to hunt buffalo. During the summer and winter months, the men hunted and fished while the women gathered berries and herbs, made buckskin clothing, and wove baskets out of reeds. For warmth and shelter, they made tepees out of tree branches and buffalo hide.

It was customary for the Nez Percé to welcome those in need and to share anything they had in order to help others. They earned a reputation for peacefulness toward whites when Lewis and Clark (accompanied by the Shoshone translator Sacagawea) passed through their territory in 1805 on their way to the Pacific Ocean. The Nez Percé welcomed the white explorers, offering them food and a place to store their horses for many months. For seventy years, the Nez Percé had never shed a white man's blood—until they were forced to battle for their homeland.

Old Joseph. Joseph's father, Old Chief Joseph, struggled for many years to resist white influence. In 1855 Washington Territory governor Isaac Stevens asked Old Joseph and the Nez Percé to join a peace council. There Stevens asked the chief to sign a treaty giving over Indian land in exchange for blankets. Old Joseph refused because he believed that "no man owned any part of the earth, and a man could not sell what he did not own" (Howard, p. 25). Stevens again urged Old Joseph to sign. "Take away your paper," he replied. "I will not touch it with my hand" (Howard, p. 54). This first treaty had guaranteed the homelands of the different bands of Nez Percé, establishing a reservation of about 12,000 square miles (out of their original 30,000) that spread across Idaho, Oregon, and Washington.

The whites came back in 1863 with a new treaty. This one took away the beautiful Wallowa Valley and three-fourths of the remaining Nez Percé land, leaving the Indians with a very small reservation of about 550 square miles in what is now Idaho. Again Old Joseph refused to sign the treaty. To show his disdain for the treaty and all things related to white culture, including Christianity, he tore up a Bible he had received from a white missionary. Old Joseph also planted poles around the boundaries of the Wallowa Valley, parceling off the territory on which his people had lived peacefully for so many years.

Unfortunately, not all the Nez Percé agreed with Old Joseph. Several members of the tribe, including other chiefs, signed the treaty despite Old Joseph's warnings that the whites would take everything away and leave nothing. In 1871, shortly after his brave protest of the 1863 treaty, Old Chief Joseph died, passing his chieftainship on to his son, Young Joseph, who was about thirty years old at the time.

Participation: Indian Resistance

The new chief holds his ground. Not long after Joseph settled into his new position as chief, officials from the U.S. government came to him and ordered that his people leave the Wallowa Valley and live on the Lapwai reservation in Idaho, a place that the whites had chosen for the Nez Percé. Joseph refused, telling the officials that "we will defend this land as long as a drop of Indian blood warms the hearts of our men" (Brown, p. 318). Joseph petitioned President Ulysses S. Grant, whom he called the Great Father, to allow his people to stay in the valley. The petition convinced the president to serve an executive order on June 16, 1873, excluding the Wallowa Valley from white settlement.

Despite this triumph, more government men came and attempted to organize an Indian agency in the area. They offered to run schools for the young Nez Percé children. Again Joseph refused, knowing that the schools would teach the white man's religion. Committed to his own religious beliefs, he told the commissioners, "We never quarrel about God. We do not want to learn that" (Howard p. 93).

Greedy eyes. It seemed to Joseph that the whites would not take no for an answer. More officials and settlers came, feasting greedy eyes on Nez Percé land. Gold had been found in the mountains nearby, and settlers flocked to the area in search of riches. For years, Nez Percé horses and cattle had wandered through the area, but suddenly they were being stolen and branded by newcomers. Some whites went so far as to make the brazen claim that the Nez Percé were livestock thieves and a threat to peace in the area.

Thirty days. When the president heard these stories, he sent General Oliver Otis Howard to the area in 1877. Howard, whom the Nez Percé called One-Armed Soldier Chief, was instructed to force the band out of the valley and onto the Lapwai reservation, despite Grant's earlier order to keep settlers out of the Wallowa Valley. Joseph agreed to meet with Howard at Lapwai. Accompanying the chief were Ollokot, the prophet Toohoolhoolzote, another chief the whites called White Bird, and several more from his tribe. Both sides held strong to their convictions and, after many hours of arguing, Howard impatiently ordered the arrest of Toohoolhoolzote and informed Joseph that he had thirty days in which to remove his people from the valley they called home.

Joseph pleaded that thirty days was not enough time. Howard answered that if they took any longer, soldiers would move in to force the Indians out. Joseph called a council immediately, informing his people that they had no choice but to move. Some Nez Percé, including the newly released Toohoolhoolzote, were angry and called for war. Yet Joseph continued to speak for peace: "I said in my heart that, rather than have war, I would give up my country. I would give up my father's grave. I would give up everything rather than have the blood of white men on the hands of my people" (Howard, p. 134).

Under Joseph's urging, the Nez Percé hastily began the difficult trek toward Lapwai. As they were crossing the Snake River on the border of what is now Idaho and Washington, several white men snuck up and stole some of their cattle. In an attempt to hurry the rest of the cattle across the river, some Nez Percé were lost in the swift current.

Battle of White Bird Canyon. Although Joseph continued to preach peace, the frustration of the loss of their home and livestock finally took its toll on some of the Nez Percé on the night of June 15, 1877. While the tribe camped in Rocky Canyon, several Nez Percé warriors snuck away and killed eleven whites. Reflecting on the June 15, 1877, incident, Chief Joseph later confessed: "I would have given my own life if I could have undone the killing of white men by my people. I know that my young men did a great wrong, but I ask, Who was first to blame?" (Howard, p. 143).

Two days later, after Joseph had moved his tribe sixteen miles to White Bird Creek, Howard's soldiers attacked in retaliation for the murders. Joseph's men killed one-third of the soldiers and captured the rest, despite being severely outnumbered by the army. More soldiers were sent to the area, but the Nez Percé managed to escape to Clearwater, where they joined A-push-wa-hite, another Nez Percé chief, and his warriors. A-push-wa-hite was known to the whites as Chief Looking Glass because he hung a mirror, fastened to his hair, in the middle of his forehead. Like Joseph, this chief pleaded for peace but was prepared for war.

The joining of the two bands made for a substantial Indian force. Together the two chiefs decided they might have the strength to flee the Northwestern Territory with their warriors, women, and children and head for Canada, where they could pursue their own peaceful life style.

On July 25, the Nez Percé spotted U.S. soldiers constructing a barricade directly in their path. Carrying a white flag, Joseph, Looking Glass, and White Bird approached the soldiers on horseback and announced their intent to pass without incident. Waiting for reinforcements, Captain Charles Rawn tried to stall the Nez Percé by assuring them of the possibility of passing through the barricade in a few days. Joseph and the others grew impatient, however, and on July 28, he and Looking Glass prepared for more fighting. Joseph led the women, children, and livestock to safety while Looking Glass prepared the warriors for an encounter.

Wives and Children

As was the tradition for Nez Percé chiefs, Joseph had several wives. In all, he married four women, including two widows of Chief Looking Glass. He fathered nine children. Many died in infancy, but a few survived long enough to accompany Joseph on his journey throughout the Northwest. When whites protested his having more than one wife, he countered, "I fought all through the war for my country and these women. You took away my country; I shall keep my wives." (Dockstader, p. 130)

After a few battles between the two groups, Joseph and Looking Glass abandoned the idea of fleeing to Canada and decided to head south, hoping that they would not be pursued by the white soldiers.

Battle of the Big Hole. Several days later, as the Nez Percé camped along the Big Hole River, Colonel John Gibbon, whom the Indians called One Who Limps, executed an unprovoked attack on the tribe at dawn. His soldiers riddled tepees with bullets, killing many Nez Percé instantly. Once again, Joseph scrambled to save the women and children, while Looking Glass attempted to organize the warriors for a retaliation. "These soldiers mean battle," he shouted. "Now is the time to show your courage and fight" (Howard, p. 247).

Eventually the warriors were able to fight back, but when the smoke of battle cleared, eighty Nez Percé were dead, the majority of them women and children. Thirty white soldiers were killed, and a bullet in the leg turned One Who Limps into One Who Limps Twice.

▲ **Big Hole, where U.S. government troops fought Chief Joseph and the Nez Percé**

By August 22, the Nez Percé had fled farther south, surviving yet another attack by Howard. They entered Yellowstone Park to find General William Tecumseh Sherman and the Seventh Cavalry ready for battle. In an attempt to flee war altogether, the Nez Percé escaped the Seventh Cavalry and headed back north again, toward Canada.

Faced with massacre, surrender, or retreat, Joseph chose the last option. His retreat is still considered one of the most skillful in U.S. military history. He escaped oncoming troops, often by rearguard ploys in which a few sharpshooters held off many more soldiers. Joseph led roughly 750 of his band twice across the Rocky Mountains through Yellowstone Park and across the Mis-

William Tecumseh Sherman—A Viewpoint
"The more we can kill this year, the less will have to be killed the next war, for the more I see of these Indians, the more convinced I am that they will all have to be killed or be maintained as a series of paupers." (Warren, p. x)

souri River, a journey of 1500 miles. Forty miles from Canada, at Bear Paws, Montana, his people paused to rest, worn out and close to starvation.

Battle of Bear Paws. Early the next morning on September 30, the Nez Percé were attacked by uniformed white, Sioux, and Cheyenne soldiers under General Nelson Miles, known to the Indians as Bear Coat. Joseph later revealed what his thoughts were when the firing began: "I thought of my wife and children, who were now surrounded by soldiers, and I resolved to go to them or die. As I reached the door of my lodge, my wife handed me my rifle, saying: 'Here's your gun. Fight!'" (Howard, p. 320). He went on to describe the battle: "We fought at close range, no more than twenty steps apart.... We lost, the first day and night, eighteen men and three women" (Howard, p. 320). One of the men lost was Joseph's brother, Ollokot. Another was Toohoolhoolzote the prophet.

The Nez Percé men and women spent the remainder of the night digging trenches in preparation for another attack, some using knives and sharpened frying pans as tools. When the sun finally rose, Joseph and his people expected another day of war. Instead of sending soldiers, Miles sent a messenger carrying a white truce flag and demanding Joseph's surrender. Joseph sent him back with the message that he had not made up his mind but would think about it. A little later, Miles sent some Cheyenne scouts with another message: Miles was sincere and really wanted peace.

Imprisonment, freedom, and surrender. Joseph believed Miles's promise and walked with the scouts over to his tent. Upon arriving, Miles took him prisoner and kept him restrained in a damp, underground passage for two days, still demanding his surrender. The general then resumed his attack on the Nez Percé, and, despite Joseph's absence, the warriors held the soldiers at a reasonable distance for another day. Meanwhile, Joseph refused to surrender.

During the third day of fighting, a Nez Percé warrior captured an officer in Miles's army and threatened to kill him if Joseph was not released unharmed. When Joseph heard this, he sent a message to his people: "I do not know what they mean to do with me, but if they kill me you must not kill the officer. It will do no good to avenge my death by killing him" (Howard, p. 325).

▲ **General Oliver Otis Howard and Chief Joseph meet again in 1904**

By the fourth day, the respective prisoners were exchanged, unharmed, and Joseph met with the rest of the Nez Percé chiefs. Although Looking Glass and White Bird wanted to continue fighting, Joseph leaned toward surrendering. He was persuaded by his fellow chiefs to postpone the surrender for a little while. Just a few hours later, Looking Glass was shot and killed in battle by a sharpshooter.

Joseph surrendered immediately the next day, relying on Miles's promise: "If you will come out and give up your arms, I will spare your lives and send you to your reservation" (Brown, p. 328). As he turned his gun over to General Miles on October 5, 1877, Joseph delivered a powerful speech:

Tell General Howard I know his heart. What he told me before I have in my heart. I am tired of fighting. Our chiefs are killed.

Looking Glass is dead. The old men are all dead. It is the young men who say yes or no. He who led on the young men [Ollokot] is dead. It is cold and we have no blankets. The little children are freezing to death.... Hear me, my chiefs! I am tired; my heart is sick and sad. From where the sun now stands I will fight no more forever. (Beal, p. 229)

The escape and the broken promise. As the surrender was being finalized that evening, a band of Nez Percé, led by White Bird, finally realized the dream of escaping to Canada, stealing off into the night and crossing the border the next day to be welcomed by Sitting Bull and his tribe of Sioux Indians. Meanwhile, Miles's promise of a safe home at Lapwai for the Nez Percé was broken as quickly as it was made. Joseph and the Nez Percé who had not escaped to freedom with White Bird were sent to live in Fort Leavenworth, Kansas, as prisoners of war. They lived in unhealthful swamplands where many fell ill and died. The survivors were finally moved to the Indian Territory, where disappointment and harsh conditions led to more deaths.

An Artist's Reflection

Frances G. Hamblen of Spokane, Washington, was a sculptor who received a rare visit from Chief Joseph in 1893, so that she could study his features for a likeness. In her journal she remarked:

"Moderately tall and heavily built. Hand that felt as big as a ham when shaking hands. Eyes small but particularly bright.... He told us how he lived away from his people—how his wife had died, his children, all his family and putting his hand on his heart, he shook his head, 'Sick-sick.'" (Howard, p. 377-78)

Joseph was able to travel to Washington, D.C., in November of 1877 in order to make a plea for his people. He protested that he had believed Miles, or he never would have surrendered. No one seemed to hear Chief Joseph. He was sent back to Indian Territory to remain a prisoner with the rest of his captive tribe until 1885, the year he turned forty-five.

Aftermath

"Let me be a free man." Joseph had pleaded many times with the U.S. government to allow his people to live their lives in peace and freedom. His final official words to the whites were a plea to set him free so he could travel, trade, follow his own religion. Given such freedom, he promised, he would obey the white men's laws or pay the penalty. But Joseph would never be free. He and 150 other Nez Percé were moved from Indian Territory in 1885 and exiled to the Colville Reservation in Washington. They were considered too dangerous and influential to stay with the rest of the tribe, which had dwindled to less than 300 members. Some of the remaining Nez Percé were allowed to live out their lives at Lapwai, though their bands, families, and chiefs had been destroyed or broken apart.

In 1903 Joseph, escorted by Miles, again visited Washington, D.C., and met President Theodore Roosevelt. Joseph died in exile on September 21, 1904, at the age of sixty-four. The cause of death, reported a doctor at the reservation, was a broken heart. A peace-loving chief forced into fighting, Joseph had seen the failure of his dream that all the peoples of America could live in harmony under one sky, in one country, and with one government for all.

For More Information

Beal, Merrill D. *"I Will Fight No More Forever": Chief Joseph and the Nez Percé War.* Seattle: University of Washington Press, 1963.

Brown, Dee. *Bury My Heart at Wounded Knee: An Indian History of the American West.* New York: Holt, Rinehart and Winston, 1970.

Dockstader, Frederick. *Great North American Indians.* New York: Van Nostrand Reinhold Co., 1977.

Howard, Helen Addison. *Saga of Chief Joseph.* Lincoln and London: University of Nebraska Press, 1965.

Warren, Robert Penn. *Chief Joseph of the Nez Percé.* New York: Random House, 1982.

Labor Movement

1859
U.S. industry earns more than U.S. agriculture.

1866
National Labor Union becomes first nationwide collection of unions.

1867
George Pullman organizes the Pullman Palace Car Company.

1877
Railroad workers stage the first nationwide strike. President Rutherford B. Hayes sends troops to end the strike.

1873
The Panic of 1873 leads to six years of depression.

1870
John D. Rockefeller forms Standard Oil Company of Ohio.

1869
Workers organize the Knights of Labor. Railroad laborers complete America's first transcontinental railroad.

1886
Samuel Gompers forms the American Federation of Labor. A peaceful protest turns into the Haymarket Riot.

1888
Andrew Carnegie organizes Carnegie Steel Company at Homestead, Pennsylvania.

1890
Miners form United Mine Workers union.

1892
Silver miners go on strike in Idaho. Steel workers stage the Homestead Strike.

1897
Mary "Mother" Jones organizes miners' strike in West Virginia.

1894
Pullman Palace Car Company workers go on strike.

1893
The Panic of 1893 leads to four years of depression. Eugene V. Debs forms American Railway Union.

LABOR MOVEMENT

Before the Civil War, most Americans had earned their living at agriculture. Industry was limited mainly to textile, clothing, and leather goods production or to the processing of crops, lumber, and other natural resources. After the war, however, heavy industry boomed, and businesses involved in steel, iron, and oil production appeared.

The spectacular growth in American industry in the postwar era led to its being called the Gilded Age. Yet behind the flash and glitter were misery and hardship. While a few Americans climbed from rags to riches in the late 1800s, the rapid rise of industry plunged thousands into tedious, dangerous jobs sixty hours a week for ten or twenty cents an hour. Out of struggles between these industry owners and workers came the birth of the American labor movement.

Despite miserable working conditions, there was no shortage of labor because of the steady supply of immigrants; 3.25 million immigrants arrived in the decade after the war, settling mostly in cities. In Chicago, for example, they and their children made up 87 percent of the population. Their interest in changing working conditions was limited since many planned to earn some money and then return to their homelands. Also, a ten-hour factory job, even at a few cents an hour, was seen as better than farmwork in

Europe. Yet an eight-hour movement was begun after the war, which called for government laws to limit the workday to eight hours without lowering wages.

Business in the post–Civil War years alternated between good times and hard times, the Gilded Age lasting from 1865 to 1873. Panics in 1873 and 1893 began six and four years of depression respectively, in which wages were cut.

The railroad industry became the nation's first big business. Built frantically during the war, railways soon spanned the country. The first transcontinental railroad was completed in 1869, and four more were constructed over the next two decades. Suddenly Americans could transport wheat from the Midwest, cotton from the Mississippi Delta, and fruits from California to any other region of the country.

The growth of the railroad industry had far-reaching effects. Huge factories that employed thousands of workers and used the latest machinery were built. Chicago, at the crossroads of different rail lines, grew to more than half a million people. And a few individuals, such as **George Pullman,** grew very wealthy in the business. Pullman built a company town for his workers. They occupied houses, churches, and schools that he owned. In other words, Pullman arranged their living as well as their working conditions.

The Rags-to-Riches Dream— A Few Who Struck it Rich		
	First job	**Company that led to industrial power**
Philip Armour	Miner	Armour and Co., 1870
Andrew Carnegie	Child laborer— bobbin-boy in cotton factory	Carnegie Steel Co., 1888
Marshall Field	Boy store clerk	Marshall Field Co., 1886
J. P. Morgan	Clerk in drygoods store	George Peabody and Co., 1854
George Pullman	Carpenter	Pullman Car Co., 1867
J. D. Rockefeller	Farmhand	Standard Oil Co., 1870
Leland Stanford	Miner	Central Pacific Railroad, 1860

Pullman was one of a few businessmen who rose to control a large share of the industrial wealth of the nation. They financed their companies by forming them into corporations and selling stock, or shares, in the business. The industrialists paid a great deal of attention to their stockholders but showed little regard for their employees. Workers received no protection from unfair labor practices. Boys and girls, for example, began at young ages to work in damp, dirty mines. Not only did workers suffer long hours, low wages, unsteady employment, and poor conditions, but those who protested were blacklisted as undesirable workers.

Laborers felt entitled to a larger share of the new wealth and to equality in the workplace, especially after their sacrifices to preserve the Union in the Civil War. They began joining together to demand better treatment. The American labor movement grew slowly at first. The immigrants had little in common in the beginning, as they came from different lands and did not even speak the same language. Sometimes an employer made them sign yellow-dog contracts, agreements not to join a union, or workers association. And in years of depression, union dues were difficult to pay.

Yet 1866 saw the appearance of the first workers organizations on a national level. The National Labor Union collapsed after the Panic of 1873, but by then over 300,000 workers belonged to about 1,500 trade unions. The American Railway Union survived and in 1877 staged the first nationwide strike. Workers decided to go on strike, or stop working, until their demands were met. When the trains stopped running, business came to a standstill, and federal troops were called in to end the strike. The strikers fought back by looting and burning railroad yards; over 100 people died before the troops managed to end the incident.

Thousands of strikes in other industries followed. The tactic of striking was looked upon with disfavor by a second national workers organization, the Knights of Labor. Led by Terence V. Powderly, the Knights welcomed skilled and unskilled, male and female, and black and white workers. It grew to 700,000 members in 1886, its membership soaring after a riot at Haymarket Square in Chicago. Some 2,000 workers had been listening to a protest against police brutality in a demonstration the day before at the McCormick Reaper Works company. A bomb exploded during the protest, and the Haymarket Riot followed, killing seven policemen and ten others. After the riot, business owners set out to weaken the workers by breaking up the Knights of Labor. It finally dissolved but two other national organizations survived: the American Federation of Labor (AFL), founded by **Samuel Gompers,** and the United Mine Workers (UMW), whose aims were furthered by **Mary "Mother" Jones.**

Unlike the Knights of Labor, the AFL was limited to unions of skilled workers. It made little attempt to organize women and, in time, accepted member unions that excluded blacks, though at first it refused to do so. Also unlike the Knights of Labor, the AFL focused on immediate needs such as higher wages and an eight-hour workday. Labor organizers such as Gompers and Jones traveled the country, recruiting members and exhorting them to act in accordance with union plans. Gompers brought millions of skilled workers together in the AFL. Jones recruited thousands of miners, leading them in the fight for reasonable work hours and the elimination of child labor in the mines.

In 1892 silver miners went on strike in Idaho when machine drills were brought in to do their work; the miners were reduced to shovelmen, and their wages were cut. The mine owners broke the strike by hiring strikebreakers, or nonunion workers, which led to armed fighting. Violence often followed the entrance of strikebreakers, typically immigrants in need of work and money. Prejudice against immigrant groups, such as the Chinese, resulted. At the same time, immigrants and their children occupied so many of the jobs in industry that middle and upper class citizens tended to dismiss protests made by workers in industry as unpatriotic and un-American.

Besides the silver miners' strike, 1892 saw a standoff that ended in violence at the Homestead steel mills near Pittsburgh, Pennsylvania. Due to wage cuts, workers went on strike, whereupon the business manager Henry Clay Frick hired strikebreakers and private policemen from the Pinkerton Detective Agency to protect the new workers. When 300 Pinkertons arrived on barges in the thick of the night, the old workers were waiting for them. Gunfire and dynamiting followed, killing nine strikers and seven Pinkertons. The governor sent in state troops to end the violence and, though the strike continued for over four months, the workers won nothing except new public support for the cause of labor.

Two years later, during a depression, workers at the Pullman Palace Car Company went on strike. Their wages were cut five times while their rents in Pullman Town remained the same, as did prices in the town stores. Eugene Debs, leader of the American Railway Union, led his members in a sympathy strike for Pullman workers. Meanwhile, the General Managers Association, which ran 24 railroads centered in Chicago, sided with the employer, Pullman. The managers hired 2,500 strikebreakers and persuaded President Grover Cleveland to send federal troops to crush the strike. Also, the Supreme Court authorized an injunction, a court order forbidding an action, that prohibited any interference with trains. Thereafter the injunction was used to defeat unions.

Victory, then, did not come easily to American workers. Business owners tried to put down strikes with company-hired thugs. When these proved inadequate, they enlisted the aid of the courts, local police, state militia, and federal troops, and violent confrontations followed. The laborers needed to gain strength, which finally came from numbers and from operating their unions in businesslike fashion, collecting and saving money to support workers who went on strike. Progress was slow. Although the early union leaders had some success, they were not equipped to fight leaders in industry and government. Employers felt it was their right to make business decisions as they pleased, and judges tended to agree. Overall there were few successes for workers from the 1860s to the end of the century. It was mostly a time of consciousness-raising and preparation for a future day when labor would have a voice in the economy. Not until well into the twentieth century would the federal government begin to recognize and respond to the demands of labor organizations.

George Pullman

1831-1897

Personal Background

The Pullman family. James Lewis Pullman and his wife, Emily Minton Pullman, lived in Brocton, New York, where James earned a comfortable living as a carpenter. They had five children, the third of whom was George, born March 3, 1831.

James and Emily were religious people although they shared different Christian faiths. During the early years of their marriage, James became a devoted Unitarian and eventually became a minister. While the children were young, however, he contented himself with studying the Bible and with raising his children to be obedient, to detest idleness, to avoid extravagance, and to be absolutely honest.

George Pullman, early life. The Pullman children attended the country school in nearby Portland. George grew to be five feet seven inches tall and had a round face that would always make him look younger than he was. He would later try to hide his young looks by growing a beard. At fourteen, George left school to contribute to the family income. He took a job as a clerk in an uncle's store in Westfield, earning forty dollars a year plus room and board. Three years later, in 1848, his parents decided to move the family to Albion on the Erie Canal. George moved with them.

There was much for James to do at Albion. The Erie Canal was being expanded, and houses that had been built on its banks had to

▲ **George Pullman**

Event: The building of Pullman, a model town.

Role: The son of a carpenter, George Pullman earned a reputation as the builder of the finest railroad sleeping cars in the world. As his company grew, he built a model city and a factory on the outskirts of Chicago. Pullman was torn between his obligations to his employees as owner of the company and his duties as their landlord; the conflict led to difficulties with the workers and eventually to a strike that disrupted mail and transportation across the nation.

be moved so that the canal could be widened. James began to apply his building skills to moving houses, but, in 1853, while still under contract, he died. Now George had to care for his mother. Though he had been working as a cabinetmaker, he gave up his job to fulfill his father's house-moving contracts, which he managed to do very capably.

Chicago, 1855. The widening of the Erie Canal would not, however, continue forever. By 1855 work in the area was beginning to dwindle. Casting about for another way to support the family, Pullman learned of opportunities to do similar work in the growing town of Chicago. Early builders there had constructed buildings along the lakefront, too close to the lake. As time passed, the waterfront eroded and the buildings and some roads became endangered. It was necessary to raise the roads several feet to keep them from becoming mud bogs. In the process, the buildings would then have to be raised to the new street level.

At the time Pullman heard of this opportunity, bids were just being taken to raise the second most important hotel in the town. He rushed to Chicago and won the bid, stopping first to arrange for shipment of the 1,000 screw jacks he would need for the job. Jacks were placed around the six-story brick building and raised one turn at a time until the whole building was at the desired height. It was the first of many successful building raisings. When the job was finished, Pullman joined other Chicago contractors in raising a whole block of brick buildings at once.

More contracts followed, and Pullman soon found himself supervising the raising of the Tremont Hotel. This four-story, all-brick hotel was the finest in Chicago and needed to be raised six feet. Legend tells how George arranged 1,000 workers and 500 jacks around the building and signaled the turning of the jacks together, raising the hotel with the furniture and people still in it— to the desired height in one hour. In reality, the raising took considerably longer than an hour, and by the time Pullman had won this contract he was so busy that his brother Albert supervised the job. Nevertheless, the story illustrates Pullman's success. He was soon in demand around Chicago and by the age of twenty-seven had amassed a small fortune of $20,000.

All the while, family obligations took Pullman frequently from Chicago to Albion and back. Perhaps one of these uncomfortable train trips started him thinking about ways to make travel more comfortable. At the time, trains were jarring, noisy, and smoky. Travel was so miserable that travelers took extra time so that they could stop each night in a hotel rather than try to sleep on the trains.

Sleeping cars. The idea of sleeping on a train was not new. R. F. Morgan had experimented with sleeping cars as early as 1829. By 1836 the Cumberland Valley Railroad had put bunks in some train cars. These were in regular use even though the bunks made the cars useless for daytime travel. By 1855 two companies were already building sleeping cars. Their popularity had grown the year before, when H. B. Mayer hooked pulley systems to raise the top bunks out of the way during the day, leaving the bottom bunks as hard benches to sit on.

This was how far the sleeping car had developed in 1856, when a Chicago businessman, Benjamin Field, contracted with two railways to build and operate sleepers on their tracks. He and his brother, Norman, joined with Pullman to form a company to build the special railway cars. Pullman designed and built a sleeper that could be changed during the day to a chair car. The chairs were hinged so that they could be made into lower berths, and upper berths were hung by pulley systems so that they could be raised to the ceiling during the day. The Pullman car, as it became known, carried still another new feature, toilets at each end of the car.

The Pullman cars grew quite popular, and business was beginning to build as the Civil War broke out. The army immediately took charge of all the railroad stock, which forced the Pullman/Field company to break up. Pullman then moved to Central City, Colorado, and established a trading post.

The Pullman Pioneer. In 1864 Pullman returned to Chicago with $20,000 and an idea. He planned to build the most beautiful and comfortable sleeper cars ever and keep the rights to those cars himself. Railroad companies could charge their regular fees for traveling in one of his cars, and he would charge travelers an extra fee in return for his taking responsibility for the fancy sleepers. His Pullman Pioneer was sensational. Instead of eight wheels, the car sat on sixteen, making the ride smoother and more comfortable. The longer and wider car was mounted on coiled springs and large blocks of rubber to cushion the ride and make it less noisy. He replaced the pulley system with hinges that allowed upper berths to be folded away during the day. Carpets, mirrors, rich woodwork, and even coal-oil lamps were installed, and fine drapes covered the windows at night. The Pioneer was a masterpiece, but it required the railroads to change the widths of bridges and other passage ways, something few seemed willing to do—until the death of Abraham Lincoln.

Lincoln's assassination. A special train was put together to carry Lincoln's body from Washington to its burial place in Illinois. Pullman's car was chosen to be part of the funeral train. All along the path, thousands of people lined the rails to see the Lincoln train, and Pullman's car became immediately popular. Now railroad companies were interested in making the changes needed to run the Pioneer. Thus Pullman influenced the railroads to standardize their rail lines.

In 1866 Pullman had twenty-one cars running on various railroads; by 1868 Pullman cars were running on ten major railroad lines. Pullman's company, which had been incorporated in 1867, always maintained control of its own cars. Soon porters were hired to see to the comfort of the passengers.

During this time, in 1867, Pullman married Harriet Singer. The couple would live in a magnificent gray-stone, three-story house in Chicago, where they would raise two daughters and twin sons.

Pullman Company expands. The cars grew so popular that Pullman's company contracted with other companies to do the building. By 1875 the Pullman Company had decided to add day coaches to its luxury line and to build baggage cars to sell to the railroad companies. To do this, Pullman built a factory in Detroit. Pullman meanwhile lived in Chicago, which was rapidly becoming the most important railroad city in the Midwest. He built a factory in Calumet, just outside the city. Every day, Pullman went to his office at 8:00 a.m. and stayed until 1:00 p.m. Then he had lunch with other Chicago millionaires at the Chicago Club, returning to work from 3:00 till 6:00 p.m. He was very active in Chicago affairs, serving for example, as president of the YMCA board of directors for three years.

By 1880 the company had become so successful that Pullman was ready to complete another dream. He would build a new factory and around it a model city where his workers would live in better conditions than could be found anywhere in the Chicago area, except on millionaires' row.

Participation:
The Rise and Fall of Pullman, Illinois

The Pullman Palace Car Company. The new Pullman Company factory would employ 9,000 workers, most of them skilled craftsmen who commanded good salaries for that time. They could choose to live in nearby Chicago or in the new town of Pullman, Illinois. There, the Pullman Company would at first build 320 houses to rent to the workers.

Building a company town was not a new idea. Miners, who generally worked far from towns, had often been housed in company-owned shanties near mines and usually purchased supplies at company stores. Mine owners, such as John D. Rockefeller, Jr., often paid their workers not in money but in scrip, which was only good at the company store. They also let workers buy goods using company-store credit, since the small salaries would often not last from pay period to pay period. The credit system plunged the workers into debt. Mine workers in company towns became indebted to the mine owners for food, clothing, medicine, and housing. Pullman planned to make his town different.

> **George Pullman on Why He Built His Model City**
>
> "[I am] paying more attention to the Town of Pullman than anything I have on hand. I am studying the effect of improved homes upon the laboring society." (Buder, p. 77)

The workers in his factory would be paid in money. In Pullman, there would be parks and two shopping centers along with a library, which company employees could use for three dollars a year. Schools would be provided for the children of the workers.

Everything a worker might want, including medical care, was readily available in the new model city. To make it even more attractive, an artificial lake was built for recreation, and the Pullman factory was separated from the city by a broad highway. Although the

▲ An advertisement for the Chicago & Alton Railroad

rent in Pullman was higher than in Chicago, the attractiveness of the new town drew many of the most skilled workers to live there. The company grew and so did the town. By 1883 the factory employed 14,000 workers, of which nearly 6,000 lived in the model town. In that year, the Pullman Company earned $4 million and the average worker was being paid the annual salary of $613, a fair sum for that time.

By 1889 the city of Chicago had grown so large that it surrounded the town of Pullman. Then came the World's Fair. Held in Chicago in 1893, it drew thirty-five million visitors who traveled by train to see the great exhibition. The railroad companies expanded rapidly to carry the added customers. This led to trouble later when reduced numbers of passengers did not fill the new trains.

Changes in the railroads. The end of 1893 saw great changes in the railroad business. Eugene Debs organized the American Railroad Union. Meanwhile, the Pullman Company grew to such size that Pullman could no longer oversee everything. More and more, the day-to-day workings of the company were managed by selected workers appointed as foremen. At the same time, a great panic erupted in the country when one of the great eastern financial companies declared bankruptcy.

1885 Population of Pullman	
U.S. citizens	4,013
Immigrants	
German	1,088
Swedish	1,024
Irish	563
Canadian	557
English	406
11 other countries	952

The traffic to and from the fair had caused the railroads to overbuild. The West Shore Railroad, facing declining profits, canceled its order for 200 new Pullman cars. A company survey indicated that, as depression set in, the railroads had enough cars to last for three years. Pullman was forced to close his Detroit factory and concentrate the work at Pullman. Even so, it was necessary to lay off many workers and reduce the wages of the rest. As a final cost saving, the company began to pay the workers per piece of material completed rather than per hour. It was an awkward arrangement, and paying for piecework did not suit many of the complicated jobs of building Pullman cars. The company worked that out by assigning the needed craftsmen to a foreman and paying per section of car. After the crew completed one part of the car, the foreman would be paid, and he would divide the pay among the workers. As times grew worse, the amount to be distributed became less and less, and the arrangement made the foremen the most powerful people in the Pullman Company.

American Railroad Union. Meanwhile, Debs's American Railroad Union was gaining strength. One set of craftsmen after another attempted to strike for better conditions. The Pullman Company responded by strengthening the positions of the foremen, hiring spies to watch the union, blacklisting union members who threatened to strike, and hiring strikebreakers from the heart of Chicago, where the depression had struck even worse than at Pullman. One reason that conditions were a little better at Pullman was that the company officers decided to try to delay more wage cuts and layoffs by contracting to build railroad cars even if it was necessary to bid the jobs at a loss to the company. While the company work force dropped to just over 1,000 employees by the end of 1893, the policy of taking company losses on contracts brought in enough new business to restore the number to 3,100 by April 1894.

Pullman, however, did not see any relationship between his position as owner of the Pullman Company and as landlord of the town of Pullman. He steadfastly declared that, as landlord, he could not afford to reduce the rent his employees paid to live in the town. Workers whose wages had been cut could no longer afford to pay the high rents. Soon they were, as a whole, $70,000 behind in rent payments. Pullman and his company officers realized that the workers were struggling, so they did nothing to collect this money or to evict those who were in debt.

It was a time, however, when American laborers were beginning to feel the pressure of the depression. The Pullman workers decided to send a delegation to the company headquarters to ask that wages not be cut further and that the rent on company houses be cut to match the wage cuts. By this time, they owed the Pullman Land Company more than $100,000, which Pullman still had not tried to collect. Pullman had tried to protect his workers and his company by secrecy. None of the workers had been told that he was taking contracts at a loss in order to create jobs and preserve the company. The union delegates and company officers met from May 7 to May 9, 1894. Pullman, himself, did not join the talks at first. Here, for the first time, the employees learned that the company had been operating at a loss. Its officers steadfastly maintained that the company could not afford to meet the wage demands of the workers. They also maintained that they had no authority over rent fees. On the last day, Pullman, who had not yet taken part in the talks, spoke to the union delegates. He offered to open the company books to them so that they could see for themselves the condition of the Pullman Company. The union workers refused his offer.

Pullman strike. On May 10, probably without the knowledge of Pullman or his officers, three of the negotiators for the union were laid off. This may have been a necessary action or it may have been the whim of one of the powerful foremen. Whatever the reason, the American Railroad Union voted to strike the Pullman Company. The next day, all work at the Pullman Company stopped. Within a month, the union had expanded its pressure on the company by refusing to handle any trains anywhere that included Pullman cars. It amounted to a strike threat against all the railroads.

However, the railroad companies had their own organization, the General Managers' Association, to protect them from any problems. The association decided to resist the union boycott. When strikes spread from Baltimore throughout all the railroads, companies brought in strikebreakers to take the place of union workers. Violence erupted everywhere and millions of dollars of railroad equipment was destroyed by the striking workers. The companies, for their part, used brutal methods to stop the strike, such as hiring thugs to beat up picketers. By July 2, conditions of war existed in many spots, threatening transportation everywhere. Delays in mail transportation upset the federal government. The railroad companies succeeded in getting a federal injunction that forbade the union from forcing workers to quit working. The next day, 50,000 federal troops assigned to keep peace on the railroads confronted the workers to protect railroad property. Debs and other union officers were arrested and eventually convicted of interrupting a vital national service. Debs went to jail for six months, the union collapsed, and peace was restored.

On August 2, the Pullman Company began operation again. It

did not rehire the workers who had led the union organization. Though the strike had seemingly failed, it had raised important questions about the methods of the men who had built the country's great industries and grown rich in the effort. On August 15, the federal government began to investigate the strike that had stopped the Pullman Company and resulted in 66,000 workers losing their jobs in Chicago alone.

Meanwhile, pressure was growing to correct conditions in the city of Pullman. The mayor of Chicago had decided that he could resolve some of that city's financial problems by charging higher water rates to Pullman. When he raised the water rates by more than one-third, the Pullman Land Company offered to give Chicago control of the Pullman water system. This had been the beginning of the end of the town of Pullman. Shortly thereafter, the federal government ordered Pullman to rid himself of the property on which the company employees lived. Although it was some years before all the property could be sold, the model town of Pullman, a separate community from 1880 until 1893, eventually became part of the greater city of Chicago.

Aftermath

Recovery. The Pullman Company continued to build railway cars and to maintain them. As the depression wore to an end, the company again became one of the giants of the railroad industry. However, conditions for Pullman began to deteriorate.

Always working, he had taken little active interest in his own family. His twin boys, both twenty-one years old, were active in business; one of them worked for Marshall Fields, another Chicago millionaire merchant. The two boys later gave up their jobs and began to live the lives of luxury made possible by their father's wealth. By 1897 Pullman had become so disgusted with them that he changed their allowances in his will.

Final days. Pullman meanwhile continued to have expensive parties for the wealthy of Chicago. In 1897 he entertained the executives of the Pennsylvania Railroad in Chicago and at the factory in the barely alive community of Pullman. He complained about the heat of Chicago and wrote to his wife that he was not feeling well. Nevertheless, he went to work on October 18, and that night called for a doctor. Shortly after the doctor arrived, on October 19, 1897, Pullman died of a heart attack.

Pullman the industrialist. Like other leading industrialists of the late 1800s, Pullman played a key role in the growth and expansion of American industry. The builders of this industry, John D. Rockefeller, Andrew Carnegie, Cornelius Vanderbilt, Marshall Field, and others, had developed huge steel, coal, railroad, and merchandising corporations with money raised through the sale of stock. They felt their first obligation was to these stockholders. Few had thought much about the workers themselves, who often labored twelve to eighteen hours a day, six or even seven days a week to make the new industries grow. Pullman, however, showed some interest in his workers and tried to improve their living conditions. Yet his own stubborn quietness about taking low-paying contracts to keep the company operating led to problems with his employees. Like many industrialists of the time, he had not recognized the importance of giving workers a voice in running the company. It would be many more years before American industry would begin to address the needs of its workers.

For More Information

Buder, Stanley. *Pullman: An Experiment in Industrial Order and Community Planning, 1880-1930.* New York: Oxford University Press, 1967.

Husband, Joseph. *The History of the Pullman Car, 1917.* Grand Rapids, Mich.: Black Letter Press, 1974.

Leyendecker, Liston E. *Palace Prince: A Biography of George Mortimer Pullman.* Niwot: University of Colorado Press, 1992.

Samuel Gompers

1850-1924

Personal Background

London in 1850. Life was difficult for the majority of laborers in London, England, in 1850. Children worked long hours in dismal factories that had sprung up as a result of the Industrial Revolution. Workers often toiled twelve to eighteen hours a day to earn even the most basic necessities for living. It was a particularly difficult time for those who had just moved to London from the European mainland—and even more difficult for Solomon Gompers and his family because they were Jewish.

The Gompers family. Solomon Gompers and his wife, Sara, had emigrated from Holland to London, where they lived in a two-room apartment that also served as Solomon's workshop. Solomon was a cigar maker, a highly skilled but not highly paid occupation. He bought the raw materials himself and was paid a set amount for each cigar he delivered to his boss. In other words, he was paid by the piece. In time, Solomon joined other craftsmen in dimly lit factories where row after row of cigar makers sat on wooden benches before rickety tables to roll their cigars.

Samuel Gompers was born into this poor but hardworking family in June 1850. His playground was the streets of London, where he learned to fight and to play with the sons of other laborers. As soon as he was old enough, he was sent to the local Jewish

▲ Samuel Gompers

Event: Founding of the American Federation of Labor.

Role: Samuel Gompers was a leading figure in the American labor movement. A cigar maker at the age of ten, Gompers became involved in craftsmen unions at an early age. He fought to improve the working conditions of laborers and was instrumental in the formation of the largest of American labor unions, the American Federation of Labor.

school, where he eagerly pursued his studies. His time in school was short, however. As more children were born into the family, it became necessary for Samuel to contribute to the household income since his father's salary rose and fell with the demand for cigars. So, when he was ten, his father apprenticed him to a shoemaker. Eight months later, father and son agreed that Samuel should instead work with Solomon and learn the cigar maker's trade. Like many young boys in London at the time, Samuel had to forego regular schooling because of work. He refused to give up his education, however, and began to take classes at the local night school. Roaming the streets of London at night was no problem for Samuel, for despite his small stature he had grown to be a powerful young man.

London in the 1860s. The 1860s were as exciting as they were difficult. New ideas were flowing from mainland Europe, particularly from Germany. European workers, frustrated by poor working conditions and low pay, were beginning to talk of a workers' revolution that would result in everyone, not just a wealthy aristocracy, controlling and sharing in the wealth. Political philosopher and workers' advocate Karl Marx had proposed that an international workers group organize to help release laborers from the control of wealthy capitalist business owners. Banned from his home town, Marx was writing and teaching in London. He had begun writing a document that would later be known as the *Communist Manifesto.*

Across the Atlantic, America was bursting with talk for and against slavery, an institution that had been officially abolished in England in 1838. In London, people also entered into debates about the American problem. Most English workers sided with the slaves in their quest for freedom. They could sympathize with those who, like themselves, were oppressed by labor lords, even though the struggle was thousands of miles away and the people involved were of a different race. Through his night school classes and various meetings he attended, Samuel learned of the dreams that people were trying to realize in America and the issue of slavery there. He heard also about Marx's ideas.

Conditions only grew worse in London. More immigrants flooded into the city daily to escape an even more difficult life in

Holland and Germany. Competition for skilled-labor jobs increased until the union of cigar makers established a fund to help the unemployed. The fund was used to cut down on England's number of workers by paying out-of-work cigar makers five or ten pounds to leave England. Most dreamed of the new opportunities in America. In 1863 Solomon decided to use the money offered by the union to help move his family to America. On June 10, the family sailed on board the *City of London.*

New York. The Gompers moved into a four-room apartment in New York. Already their lives had improved. Solomon and Samuel soon found work and joined other cigar makers in Local 15 of the Cigar Makers' Union. At age fifteen, Samuel seems to have been a member in good standing of this union in spite of a rule that only white males eighteen or older could join. Meanwhile, he continued to further his education by attending club meetings of The Ancient Order of Foresters and the International Order of Odd Fellows and by attending lectures and discussions at Cooper Union. Before long, he was ready to fight with fists or brain for any cause that would improve the working man's condition.

Marriage. Samuel was a dependable, thoughtful young man. It was not surprising, then, that an older friend who had to leave town for awhile asked Samuel and a friend to look after his teenage daughter while he was away. The girl lived in Brooklyn, a place not easily reached in the evenings after work. But Samuel carried out his responsibility faithfully, catching ferries to reach Brooklyn, arranging for a ride from the ferry-landing to town on the back of a milk wagon, and sometimes walking the five miles from the ferry to his house in the early hours of the morning. Samuel was just under seventeen and the girl, Sophia Julian, barely sixteen.

In 1867, on Samuel's seventeenth birthday, he, Sophia, and their best friends, also a couple, cast about for a way to celebrate the

> ### Samuel Gompers and America
>
> Gompers' description of the Fourth of July celebration aboard ship reveals his belief in and love for America: "The festivities ended in which we all saluted the Stars and Stripes—this beautiful emblem of America that was then in a mighty contest for human freedom. In the years that followed there grew in me a feeling of pride and ownership in the Red, White, and Blue....
>
> "America is more than a name. America is an ideal. America is the apotheosis [exalted example] of all that is right." (Gompers, p. 11)

day. Someone suggested that the two couples get married, and they did. A justice of the peace performed a double wedding. Sophia later would support Gompers in his struggles to form a workable labor union.

Meanwhile, the two raised a large family—twelve or fourteen children. (Gompers could not remember the exact number in his later years.) Due to the poor living conditions of the 1860s and 1870s, only five of the children lived to adulthood and only four reached the age of forty.

Early labor involvement. When Gompers found a job in the cigar factory of David Hirsch, he encountered fellow workers from Europe who were well acquainted with the teachings of Marx. He also stumbled upon an unusual work place. Hirsch had himself been a cigar maker, and he allowed his workers time to study and learn. One worker would be chosen to read aloud for an hour or two at a time to the room full of cigar makers. Later, small groups of workers would gather to discuss the readings. From two of these workers, Adolph Strasser and Ferdinand Laurrell, who had come from socialist Europe, Gompers learned more about Marx's philosophy.

An American labor movement. As he learned more, Gompers began to believe that Marx's socialistic and revolutionary ideas would not work in America. After all, the average American dreamed of becoming one of the wealthy, not of revolting against them. Gompers looked for a way to shape an American labor union. Laurrell guided him in this search, advising him to read the *Communist Manifesto,* but to always compare it with the meaning of his union card. "Study your union card, Sam," he would say, "and if the idea doesn't square with that, it isn't true" (Livesay, p. 40).

Events of the early 1870s added to Gompers's education. He watched as the workers of the Tenth Ward organized strikes for an eight-hour workday. He saw how the poorly planned strikes were broken by the government, whose officers were controlled by large business owners. He watched as the great steel and railroad strikes of the mid-1870s resulted in injuries and deaths to workers for little gain. In his own craft, the invention of the cigar mold was turning cigar making into a cottage industry to be exploited by greedy owners. Gompers watched as these owners bought rundown tenement houses to rent to unskilled workers, where they could live and use the molders. The workers were trapped, in debt to their bosses for housing, and often dependent on the boss's store for food and other necessities.

The Cigar Makers' Union, of which Gompers was a local vice president, sought to make these conditions illegal. Although the union spent $40,000 to encourage laws against the sweatshops, it was defeated by the National Manufacturer's Association, which locked skilled workers out of the larger factories. For his effort, Gompers was blacklisted and therefore unable to find work in New York.

Through these experiences, Gompers came to believe that a successful union must be highly organized and disciplined. It must operated as efficiently and with as well-prepared plans as any business. Business unionism, he called it. By 1881 he was prepared to act.

Participation:
Building the American Federation of Labor

The Knights of Labor. There had been other large worker unions. In 1869 Gompers had been invited to a secret meeting on condition that he never reveal what took place there. It was a meeting of the Knights of Labor. Though Gompers took an interest in the movement's plans, he never fully accepted it. He continued to work for Local 144 of the Cigar Makers' Union. Meanwhile, the Knights of Labor became an open labor union. By the late 1870s, it had 700,000 members but no real strategy for improving their lives.

Eventually, the Knights tried to organize a competing union for cigar makers. The old Cigar Makers' Union was just beginning to take advantage of its reputation for having the most skilled workers. Each cigar made by a Union member was identified by a blue label. The Knights tried to take advantage of the other union's reputation by putting a white label on their own cigars. Gompers joined the Knights for the sole purpose of getting some of these white labels so that Local 144 could identify their cigars both with their own blue label and with the white label of the bigger union.

But such shenanigans only served to split labor and upset any good the unions might do. In 1881 Gompers and some friends used

▲ **Sophia and Samuel Gompers**

their own Local 144 to start a larger organization—the Federation of Organized Trades and Labor Unions.

Federation of Organized Trades and Labor Unions. From the start, the federation worked only with craft unions in order to set itself apart from the growing industrialization and its emphasis on unskilled workers. The new federation invited the unions of skilled workers to unite. Gompers insisted that membership in the organization be voluntary; no trade union would be forced to join the larger organization.

At first, the federation had little power; it still did not have enough of the business-union attitude that Gompers wanted. Some leaders of member unions, such as Peter J. McGuire of the carpenter's union, demonstrated this businesslike attitude. McGuire led construction workers to win the first agreements for an eight-hour workday. But the ironworkers of the same period did not have such strong leadership. In 1886 some of these workers went on strike against the International Harvester Company in Chicago. When police were called to break up the demonstrations, someone threw a bomb that killed one policeman instantly and injured sixty others. The militia was called out, some workers were killed, and the strike was broken. Called the Haymarket Riot, this incident stirred the labor leaders to action. McGuire called for a meeting of the Federation of Organized Trades and Labor Unions in Philadelphia.

American Federation of Labor. This conference first tried to form a more solid labor front by uniting the federation with the Knights of Labor. When that failed, the labor representatives abolished their own ineffective Federation of Organized Trades and Labor Unions and replaced it with a new American Federation of Labor (AFL) open to all trade and labor unions of skilled workers. The AFL was to have a powerful president and a fifteen-man board of directors that would approve and coordinate all union activities. Scattered and wildcat strikes, as well as legal or civil actions that were not carefully planned, would be discouraged. The new union would build a fund to support workers in well-planned strikes, boycotts, and legal actions by charging each member a small annual fee. At age thirty-seven, Gompers became president of this new association of unions. His office, a room donated by his own union, Local 144, had one piece of furniture—a box that served as both a chair and a writing surface.

Building an organization. Gompers believed his first task was to enlist a large number of unions in the organization. The AFL would grow only if its leader was persuasive, and Gompers was. In the 1890s, he convinced every established union, except for the railroad unions, to join the AFL. He also created new unions within the federation for musicians, painters, streetcar workers, and teamsters. Now he could begin to carry out his plan for business unionism.

First he worked to make the AFL financially sound by building up a fund, collecting one-half cent per worker each week. Gompers planned to raise the same kind of reserve fund for action that large businesses maintained. He felt that laborers could make important gains by striking, but only if strikes were carefully timed to have the greatest impact on business. Furthermore, strikes would be used only as a last resort and only when carefully prepared for. Funds in the federation also would be used to oppose any antilabor legislation. Gompers hoped, above all, to make business leaders see that cooperation with the federation would be more profitable than quarreling with it. He planned to direct the money and energy of the AFL to three "bread and butter" goals: higher wages, shorter hours, and safer working conditions.

With some federation money, Gompers founded and edited a newspaper, the *American Federationist,* which became the voice of the AFL. He used the paper for many purposes. For example, in 1906, the *Federationist* recommended a boycott against Buck Stove Company. When that company secured an injunction from the courts barring such a published recommendation, Gompers continued to write against the company, for which he was sentenced to a year in jail. By now, however, he had learned to use the legal system. Gompers appealed the Buck Stove verdict, and the case lingered in the courts until the federal attorneys finally asked that it be dropped. The *Federationist* continued to publish its "We don't patronize" list, recommending boycotts against uncooperative companies. It became a major tool of the Federation.

Out of step with society. As president of the AFL, Gompers made what later would appear to have been mistakes. He refused to admit the machinist union and the blacksmiths' union into the federation because they included black members. He thought blacks should come into the federation only through all-black unions. Moreover, Gompers applied the same reasoning to the growing number of unskilled factory workers and to women. Wives, Gompers said, should not even work because "in our time, in our country ... the wife as wage-earner is a disadvantage economically ... and socially is unnecessary" (Livesay, p. 156).

Gompers also opposed pensions, unemployment compensation, management-paid health insurance, and maximum or minimum wage laws. He felt that these actions made workers dependent on government and capital.

Politics and growth. Gompers had seen that political control was in the hands of the wealthy and that political actions had gained little for the laborer. He refused to use the AFL to support any political party. Rather, organization members were told to vote for their friends and vote against their enemies.

Gradually, the federation made strides in improving working conditions for laborers. Various unions won shorter workdays, edging toward the eight-hour limit. Wages in many crafts improved. A few representatives and senators who favored laborers' causes were elected to office. In 1890 the government had begun to monitor large businesses and had passed antitrust (antimonopoly) laws, forcing companies such as Standard Oil of Ohio to allow for fair competition. In the early 1890s, as Gompers traveled around the country adding members to his federation, those same large businesses tried to use the antitrust laws against the federation. By 1914 labor-friendly representatives were strong enough to push through the first major favorable labor legislation. Congress, pressed by these representatives, passed a law that eliminated labor organizations from the antitrust laws. Gompers and his AFL could continue to add unions and members to its roster, and it did.

Fame and decay. As the union grew, so did Gompers's fame and popularity. At the end of World War I, he was seen as the spokesman for American labor and represented labor at the peace conferences between the Allies and Germany. However, by that time, he had become less of a militant champion of labor causes and more a defender of the federation he had built. He spent much time in his later years trying to hold the membership at a high level. When more women became involved in labor movements, he actively sought women's membership through support of an all-women trade union. However, he steadfastly refused to organize the unskilled laborers employed in the new machine-driven factories. In this respect, Gompers was

American Federation of Labor Membership	
1897	264,000
1900	548,000
1904	1,700,000
1917	2,400,000
1920	4,000,000

marching against the tide of history. In his last years, he argued against the leader of the United Mine Workers, John L. Lewis, who wanted to actively recruit unskilled workers to the labor cause.

Perhaps as a result of Gompers's concentrating on preserving the federation rather than advancing labor causes, or perhaps because the good economy of the early 1920s made labor causes seem less important, membership in the American Federation of Labor began to decline. By 1924, when Gompers died, the federation was reduced to 2.9 million members.

Aftermath

Respect for labor unions. Under Gompers' direction, workers had benefited greatly in terms of wages, working hours, and working conditions. Nevertheless, labor unions continued to represent only a small percentage of the workers. The AFL continued to ignore the direction American industry was taking and refused to admit unskilled factory workers within its ranks. The federation, therefore, had little influence in Congress, where this trend was recognized. It was not until the Great Depression caused a flood of social legislation that organized labor began to have a real influence in national politics. In 1935 Congress created the National Labor Relations Board to oversee labor elections and handle claims of unfair practices of employers against unions. Thereafter, unions had a voice within the national government.

Competition. The AFL continued its focus on crafts unions and on skilled labor. Meanwhile, the number of unskilled factory workers increased as American industry grew more mechanized. John L. Lewis moved to organize the steelworkers, who had never been included in the AFL. To do this, he organized the Committee for Industrial Organization (CIO) in 1935. At first, he tried to keep this organization within the AFL but the federation leaders disapproved. In 1937 the CIO was expelled from the AFL. Lewis changed the name to the Congress of Industrial Organizations and recruited many unskilled workers. Women and men of all races were accepted in the new union.

In its first year, the CIO initiated 4,720 strikes. Some of these used a new technique to ensure that nonunion workers could not replace the strikers. Striking workers "sat in" their work places. This tactic was declared illegal, but the CIO pressed its strike tactics. Several major manufacturers—including General Motors, Chrysler, Firestone, and General Electric—were forced to sign agreements with the CIO.

As a result, leaders of Gompers's American Federation of Labor were stirred to action. They began to send recruiters into the field again. Between the two giant labor organizations, membership grew from 4 million in 1936 to 6 million in 1938. Eventually, the two organizations merged into the single AFL–CIO, and labor became a powerful force to be reckoned with in American industry.

For More Information

Dick, William M. *Labor and Socialism in America: The Gompers Era.* Port Washington, New York: Kennikat Press, 1972.

Gompers, Samuel. *Seventy Years of Life and Labor.* Edited by Nick Salvatore. New York: ILR Press, 1984.

Livesay, Harold. *Samuel Gompers and Organized Labor in America.* Boston: Little, Brown and Co., 1978.

Mary "Mother" Jones

c. 1830-1930

Personal Background

Ireland. Life in Ireland in the early 1800s was miserable for the average peasant. Wealthy landlords rented small plots to peasant farmers and collected the rent in labor on their own large farms. Richard and Mary Harris were typical of these renters. They lived and raised Mary and her two brothers in a windowless one-room house made of mud and straw and covered with a thatched roof. There was not much warmth and little hope in the homes of these cottage tenants, or "cotters," as they were called. Heavy rains sometimes spoiled the potato crops on which all of Ireland depended. When the rains came and the cotters could not pay their rent, they were cruelly evicted. Thousands of ex-cotters begged on the streets and turned to thievery to support themselves. When they did steal for food, they were hunted down and destroyed like animals. One of Mary's earliest memories was of the landlord's soldiers riding into her village carrying the heads of cotters-turned-beggars-and-thieves on their lances.

Mary had been born a cotter early in the 1800s. In later life, she claimed to have been born May 1, 1830. Other records suggest that the year may have been 1837 or 1843. No matter the year, conditions for the Irish cotters were dismal. By the time Mary was five years old, the Harris family, although still able to live in their little cottage, had begun to feel the desperation and hunger that ran

▲ Mary "Mother" Jones

Event: Organizing the coal miners of West Virginia.

Role: Inspired to fight for the poor from the very start of her life, Mary Harris Jones championed the rights of workers throughout America. One of her weapons in the fight was the newspaper *An Appeal to Reason,* which grew out of her efforts to organize the coal miners of West Virginia. She served as a union organizer for most of her life.

through the land. Mary's father was accused of stealing food and raiding a military camp to free some poor prisoners. As punishment, he was ordered hanged. However, he escaped this fate, most probably by joining a boat of friendly fishermen, and managed somehow to reach America. From there, he wrote that he would send for the family as soon as he had earned enough money from the dollar-a-day job he had already found.

The family reunited. Six years later, Mary Harris and her three children arrived in North America, where Richard had a job as a railroad worker near Toronto, Ontario, Canada. They rented a small four-room house and owned two pigs. Mary was eleven when the family was reunited; two years later, the growing Canadian city opened its first public school, which Mary attended. She then spent one year in the newly established Toronto Normal School studying to become a teacher. No one now knows what happened in that year, but at the end of it, Mary quit school and also left her family. As far as the records show, she did not contact her mother and father again.

Marriage. For a short time, Mary taught elementary school, first in Maine, then in Monroe, Michigan. After a couple of years, she found the need to discipline the children distasteful and left teaching to become a seamstress in Chicago. After two years of sewing beautiful gowns for rich people in the city, she grew restless again and moved to Memphis, Tennessee, amid the 1860 talk of secession.

There she met George Jones, an iron molder. His was an important craft. Melted iron was poured carefully into molds to make many of the necessary tools of the day. By 1860 the craft had grown more important because of the expanding railroad system and its need for tracks. George was a proud member of the Iron Molders Union. Soon he was also working as an organizer, assigned with the task of signing up new members. He must have been dedicated to his job and good at it: in 1860 there were 1,000 members in the union; seven years later, there were 8,615.

George and Mary lived comfortably on his salary. By 1867 Mary had borne four children. (Because of Mary's tendency to tell stories, the number of children has also been questioned. She later said four, but there may have been any number from one to four.)

However large the family, it fell victim to the great yellow fever epidemic of 1867. All of Mary's children died in the epidemic. In the same year, George died in an industrial accident.

Alone again. With her family gone, Jones returned to her work as a seamstress in Chicago. She set up her own shop and prospered by sewing for the rich. Her bad luck continued, however. Just as she was gaining financial success, the great Chicago fire of 1871 erupted. One-sixth of the city burned, including Jones's shop and apartment. After a short time spent wandering through the rubble, Jones borrowed a sewing machine and soon was back at work doing some sewing. However, sometime during her stay in Chicago, she happened to attend a meeting that set her on the path of her main work in life. While wandering the burned streets, she noticed an old building that seemed to be housing a meeting of some sort. After talking to the lookout person, she was admitted to a secret meeting of a new labor organization, the Knights of Labor. Although Jones later objected to the Knights' dislike of violence and of striking to win a labor point, she was impressed with its goal to turn America into a socialist state ruled not by wealthy industrialists but by the workers. Jones soon joined the Knights of Labor.

Although she talked little about the next few years in her own autobiography, her attitudes toward the big businessmen of her time and toward the difficult working conditions of the average laborer must have been strengthened by the struggles she saw around her. She saw firsthand the difficulties of the average worker in the great panic of 1873. She noticed the cooperation between the bosses and government as the great railroad strike of 1877 was put down by President Rutherford B. Hayes and 50,000 federal troops. And she knew of the violence that erupted when workers in Chicago struck the McCormick Harvester Company, demanding an eight-hour work day: many workers and police had been killed in the 1886 Haymarket Riot that ended the strike, and its leaders were hanged.

Through all this, Jones watched the Knights of Labor stand by without taking part in the strikes or in the battles with militia and police. She was now convinced that the workers needed to become more unified and more resistant. She left the Knights of Labor, but her commitment to unions to strengthen the position of laborers was now firm. Jones was ready to begin her life's work.

▲ **Government troops defending the railroad against strikers**

Participation: The Coal Miners' Strikes

Mother Jones. By the 1880s, Jones had been working with a labor union for nearly ten years and had become known for her fiery speeches. She was able to lecture to prospective union members as if she were their mother, and the mine workers even called her "mother." Her age commanded respect and her speaking skills held the workers' attention. Jones spoke the language of the streets, and her speeches were dotted with swear words. The rough and unskilled workers in the newly developing factories loved her style.

Mine workers. One group of oppressed workers was the miners. Miners everywhere worked very long hours in the dark, stuffy, unsanitary, and cramped conditions. Often they were forced to shovel and pick coal and metals out of small shafts in which they could not even stand up. Sometimes the openings were so small that the ore could not even be taken out by mule—instead, dogs were used to pull the heavy carts. In the narrow coal mines, too much digging often resulted in cave-ins that trapped the workers, or in poisoning from methane gas, which was freed from the loosened coal. There were already two unions organizing the miners to demand better working conditions.

Working far from towns, most of the miners lived in hovels provided by the mine owners. They were paid in scrip, or company money, and were forced to shop at the company store. Thus they were bound to their low wages and poor housing. To make ends meet, boys of the families often went to work in the mines at a very young age, at first sitting on ladders along the chutes through which the coal tumbled to the railcars. There they hunched over the coal, sorting out the shale rock that sometimes mixed with it. If these boys lived long enough, they too would become miners as they grew into their teens.

Many mining families did not earn enough income, and industrialists saw another opportunity for more cheap labor. They built textile mills near the coal-mining villages. The girls of the mining families were brought in to tend the weaving machines. This was the setting in Norton, Virginia, in 1891, when the miners decided to strike against the great Dietz mines.

Mine strike in Norton, Virginia. Striking was difficult in those days. Police, the national guard, and even the federal army were ready to protect the owners' properties and to put down any rebellion. A striker or union member could expect to be fired, threatened, and maybe beaten by police or by thugs hired by the company. If the miners in Norton were to strike, they would need someone to rally them and hold up morale. The United Mine Workers of Norton sent for Jones.

Jones and union organizer Dud Hado met with trouble the minute they set foot in Norton. They were met at the train station by a company messenger, who told them that the mine superintendent

▲ **Children in the mines**

intended to blow their heads off. Jones sent back a message saying she had come to talk with the workers, not with the superintendent. Although no building in the company town would allow a meeting, and the black church that at first agreed was frightened into withdrawing, Jones spoke to the workers at the largest street intersection outside of town.

Dud Hado had prepared himself by carrying a concealed gun. As they made their way first to the black church and then to the street rally, Jones was glad for the protection but thought that Hado should not hide it since concealing it was against the law. Hado agreed and took the gun out in full view after the two left the meeting. They were immediately pounced on by eight or ten armed men and taken before a justice of the peace to be tried for carrying a concealed weapon.

The mine manager appeared and expressed surprise that Jones would carry a gun into a church. As always, Jones was neither frightened nor speechless. She reminded the manager that the land on which the church was built was company property. The church was, therefore, a company house, and "God Almighty never comes around to a place like this" (Jones, p. 26).

Jones was acquitted of the charges and Dud Hado was fined $25, which Jones paid out of union money. Later, she was told that the coal company had expected her to stay in jail while she appealed the fine. They planned to kill her and Hado in jail and dispose of their bodies, telling others that they had been released early in the morning and disappeared. True or not, this story accurately describes the strength of the mine bosses of the 1890s.

The strike at Norton failed to accomplish its goals, but it resulted in several positive aftereffects. Jones had become well acquainted with Mr. J. Wayland. In 1893 the two joined with three others to write and print the first United Mine Workers newspaper, *An Appeal to Reason*. Jones used this newspaper in future efforts to rally the mine workers throughout the country.

Birmingham strike. In 1894, 8,000 union members decided to strike the mines around Birmingham, Alabama. Eugene Debs, a popular politician who was famous for organizing the American Railroad Union, went to Birmingham to speak to the workers. The mine companies called the national guard to prevent Debs from using a meeting hall. Meanwhile, Jones rallied the workers, convincing 2,000 to go to the train station to meet Debs. They carried Debs on their shoulders to the center of town. The show of strength held back the national guard, and Debs was allowed to speak.

Although, in the end, the Birmingham strike failed, Jones and Debs had once again called attention to the miners' dismal working conditions.

Child labor. While visiting the coal fields of West Virginia, Jones had noticed very young boys at work in the mines. She also visited one family where an eleven-year-old girl lay dying of tuberculosis, the result of working long hours in dismal conditions at the textile factory. During Jones's stay, the girl died, not from the disease, but from being so tired that she could not hold up her head while working—her hair caught in the fast-moving machinery at the mill, and she was killed.

The textile mills. Jones decided to see for herself what conditions were like in the textile mills. In 1894 she went to Cottondale, Alabama, a textile town in the coal mining area. Her suspicions of what she would find were confirmed as soon as she applied for a job. The textile boss told her he would hire her only if she had children who could also work in the mills. Jones lied, saying that she had six children who would soon be coming to town with their father. She was hired, and she watched as girls ten and eleven years old were forced to work in damp and cold conditions for twelve hours a day. Some worked washing the threads and textiles in rooms that were always wet. Some grew so weary that they fell asleep on the job, only to be brutally roused by the foremen.

When two weeks passed and the six children did not show up, the boss became suspicious. Jones quit, saying her husband was ill, and moved to Tuscaloosa, Oklahoma, to work in a rope factory. There she saw the same conditions. From that time on, Jones would have two great concerns—improving conditions for the miners and eliminating child labor.

Aftermath

Union organizer. Now a paid organizer for the United Mine Workers, Jones toured the country, appearing to rally the forces wherever miners rose up in strike. In 1897 she organized strikers in Wheeling, West Virginia, for another losing strike effort. It was not until 1899 that Pennsylvania miners would win a first victory over the owners, gaining a shorter workday and a ten percent raise.

By 1900 Jones was earning $494 a year as a United Mine Workers' organizer, probably as much as she had ever earned from the union. She traveled wherever she was needed, often by hitching rides from sympathetic railroad conductors. She lived in cheap hotels or with mine-worker families. Usually, she carried no extra clothes or baggage with her. Baggage was too awkward for her job, which she defined as being a hell-raiser.

Southern Colorado. In 1903 Jones was called to Colorado to help miners in their strike against mine owner John D. Rockefeller, Jr. The governor had called out the national guard to protect the mines. Both coal and metals were mined in the West. The efforts of the miners were undermined because they had organized into two unions. Coal miners had not yet learned to accept metal miners into the United Mine Workers (UMW). The UMW president, John Mitchell, did not really accept the metal miners' union and proved reluctant to call on the combined strength of the UMW to settle the Colorado strike. In the end, the strike failed. Jones was never again friendly with Mitchell.

The textile children. In 1903 Jones again visited the textile workers and decided that something had to be done to help the children. Too many of them were working long hours in the mills, and too many of them were being permanently injured by the work. She decided to organize a march from Philadelphia to New York City and then to Oyster Bay, New York, where she hoped to speak with President Theodore Roosevelt.

The march began with 300 people, 200 of them children. They marched from Philadelphia to Bristol and then finally to New York. By that time, weary children had been sent home, and only about fifty marchers remained, ready to parade in New York. After marching through the city, they went on to Oyster Bay. Jones chose just three children to meet the president, hoping not to overwhelm him. But Roosevelt refused to see even this small group, claiming he had no authority to interfere with child labor laws. In spite of his negative response, Jones's march had been successful; it had called nationwide attention to the plight of children and to the state officials who refused to enforce laws against child labor.

> ## Workers Helped by Mother Jones
>
> West Virginia miners
> Pullman Palace Car Company workers
> Pittsburgh, Pennsylvania, workers
> Scranton, Pennsylvania, silk weavers
> Scranton housemaids
> West Virginia textile workers
> Colorado miners
> Idaho miners
> Michigan copper miners
> Roosevelt, New Jersey, chemical workers
> Bisbee, Arizona, miners
> Homestead steel workers
> Chicago, Illinois, dressmakers

Victory in West Virginia. Back in West Virginia in 1912, Jones found the miners again on strike and the governor again calling out the militia to protect the mine owners. But now the union was stronger. The mine owners saw that they would lose the battle and were desperate. Now about eighty years old, Jones was arrested to keep her from speaking to the miners. She was held in a jail for twenty-two days awaiting trial by a military court. The new governor, Henry Hatfield, heard about this and went to the jail to find Jones sick with pneumonia. He ordered her taken to a hospital until she was well and then returned her for trial. By this time, however, U.S. Senator John Kern had learned of the situation and demanded that Congress intervene.

The mine owners now saw that they would lose the battle. They arranged to save face by having Hatfield impose state rules that would give the mine workers a nine-hour day and the right to shop in stores other than the company store. Thus the union won its demands, but the mine owners did not appear to be losers.

Ludlow and Pancho Villa. A great strike was on to protest the conditions at the mines owned by John D. Rockefeller, Jr., near Ludlow, Colorado. Nine thousand striking workers had moved out of company towns and established tent cities. They were striking for work conditions already guaranteed by state law. Still the miners were treated brutally. One camp was visited by company thugs under a flag of truce; the thugs pulled out firearms and fired randomly into the crowd gathered to hear them. Another camp woke up one morning to find company militia mounting machine guns on a hill above the tent city. The militia fired, scattering the people and allowing company hoods to destroy the camp. The incident triggered a nationwide outrage.

Jones, who had come to Ludlow to help the workers, had been met by police and escorted out of the area. As soon as possible, she had returned, only to be arrested and held in a cellar of the county courthouse for twenty-six days. Now she received publicity and help from an unexpected source.

General Francisco (Pancho) Villa was a Mexican revolutionary whom Jones had previously helped. He had run from government forces and escaped into the United States. One day, some men in a big black car had come to his home, kidnapped him, and returned him to Mexico. Hearing of this, Jones had raised a national outcry over Mexican officials being allowed to kidnap people living peacefully in the United States. She raised such a ruckus that seven days later the big black car drove up to the border and deposited Pancho Villa back in the United States.

Hearing of Jones's imprisonment, Villa offered to trade some prisoners in Mexico who were wanted by the United States for Jones's freedom. The accompanying publicity convinced the military that they should not hold Jones for trial.

Women's rights. Although other causes arose during her long life, Jones was concerned only with union matters. Women sought the right to vote, but Jones would have nothing to do with this fight. "You don't need a vote to raise hell," she said (Jones, p. 195). Throughout her life as a union organizer, she demonstrated the power of women. Often, when conditions threatened to become violent, she had organized the striking men's wives into noisy pan-and-broom brigades in such numbers that the would-be thugs were turned away. The broom brigades became a part of her union strategy. They relieved the men and proved to the downtrodden women that they had power. They listened to her because she was a successful union organizer, a profession that had been almost exclusively male.

> ## The Words of Mother Jones
>
> "I asked a man in prison how he came to be there and he said he had stolen a pair of shoes. I told him if he had stolen a railroad he would be a United States Senator."
>
> "[To women] No matter what you fight, don't be ladylike! God Almighty made women and the Rockefeller gang of thieves made the ladies." (Jones, pp. 81, 204)

Final years. By 1920, and by her count nearing ninety years old, Jones was penniless. She had worked for the unions for sixty years and had little to show for it except many friends, who now came to her aid. She lived with one friend after another until her death on November 30, 1930. Jones was buried in the Union Miners' Cemetery at Mount Olive, Illinois.

For More Information

Atkinson, Linda. *Mother Jones, The Most Dangerous Woman in America*. New York: Crown, 1978.

Jones, Mary. *The Autobiography of Mother Jones*. Chicago: Charles H. Kerr, 1990.

Long, Priscilla. *Mother Jones, Woman Organizer*. Cambridge, Mass.: Red Sun Press, 1976.

Struggle for Civil Rights

1864
Blacks hold the National Convention of Colored Men at Syracuse, New York, planning to gain political rights.

1875
Congress passes the Civil Rights Act of 1875.

1890
Blacks move to Tennessee and Kansas, continuing to found all-black towns.

1883
The Supreme Court declares that the Civil Rights Act of 1875 is unconstitutional. Economic depression begins.

1881
Tennessee passes the first Jim Crow law. **Booker T. Washington** opens Tuskegee Institute.

1877
Reconstruction ends. Southern Democrats are back in control of most of the former Confederate states.

1892
Ida B. Wells-Barnett begins antilynching crusade; her book *Southern Horrors* is published. Populist party forms.

1893
Supreme Court upholds segregation in *Plessy* v. *Ferguson* ruling.

1895
Washington makes his Atlanta Compromise speech. Wells's second book about lynching, *A Red Record,* is published.

1910
Du Bois begins to publish monthly magazine for the NAACP, *The Crisis.*

1909
National Association for the Advancement of Colored People (NAACP) is founded.

1903
Du Bois publishes *The Souls of Black Folk,* a book that criticizes the strategy of Washington.

1900
W. E. B. Du Bois attends first world African conference.

STRUGGLE FOR CIVIL RIGHTS

Black leaders foresaw that freedom from slavery was only the first step in the struggle for equality in America. Anxious for political rights, they began as early as 1864 to hold their own conventions and organized to gain the vote. Hopeful signs of change followed. In 1866 Congress produced a Civil Rights Act defining American-born blacks as citizens. In 1868 the Fourteenth Amendment guaranteed their citizenship in the Constitution. By 1869 Louisiana was experimenting with integrated schools, courtroom juries were mixed, and blacks had been elected to office in several Southern states.

These changes were short-lived, however. Conservative whites, who opposed change and wanted to keep blacks in an inferior position, regained control of state governments. This accomplished, they enacted laws to deprive blacks of rights. For example, they charged a poll tax for casting a ballot, making it difficult for blacks to vote. If blacks did not pay the tax, they could not vote. And if they did not vote in one election, the cost doubled at the next election. There was a loophole in such laws, called the grandfather clause, for poor whites. It said that the laws did not apply to anyone who could vote before 1867 or to their children.

Congress made a last effort to safeguard black rights, passing the Civil Rights Act of 1875, which guaranteed to all races full and equal enjoyment of trains, hotels, and other public places of amusement. But, particularly in the South, the act was ignored. Reconstruction ended in 1877, and federal troops withdrew, leaving the conservative whites in control of state governments.

The states began passing Jim Crow laws, which segregated the South. Blacks were required to use separate public facilities—for example, schools, trains, and theaters—from whites. Tennessee, Florida, and Texas all passed Jim Crow laws in the 1880s. In 1883 the Supreme Court declared the Civil Rights Act of 1875 unconstitutional. Delighting many Southerners, the ruling meant it was legal for private businesses to practice segregation. In 1893 the Supreme Court upheld segregation in *Plessy* v. *Ferguson.* Homer Plessy, a New Orleans citizen whose ancestry was 7/8ths Caucasian and 1/8th African, sat in a railroad car reserved for whites. The court ruled that by doing so he broke the segregation law, and thus the court declared that "separate but equal" facilities were legal under the Constitution. It would take sixty-one years for the judgment to be overturned in *Brown* v. *the Board of Education.*

While facilities for blacks were separate, they were certainly not equal. This presented problems, but segregation was often not the primary concern. In education, for example, the alternative to segregation in some areas was no schools at all. The first priority in such areas was often the existence of education for blacks, so segregated schools were acceptable. There were a few blacks who even preferred the development of separate schools, churches, and other organizations, thinking they would strengthen black independence.

No matter what the strategy, however, blacks were not left alone in the South. There were beatings and killings of those who attempted to vote or exercise other rights. White terrorists burned houses of blacks in the middle of the night. Blacks were charged with made-up crimes, then hanged without a trial. Such killings, called lynchings, became increasingly common toward the end of the century. Over 1,400 black men were lynched or burned to death in the 1890s alone.

There was disagreement in the black community about

how to respond to the violence and discrimination. Some leaders, such as Benjamin "Pap" Singleton, encouraged blacks to migrate to Kansas or Oklahoma and establish their own towns, an option many blacks chose to take. Unconvinced that blacks could ever win equal rights in America, Bishop Henry Turner urged movement back to Africa. Others chose to wage a struggle for equality in America. In Tennessee, the crusader **Ida B. Wells-Barnett** protested against lynching in her Memphis newspaper *Free Speech*. After she herself was threatened by angry whites, the reporter went to New York and later Chicago, where she continued to write articles and books exposing the horrors of black lynchings in the South.

Booker T. Washington provided blacks with an alternative for dealing with conditions in the South. Wanting blacks to learn skills with which to earn a living, he founded Tuskegee Institute, a school to teach such skills. He further advised that blacks adjust to white racism for the time being. Publicly Washington called for blacks to stay out of politics, though he secretly backed activists who pushed for black rights. His approach won him much support from the white community. Whites saw him as a black man who knew his place, or accepted the realities of segregation. They liked what they heard and accepted him as the official spokesperson for blacks. Meanwhile, he had great appeal among blacks as a leader who developed independent institutions for the group.

There were, however, some educated blacks who grew frustrated with Washington's calls for adjustment and compromise. Under the leadership of **W. E. B. Du Bois,** they formed the National Association for the Advancement of Colored People (NAACP), which called for immediate integration without compromise. The NAACP became the leading black organization and the nation's most effective voice for integration, and Du Bois became editor of its journal, *The Crisis*. A respected scholar, he also helped establish black studies as an educational field and accurately predicted that race relations would become one of the country's foremost problems in the twentieth century.

Ida B. Wells-Barnett

1862-1930

Personal Background

Ida Bell Wells was born a slave in Holly Springs, Mississippi, on July 16, 1862. Her parents, James and Elizabeth Wells, were slaves. The son of a white plantation owner and a slave mother, Jim Wells had grown up on his father's plantation, where he was treated relatively well as a slave. According to law, babies born to a slave mother automatically became slaves, regardless of their father's status. Jim's father openly recognized him as his son, so the boy was not whipped, beaten, or sold away from his family. At eighteen, he was apprenticed to a nearby carpenter named Bolling. As he learned the carpenter's trade, he also met Bolling's cook, Elizabeth Warrenton, who was part black and part Indian. The two fell in love and married. Ida, their first child, was born soon after, in the second year of the Civil War.

Reconstruction childhood. Six months after Ida's birth, President Abraham Lincoln's Emancipation Proclamation freed the South's slaves. The war ended in 1865 with total Southern defeat. Ida grew up during the Reconstruction era, when victorious Northerners flooded into the ruined South, taking control of state and local governments. Defeated Southern leaders, traditionally plantation-owning Democrats, hated these Republicans, whom they called carpetbaggers because of their cloth suitcases. Blacks allied them-

▲ Ida B. Wells-Barnett

Event: Crusade against the lynching of blacks.

Role: Journalist, feminist, and civil rights worker, Wells-Barnett wrote articles that exposed the lynching of blacks by white mobs. She carefully gathered evidence on hundreds of lynchings—murders, without legal trial, of blacks supposedly guilty of some offense—and worked to win greater civil rights for blacks and women.

selves to the carpetbaggers, helping to vote Republicans into power throughout the South.

Carpentry success. When Ida's father, now employed by Bolling, went to vote for the first time, Bolling warned him to vote Democratic. Jim ignored his boss and returned from the polls to find the building locked against him. After this, he rented another building nearby and set up a carpentry business of his own. It did well, and his success meant that his children could all go to school. Their mother, a religious woman and a firm person, made sure they also went to church and did their chores around the house. The family grew, and by 1878, when Reconstruction was ending, sixteen-year-old Ida had six younger brothers and sisters. She attended Rust College, a high school for freed blacks in Holly Springs. A serious girl who worked hard in school, she also helped her mother with the younger children. She would give them their baths Saturday night, then lay out their best outfits for church on Sunday.

Yellow fever. In the summer of 1878, Ida went to visit her grandparents on their farm deep in the country. That summer, a yellow-fever epidemic broke out in some of the area's larger towns, including Holly Springs, and it killed many people. Out in the country, Ida heard nothing about the epidemic until a letter arrived from a friend of her parents. Jim and Elizabeth Wells had both died of the disease, along with Ida's youngest brother, Stanley. A few days later, Ida returned to the now nearly empty town. She heard from her sister Eugenia how their father had helped nurse the town's sick and then took care of his wife and children when they fell ill before catching the fever himself and dying the day before Elizabeth.

Taking charge. The Wellses had had many friends. They decided that care of the children would be divided among themselves. Ida had different ideas. She would look after them herself, she told the friends firmly. They argued that she was too young, but she didn't back down and they finally agreed. So at sixteen, Ida took full responsibility for her five younger brothers and sisters.

Teacher. The first thing she had to do was find work. Tying her hair back to look older, she took the teacher's examination. She passed it and won a teaching job at a small school six miles outside of Holly Springs. She made $25 per week, enough to support herself and the children. During the week, she lived with the family of a student, and her grandmother or someone else stayed with the children. On Friday afternoons, she rode back into town on a mule, then spent the weekend cleaning, cooking, and doing laundry at home. On Sunday afternoons, she rode back out to school for the week's teaching.

Move to Tennessee. After about a year, her father's sister Fanny, who lived in Memphis, Tennessee, asked Ida if she would like to come live with her there. Exhausted by her heavy schedule, Ida gratefully agreed. Two of her sisters were also invited to Fanny's, while Eugenia and the boys went to live with another aunt. Ida found another job teaching ten miles outside of Memphis, in the town of Woodstock. She traveled there by train in the morning and returned to Fanny's at night. During summer vacations, she took classes at Fisk University and Lemoyne Institute in Memphis.

Interests and dreams. During the early 1880s, Ida, now a pretty young woman, enjoyed the social life in Memphis's black community. She went to concerts and plays as well as church events. She also kept a diary, in which she wrote about her dreams of becoming an actress or writing a novel. As her interests grew broader, she often wondered what the future would bring. She never suspected that she would take the first step toward her life's work while in the middle of her daily routine—the short train ride to Woodstock.

Participation: Struggle for Civil Rights

Overturning Reconstruction. While Ida had been growing up, the programs and laws passed by the Republicans began to be overturned as Democrats slowly came back into power throughout the South. In the late 1860s and early 1870s, a series of civil rights Acts and constitutional amendments had promised blacks full citizenship, full voting rights (for the men), and full enjoyment of public facilities like restaurants and trains. By the time Ida moved to Memphis, however, Republicans in Washington had lost interest in enforcing these laws. Beginning in the 1880s, the Supreme Court struck down many of them. For example, in 1883, the court declared it unconstitutional for the government to prevent segregation in a case questioning the legal separation of facilities for whites and blacks.

Jim Crow laws. Meanwhile, Southern old-style Democrats who believed that whites were superior to blacks passed the Jim Crow laws. (Jim Crow was a black slave character from songs popular among Southern whites before the Civil War.) The laws made it hard for blacks to vote and kept them separated from whites in most areas of society, such as in schools and public facilities. Protected by such racist laws, whites felt free to threaten, beat, and kill blacks who behaved in ways they did not like.

Train ride. One day in May 1884, Ida took her usual seat in the first-class ladies' coach for the train ride out to Woodstock. When the conductor came to take her ticket, however, he asked her to move forward to the smoking car where blacks were now supposed to sit. Ida refused. She had paid for a first-class seat and did not want to move. When the conductor angrily tried to pull her out of the seat, she bit his hand. With the support of the white passengers, he and two other railroad employees finally succeeded in physically forcing her from her seat into the smoking car. Bruised but determined, she got off at the next stop and looked for a lawyer to help her sue the railroad.

Journalist. Ida won her case. The judge fined the railroad $300 and awarded Ida damages of $500. When the railroad appealed the decision, however, the Tennessee Supreme Court overruled the lower court. She had to return the money and pay the railroad's legal costs. In the meantime, she had done some work for local church publications. In 1887 she was asked to write an article telling her story for a black church weekly, *The Living Way*. The article was so popular that the newspaper's editor asked her to write regularly for it. She agreed and thus began her career in journalism.

Iola. Over the next several years, while continuing her main job of teaching, Ida Wells wrote regular articles for *The Living Way*. Although she sometimes covered local events like weddings and club meetings, Wells mostly wrote about social issues affecting both blacks and women. Soon she was also contributing pieces to other black newspapers and magazines throughout the United States. Like many writers of her day, she did not write under her own name but instead used a pen name, Iola. Her articles, written in a plain style that even poorly educated blacks could easily understand, were popular and successful.

Free Speech. By 1889 Wells was being called "the Princess of the Press," and in that year, the two owners of a black paper called the *Free Speech and Headlight* asked her to be their editor. She accepted on the condition that they let her buy a third share in the paper as an equal partner. They agreed, and somehow she came up with the necessary money.

Platform. Wells had found the platform from which she could express her views, and she began doing just that in her editorials. Unafraid of controversy, she did not hesitate to criticize blacks as well as whites. Black ministers in Memphis were angry with her when she exposed a black minister who was having a love affair with a member of his church. And when she blasted the poor quality of education for black children in Memphis, the board of education fired her from her teaching job. But her efforts had brought 2,000 new subscribers to the newspaper, and she now made a decent living from her job as editor.

Lynching. She also wrote an editorial supporting the use of violence to protest lynching. When blacks in Georgetown, Kentucky, outraged by the lynching of a black man, had set fire to the town, Wells wrote, "Not until the Negro rises in his might and takes a hand in resenting such cold-blooded murders, if he has to burn up whole towns, will a halt be called in wholesale lynching" (Thompson, p. 23).

"A feeling of horror." The first lynching in Memphis occurred in 1892. The victims, three friends of Wells's, owned a grocery store that had recently opened and was cutting into the business of a white-owned store across the street. The other store's owner started several fights with them. Tensions rose, and Wells's friends were told by a lawyer that, since the store was outside the city police's territory, they had the legal right to defend their property from attack. One Saturday night in March, a group of nine armed white men came walking toward the store from across the street. The black store owners fired on them, not realizing the men were actually deputies who were wearing regular clothes instead of their uniforms. Three deputies were wounded, and Wells's friends surrendered right away when they realized what they had done.

They and about twenty-five other blacks were taken to jail, and black soldiers from the national guard kept watch for two nights to make sure the jail would not be attacked. A white judge illegally had the soldiers' weapons taken away, and, on a Wednesday night, nine white men simply took the three grocers from jail and shot them to death. The murderers were thought to have been deputies. As Wells later wrote, "a feeling of horror ... possessed every member of the race in Memphis when the truth dawned on us that the protection of the law which we so long enjoyed was no longer ours" (Van Steenwyck, p. 37).

Blacks leave Memphis. The lynching of her friends would change Wells's life forever. She wrote editorials filled with sorrow and outrage, urging blacks to leave Memphis. They did so in the thousands, many going to Oklahoma. White businesses faced ruin from the loss of black customers. White newspapers, which had helped encourage the lynching, wrote articles painting a horrible picture of what awaited those who went to Oklahoma. Wells went to Oklahoma herself, returning to tell readers the truth about conditions there. As blacks continued to leave, she began to do research on lynchings, which had become common throughout the South since Reconstruction.

Rape myth. The most common reason used to lynch black men was that they had raped white women. Wells discovered that even when a white woman had chosen to have sexual relations with a black man, lynchers called it rape to give them an excuse for murder.

Crusade. When eight more Memphis blacks were lynched in May 1892, Wells wrote editorials about what she had found in her research. She attacked the idea that black men raped white women, and she implied that white women were often attracted to black men. Memphis whites were furious. The *Free Speech* office was attacked

> ## Wells on the First Memphis Lynching
>
> "The city of Memphis has demonstrated that neither character nor standing avails the Negro if he dares to protect himself against the white man or become his rival.... There is therefore only one thing left that we can do; save our money and leave a town which will neither protect our lives and property, nor give us a fair trial in the courts, when accused by white persons." (Thompson, p. 28)

and wrecked. Wells was in Philadelphia when the article was printed, and she did not return to Memphis. Instead, she went to New York City, where she joined the leading black newspaper of the day, the *New York Age*. There she continued her crusade against lynching and against whites who falsely used the charge of rape to justify lynchings. A long article in the *Age* became the basis for two books, *Southern Horrors* (1892) and *A Red Record* (1895), which told the full story about the hundreds of lynchings in the South since the Civil War.

> ## On the Excuse of Rape
>
> "Nobody ... believes the old threadbare lie that Negro men assault white women. If Southern men are not careful they will over-reach themselves and a conclusion will be reached which will be very damaging to the moral reputation of their women."
> (Thompson, p. 29)

International audience. Over the next few years, Wells became one of the black community's leading voices. She worked closely with other leaders, including Frederick Douglass, who was now in his seventies. The most influential and respected African American of the century, Douglass shared Wells's strong views on the blacks' situation. Wells also went twice to England, where her speeches won wide support for the black cause in America. On her second trip, in 1894, she stayed for six months and spoke to over 100 clubs and associations, while regularly sending articles back to a Chicago paper, the *Inter-Ocean*. One of the few white papers open to the idea of racial equality, the *Inter-Ocean* ran the articles under the title "Ida B. Wells Abroad" (Thompson, p. 54).

World's Fair. Wells had moved to Chicago in 1893, after attending the Chicago World's Fair (officially called the Columbian Exposition) earlier that year. She had gone to the fair because African Americans were not represented there at all, though other peoples from all over the world were. With Frederick Douglass's encouragement, she wrote a booklet, *The Reason Why the Colored American Is Not in the World's Columbian Exposition*. The booklet went beyond black exclusion from the fair to explore broader issues about the black situation. In Wells's words, "it was a clear, plain statement of facts concerning the oppression put upon the colored people in this land of the free and home of the brave" (Van Steenwyck, p. 46). Douglass himself wrote the booklet's introduction.

Wells also started a women's club in Chicago, like the clubs she had been speaking to in both America and England. Soon taking the name "the Ida B. Wells Woman's Club," it created the city's first black orchestra and its first black children's kindergarten, among many other projects.

Marriage and family. Meanwhile, she was contributing articles to a black Chicago paper, the *Conservator,* founded by Ferdinand Barnett. Barnett, who had helped her with the World's Fair booklet, was a lawyer who shared Ida Wells's concern for black rights. The two fell in love and were married on June 27, 1895. They had four children: Charles (1896); Herman (1897); Ida (1901); and Alfreda (1904). When they grew up, the children often helped their mother with her work, but they chose not to follow her into public life.

Changing times. After marrying, Wells-Barnett traveled less but kept up with her civil rights work. She also continued writing, as the *Conservator*'s editor-in-chief. Times were changing, however. With the death of her old friend Frederick Douglass in 1895, leadership of the black community began passing from those who shared his strong, militant views to those who followed Booker T. Washington's ideas (see **Booker T. Washington**). Washington thought blacks should compromise in dealing with whites, accommodating white society rather than opposing it. Wells-Barnett, independent and strong-willed, refused to accept any kind of compromise. By the early 1900s, she increasingly found herself outside of the black mainstream in her work for civil rights.

NAACP, Negro Fellowship League. In 1909 three days of racial violence in nearby Springfield, Illinois, led to the founding of the National Association for the Advancement of Colored People (NAACP). Wells-Barnett helped found the national organization and served on its executive committee. Yet she soon found herself in conflict with other members. She clashed with NAACP field agents, for example, while investigating lynchings and violence in Illinois and Arkansas. She had also founded her own group, the Negro Fellowship League, which she worked with more closely, helping other blacks with practical problems like jobs and homes. At the same time, she gave much of her time to the women's movement, marching in parades and organizing other activities to win the vote for women.

Aftermath

Health problems. In 1920, a year after race riots in Chicago had claimed thirty-eight black and white lives, Wells-Barnett was forced to close the Fellowship League for lack of money. A week later, she entered the hospital for a major operation. It took her several months to recover, and when she returned too quickly to her heavy schedule, she fell ill for more than a year. Now in her late fifties, she was forced to take some time off for the first time in her busy life.

State senate race. In 1922, with her health recovered, Wells-Barnett jumped back into the civil rights movement by continuing her investigation of racial violence in Arkansas. The resulting booklet, *The Arkansas Race Riot,* led the Supreme Court to free twelve black men who had been wrongly sentenced to death. Despite such victories, her sometimes harsh style hurt her popularity. In 1924, for example, when she ran for the presidency of the National Organization of Colored Women, she faced wide opposition and lost. In 1930 she ran for a place in the Illinois State Senate and lost badly, winning fewer than 600 votes. In March of the next year, she suffered kidney failure and was rushed to the hospital. Two days later, on March 25, 1931, Ida B. Wells-Barnett died at the age of sixty-nine.

For More Information

Thompson, Mildred. *Ida B. Wells-Barnett.* Vol. 15 of *Black Women in United States History.* Brooklyn: Carlson Publishing Co., 1990.

Van Steenwyck, Elizabeth. *Ida B. Wells-Barnett: Woman of Courage.* New York: Franklin Watts, 1992.

Booker T. Washington

1856-1915

Personal Background

In the spring of 1856, a slave woman named Jane gave birth to a baby boy in Franklin County, Virginia, whom she named Booker. Jane would not reveal the identity of Booker's father, a white man from a nearby plantation. Booker would never know who his father was or even his own birthday. He never showed much interest in knowing, anyway. Even from his earliest days, he seemed to make a habit of looking toward the future instead of the past.

Slave cabin. Jane's delivery bed was a few rags thrown on the dirt floor of the small cabin where she lived with Booker's older brother, John. Her owner, James Burroughs, had a farm of about 200 acres, and Jane's main job was to cook for the Burroughs family and the other slaves. The rough log cabin served as the kitchen for the entire plantation. Its windows were holes in the walls; there was also a cat hole, though Booker could never understand why, since the poorly built walls had plenty of other holes large enough for a cat. A deep, covered pit in the middle of the floor was potato storage, and cooking was done in a large open fireplace. The holes in the walls made the cabin cold in the winter, while the fire made it stifling hot in summer.

Freedom. Booker was a young boy during the Civil War. When he was big enough, one of his jobs at the plantation was to

▲ **Booker T. Washington**

Event: Founding and development of the Tuskegee Institute.

Role: In 1881 Booker T. Washington, a young teacher, was selected to start a school for blacks in Tuskegee, Alabama. The school's success, along with Washington's own personal abilities, made him the leading black spokesperson of his day.

operate the fan that kept the flies away while the Burroughs family was eating. Standing by the big table, regularly pulling the rope connected to the fan, he heard the family conversations about the war and about freedom for the slaves. The slaves talked about their coming freedom in whispered nighttime meetings. Like the others, Booker knew freedom was approaching when word of Southern defeats spread, or when blue-coated Yankee soldiers marched by on their way south.

Freedom finally came when he was nine. Washington recalled the scene in his autobiography, *Up From Slavery.* All the Burroughs family and their slaves gathered at the "Big House." A white stranger, probably a Northern officer, read from a paper, perhaps the Emancipation Proclamation, and then told the slaves they were free to do whatever they wanted. Jane, who had prayed with her children for this day, kissed them while "tears of joy ran down her cheeks" (Washington, p. 15).

New challenges. For most blacks, the joy of freedom was soon tempered by the difficult challenge of making a living in the white South. During slavery, Jane had been married to a neighbor's slave, a man in his fifties named Washington Ferguson. Called Wash, he was often hired out to people in other towns, so Jane and the children rarely saw him. After emancipation, Booker's family took his last name and moved with him to Malden, West Virginia, where Wash had previously worked as a slave in salt and coal mines. Wash got a paying job in the mines, but the pay was so low that John and Booker had to work there also to help support the family.

School. Booker, who had hoped to be able to go to school, was disappointed. He had sometimes accompanied the young Burroughs daughters to school, but as a slave he had never been allowed through the door. Still not allowed to attend white schools, Malden blacks, like others elsewhere, had organized a small classroom and hired a teacher. Many shared Booker's hopes, and the classes were filled with both young and old.

School seemed like a paradise to Booker, and the idea of learning excited him. He sensed that it offered the best hope for a better life. By starting in the mines at four in the morning, or by going to nightschool, he was usually able to squeeze in a few days of school a week.

Making a name. Another problem blacks faced after freedom was the practical matter of names. In *Up From Slavery,* Washington says that they did not think it was proper to take the names of their former masters. Wash's master had been named "Ferguson." Perhaps that was why, when asked for his last name at school, Booker blurted out "Washington" instead of Ferguson. His brother and sister later took the same last name, as did an adopted brother, James. Later, his mother told Booker that she had chosen Taliaferro (pronounced Tolliver) as his last name when he was born, but that name had not really been used. He decided to keep it as a middle name, however, and became Booker Taliaferro Washington.

Mrs. Ruffner. Soon after choosing his new name, Booker heard about a servant's job available in the household of the mine's owner, General Lewis Ruffner. Mrs. Ruffner (Viola) was known for being very strict, and none of her servants had stayed for more than a few weeks. Anything was better than the mines, though, and Booker got his mother to apply for him. He was hired at five dollars a month. The money would go to his family, and he would live with the Ruffners.

Mrs. Ruffner, a Vermont Yankee who had married a Southerner, was indeed strict. At first, Booker trembled when he went to see her. It seemed as if everything had to be perfect before she was satisfied. Several times he ran away, once joining a steamboat running between Malden and Cincinnati. Yet each time he returned. Gradually, his fear turned to understanding.

> I soon began to learn that, first of all, she wanted everything kept clean about her, that she wanted things done promptly and systematically, and that at the bottom of everything she wanted absolute honesty and frankness. (Washington, p. 31)

Careful yet capable, soft-spoken but energetic, Booker earned Mrs. Ruffner's trust, and she in turn won his lifelong affection. She helped him go to school, and more important, she taught him by example habits of cleanliness and thrift that would become the foundation of his own teaching. "The lessons I learned in the home of Mrs. Ruffner were as valuable as any education I have ever gotten anywhere since" (Washington, p. 31).

Journey. Booker stayed with Mrs. Ruffner for about a year and a half, until he was sixteen. Before taking the job, he had heard some men talking about a special school for blacks called the Hampton Institute. There they could learn a useful skill and pay for their education by working during the school year. Though he had no idea where it was or how he would get there, Booker had decided at once that one day he would go to Hampton.

Both his mother and Mrs. Ruffner encouraged him in his ambition. The school was about 500 miles from Malden, and Booker began saving for the journey. His family chipped in, and so did older blacks in the community. Booker set out, traveling by train and stagecoach, until he realized that he did not have enough money to make it all the way. Over the next few days he hitched rides and slept outside, spending one night in Richmond, Virginia, under a sidewalk made of boards. He had no money for food when he reached Richmond, but got a job there loading cargo onto a ship. After a few days, he continued on his way, finally reaching Hampton with only fifty cents left over.

Entrance examination. Dirty, tired, and hungry when he reached Hampton, Booker asked the head teacher to be assigned to a class. Clearly skeptical, she handed him a broom and told him that the classroom next to them needed sweeping. Seizing any chance to prove himself, he took the broom and swept the room three times. He found a cloth and dusted it four times. He cleaned every corner of the room, every inch of the walls, and every piece of furniture before going back to find the woman.

> She went into the room and inspected the floor and closets; then she took her handkerchief and rubbed it on the woodwork about the walls, and over the table and benches. When she was unable to find one bit of dirt on the floor, or a particle of dust on any of the furniture, she quietly remarked, "I guess you will do to enter this institution." (Washington, pp. 37-38)

Years at Hampton. Hampton was an unusual and challenging school that proved to be the most important influence of Washington's life. General Samuel C. Armstrong, the school's founder, asked much of his students. Clothes and appearance had to be neat and clean. Students were expected not only to work at academic subjects but also to learn farming, building, and other practical skills. Such work, Armstrong believed, offered the best chance for helping blacks take a place in society. He ran Hampton like an army camp, with every hour from 5:00 a.m. to 9:30 p.m. scheduled for different activities. A crisp, athletic, white New Englander who had commanded a Northern black regiment during the Civil War, Armstrong was idolized by his students. In *Up From Slavery,* Washington calls him "the noblest, rarest human being that it has ever been my privilege to meet" (Washington, p. 39).

For three years, from 1872 to 1875, Washington studied and worked at Hampton under Armstrong's guidance. He took summer jobs and worked as school janitor to help pay his fees. He visited home now and then, but his life was now centered around school. His mother, whose health had been failing, died in 1874. Washington spent that summer working in Malden to be with his family. Over these three years of work and progress, he grew from a promising but untrained boy into a purposeful, self-confident young man.

Participation: Tuskegee Institute

Teacher. After graduating from Hampton, Washington returned to Malden, where he taught school for two years. He also helped pay for his brother, John, to go to Hampton, in return for help that John had given him. He thought about becoming a minister and attended a Baptist seminary (school for ministers) in Washington, D.C., for a year. But in the end he decided to stay on the path he had already begun, believing that he could help the black cause most by teaching. Armstrong invited him to give a speech at the Hampton commencement in May 1879. Washington's speech, entitled "The Force That Wins," reflected Armstrong's ideas about the importance of hard work and self-improvement. It was a success, and a few weeks later Armstrong invited Washington to teach at Hampton.

With Washington came another former Hampton student named Fanny Smith, now Washington's girlfriend and later his wife. To pay her debts at Hampton and finish her schooling, she needed to earn money, which she did by teaching at Malden. She later returned to Hampton with Washington to finish her degree.

Plucky class. Armstrong put Washington in charge of a new program of night classes, so that students who needed to work during the day would be able to study in the evening. Washington tried to make the classes fun and interesting to keep the students awake. He succeeded so well in capturing their interest that the night students became known as "the Plucky Class." Subject matter included blacksmithing and wheelwrighting (making wheels for horse-drawn carts). Armstrong also chose Washington to take charge of a group of young native Americans who were accepted into the school.

Letter from Tuskegee. In 1891 Armstrong was asked to recommend a principal for a school for blacks in Tuskegee, Alabama, in the heart of the deep South. Though he was asked to name a white man, Armstrong replied that he knew of no one better suited for the job than his former student, "one Mr. Booker Washington," whom he called "the best man we ever had here" (Harlan, *The Making of a Black Leader,* p. 110). The officials sent a telegram back asking Armstrong to send Washington. Saying goodbye to his friends and to Fanny, who had one more year to go at Hampton, Washington left for Tuskegee a few days later.

Starting from scratch. Washington arrived in Tuskegee in early June 1881, expecting to find a building and teachers ready and waiting. Instead, he found only "that which no building and apparatus can supply—hundreds of hungry, earnest souls who wanted to secure knowledge" (Washington, p. 78). There were no teachers, no building, or even any land on which to construct a schoolhouse. The Alabama legislature had set aside $2,000 per year for the school, but that money was only to pay teachers, not to build the school itself. Disappointed but never discouraged, Washington set to work.

Early years at Tuskegee. Tuskegee had a population of about 2,000, with three-quarters of that number being black. According to Washington, the setting itself:

> seemed an ideal place for the school. It was in the midst of the great bulk of the Negro population, and was rather secluded, being five miles from the main line of railroad, with which it was connected by a short line. (Washington, p. 78)

▲ Students at Tuskegee Institute in 1902

Washington soon found that the Tuskegee townspeople, both white and black, were eager to help in whatever way they could. He arranged to use a small church and the shack next to it as the first classrooms, borrowing spare equipment—globes, maps, handwriting charts, and some library books—from Hampton. The school opened with thirty students and Washington as the sole teacher on July 4, 1881.

A few months later, Washington heard about an old abandoned plantation for sale. The price was only $500, but even that low amount was far out of reach. Although Hampton did not have the money to lend, the school treasurer offered to lend the $250 downpayment from his own pocket. The place was bought, and the students repaired its run-down cabin, henhouse, and stables to use as classrooms. After four tries, Washington and his students succeeded in making a kiln to bake bricks. The bricks were not only used to construct a classroom building and dormitories but were also sold for cash to local builders. Crops were planted and harvested, and farm animals bought. The students did almost all the work, including the building. By 1884 the Tuskegee Normal and Industrial Institute had nearly 200 students.

Washington's Educational Philosophy

"The students were making progress in learning books and developing their minds; but it became apparent at once that, if we were to make any permanent impression upon those who came to us for training, we must do something besides teach them mere books. The students had come from homes where they had no opportunities for lessons which would teach them how to care for their bodies. With few exceptions, the homes in Tuskegee in which the students boarded were but little improvement upon those from which they had come. We wanted to teach the students how to bathe; how to care for their teeth and clothing. We wanted to teach them what to eat, and how to eat it properly, and how to care for their rooms. Aside from this, we wanted to give them such a practical knowledge of some one industry, together with the spirit of industry, thrift and economy, that they would be sure of knowing how to make a living after they had left us. We wanted to teach them actual things instead of mere books alone." (Washington, pp. 90-91)

Practical approach. Washington based his educational philosophy on Armstrong's ideas, but those ideas also fit in perfectly with Washington's own character. Above all, Washington was a practical man who believed in a person doing the best he could with the tools given. This practicality is why he got along so well with no-nonsense people like Mrs. Ruffner and Armstrong. It also explains why Washington always tried to get along with Southern whites, though other black leaders criticized him for his willingness to compromise in order to achieve his goals.

Secret assistance. The story of Washington's friend, Thomas Harris, sheds some light on Washington's methods and helps to explain why other blacks sometimes disapproved of Washington. Harris, a black man living in Tuskegee, decided to become a lawyer. For Tuskegee whites, a black carpenter or builder was fine, but a black lawyer or doctor was not acceptable. Blacks were expected to know their place in society; that is, to have ambitions for only lowly worker's jobs. Some whites attacked Harris and shot him in the leg. When all the town's white doctors refused to treat Harris, the wounded man's friends brought him to Washington and asked him to have the school doctor treat Harris's leg. Washington made a show of turning them away, claiming that he could not allow the school to be endangered by a white mob.

This was the story as glowingly reported in white newspapers—the same story that led other black leaders to bitterly attack Washington. But while pretending to turn the man away, Washington had secretly arranged and paid for him to be taken to another town where he was treated in safety. Washington's solution not only saved the man but preserved the good feelings the whites had toward Washington and the school, which he felt was necessary for its survival. In the same way, Washington later secretly assisted blacks who challenged white restrictions in court, though he publicly preached cooperation with white society.

Family. Washington and Fanny Smith got married in 1882, and the following year they had a daughter, Portia. In 1884, at the age of twenty-six, Fanny died, probably from injuries that occurred when she fell from a farm wagon at Tuskegee. Still busy putting Tuskegee on its feet, Washington missed Fanny terribly. He came to rely on a young woman named Olivia Davidson, who had worked at the school almost from the beginning. She had become the Lady Principal, which meant that she was in charge of the school's female students. In 1885 the two married, and a son, Booker Taliaferro Washington, Jr. (called Baker), was born in the summer of 1886. A second son, Ernest Davidson Washington, arrived in February 1889.

By then Olivia, who had had several mysterious breakdowns in health, had given up her job at Tuskegee. Ernest's birth was a difficult one, and Olivia remained in the hospital for three months afterward. Slowly, her health seemed to fade away, and nothing Booker could do helped her regain it. She died in May. Grief-stricken, Washington did not marry again until 1892. He chose another Lady Principal at Tuskegee named Margaret Murray. While she and Washington

---

How to Ask a Millionaire for a Library

From a letter to Andrew Carnegie dated December 15, 1900:

"Such a building as we need could be erected for about $20,000. All of the work for the building, such as brickmaking, brick-masonry, carpentry, blacksmithing, etc., would be done by the students. The money which you would give would not only supply the building, but the erection of the building would give a large number of students an opportunity to learn the building trades, and the students would use the money paid to them to keep themselves in school. I do not believe that a similar amount of money often could be made to go so far in uplifting a whole race.

"If you wish further information, I shall be glad to furnish it.

Yours truly,
Booker T. Washington, *Principal*"
(Washington, p. 138)

never had any children, Maggie warmly cared for Portia, Baker, and Ernest.

Spokesman. The 1880s were thus a decade of personal tragedy and hard work for Washington. During the 1890s, however, the long effort began to pay off. Washington now had a solid achievement to his credit. He began to win financial support from millionaires in the white community, people such as steel magnate Andrew Carnegie and railroad king Collis P. Huntington. He impressed these hard-headed businessmen by telling them exactly how much he needed and what it would be used for, and then by accounting for every dollar. In raising money for the school, as in other areas of his life, Washington's personality—practical and businesslike—won him support.

In 1895 Washington rose to national fame after giving a speech at the Atlanta Exposition in Georgia. The speech, delivered before several thousand people and lasting about fifteen minutes, summarized his views, accepting the white call for segregation yet insisting on black self-improvement. The white audience reacted with loud applause, and many newspapers carried a copy of the whole speech the next day. Frederick Douglass, for decades America's most influential black leader, had died earlier in the year. The newspapers now began writing of Washington as Douglass's successor in the role of leading spokesman for the black community.

Aftermath

Tuskegee Machine. By the early 1900s, Washington had begun spending much of his time writing and giving speeches to publicize his ideas. He published *Up From Slavery* in 1901, and the autobiography soon became a best seller. He founded the National Negro Business League in 1900, based on his economic ideas. Though he often called for blacks to work hard and stay away from politics, Washington gradually became a powerful political figure in his own right. His influence was informal, rather than coming from any elected political office. Many younger black leaders had been educated at Tuskegee by this time and looked up to Washington.

Other more militant blacks, however, like W.E.B. Du Bois (see

W. E. B. Du Bois), increasingly criticized Washington's coopera-
tion with whites. They resented what Du Bois called the Tuskegee
Machine, referring to Washington's informal political influence.
Founded in 1909, the National Association for the Advancement of
Colored People (NAACP) became, under Du Bois, the most vocal
opponent of Washington's ideas.

Advisor to presidents. Despite such criticism, Washington
remained for the white community the nation's foremost black
leader. Presidents Theodore Roosevelt and William Howard Taft
sought his approval when appointing blacks (and some whites) to
office. After about 1910, as Washington saw evidence that the jobs
he believed useful for people were being taken over by machines,
his views grew closer to those who emphasized political equality.
Booker T. Washington died at Tuskegee on November 14, 1915.

For More Information

Bontemps, Arna. *Young Booker: Booker T. Washington's Early Days.* New York: Dodd,
    Mead and Co., 1972.

Harlan, Louis R. *Booker T. Washington: The Making of a Black Leader, 1856-1901.* New
    York: Oxford University Press, 1972.

Harlan, Louis R. *Booker T. Washington: The Wizard of Tuskegee, 1901-1915.* New York:
    Oxford University Press, 1983.

Washington, Booker T. *Up From Slavery.* Originally published, 1901. Garden City, New
    York: Doubleday and Co., 1963.

W. E. B. Du Bois

1868-1963

Personal Background

William Edward Burghardt Du Bois was born on February 23, 1868, in the small Massachusetts town of Great Barrington. His mother's family, the Burghardts, had lived in Massachusetts for more than a century. Her grandfather's grandfather, Tom Burghardt, had been brought as a slave from Africa and had taken his master's name. He served in the Revolutionary War and was freed, along with all other Massachusetts slaves, in 1780. His great-grandson Othello Burghardt, William's grandfather, moved to Great Barrington in the early 1800s with two brothers and a sister. There the Burghardts owned several farms and grew into a large, close-knit clan.

William's father, Alfred Du Bois, was the grandson of a white plantation owner from the Bahamas, who had two sons by one of his black slaves. One of them, Alfred's father, moved to Connecticut around 1820, where Alfred grew up. He met and married quiet, shy Mary Burghardt in 1867. They moved to Great Barrington, and William was their first child.

New England childhood. Alfred Du Bois left Great Barrington for good when William was about a year old. William never saw him again and grew up in Great Barrington among the poor but well-respected Burghardts. The quiet town is nestled in a valley sur-

▲ **W.E.B. Du Bois**

Event: Establishment of the National Association for the Advancement of Colored People (NAACP).

Role: In 1905 scholar and writer W.E.B. Du Bois helped organize the Niagara Movement to oppose the ideas of Booker T. Washington, at that time recognized by whites as the leading black spokesperson. From this movement grew the NAACP. For almost twenty-five years, Du Bois edited *The Crisis*, the NAACP's journal.

rounded by the Berkshire Hills, and through it flows the Housatonic River. Only about fifty blacks lived in Great Barrington during this time, encountering little open discrimination from the white townspeople. Until he was sixteen, William went to school with white children, like other Burghardts before him. As a result of growing up in this setting, he had little idea of the problems blacks faced elsewhere in the United States.

Work ethic. William was raised to believe that hard work would bring the reward of a secure place in society. As a boy, he worked to help support his mother, who had suffered a stroke that had crippled her left leg and hand. Before school, he shoveled coal to heat a nearby shop, and after school he worked at a local grocery store. On Saturdays, he chopped wood and did chores for two elderly women who lived nearby. During the summers, he mowed lawns.

"A power not to be despised." Though William played with his white neighbors, sometime his friends would ignore him when they met in public. When certain adults or summer visitors were around, children who normally enjoyed his company became uncomfortable being seen with him. Gradually William began to understand that it was his skin color and crinkly hair that set him apart. It was his first awareness of race and racism, and it made him think about the issue.

When he was about fifteen, William began writing occasional short articles for the New York *Globe*. The black newspaper was run by T. Thomas Fortune, at that time a leading radical voice in the African American community. When a few black families moved to Great Barrington from the South, William founded a club, the Sons of Freedom, for the advancement of the colored race. His pieces for the *Globe* began to call for blacks to organize themselves politically. Only by joining together, he reasoned, could they make their voices heard in a white, democratic society. If they could achieve political cooperation [equality], the teenager wrote, blacks could "become a power not to be despised" (Marable, p. 6).

South to college. From William's earliest days in school, his teachers recognized that he possessed an extraordinarily sharp intelligence. When he graduated from high school (the first black to do so in Great Barrington), he decided not only that he wanted to go to college, but also that he wanted to go to Harvard University. His teachers advised him to study for an extra year because of the difficulty of getting into the first-rate university. Then, for unknown reasons, they persuaded him to apply instead to Fisk University in Nashville, Tennessee, which enrolled only black students. They also raised the money to pay for his college education, which the Burghardts would not have been able to afford.

Black community. Whatever his teachers' motivations in suggesting Fisk, when he thought about it William was happy to head south to college. He realized that only in the South would he see how the vast majority of American blacks lived and worked. During his three years at Fisk, William had for the first time friends and companions who were also black. The slender young man with delicate good looks and an outgoing nature became a popular figure on campus. Never exactly modest, he enjoyed his reputation for exceptional cleverness. Having skipped the first year because of his prior studies, he was younger and brighter than most of his classmates. Aside from his social success, William excelled in his classes. History and philosophy interested him most. During the summers, he worked as a teacher in poor black rural areas around Tennessee.

Harvard. In his last year at Fisk, Du Bois decided to pursue his dream of going to Harvard. With strong letters of recommendation from his Fisk professors, he was accepted and began studies there in 1888. His goal was to win the advanced degree of Doctor of Philosophy (Ph.D.). Harvard, the most respected university in America, was a big change from Fisk. From a small, black world, Du Bois now went into a large, white one. White students generally either ignored him or were openly hostile. He mostly associated with other black students but was uncomfortable with their feelings of superiority toward common black people.

Only in his schoolwork was Du Bois truly satisfied. He met with little prejudice from his white professors, who recognized his talent and intelligence. His dissertation, the paper he had to write to earn his Ph.D., was later published as a book. Widely praised by other scholars, *The Suppression of the African Slave Trade* was the first work to examine the history of the slave trade. It remains a valuable summary of the subject today.

143

Teaching, research. Over the next decade, Du Bois held a series of teaching jobs in which he also researched and wrote about the condition of American blacks. His first post was at Wilberforce, a black university in Ohio. He held this position for two years, from 1894 to 1896, during which time his Harvard doctorate was formally finished and the dissertation published in book form. In 1896 he married Nina Gomer, a young woman he had met at Wilberforce. That same year, his book's success won him a fifteen-month job at the University of Pennsylvania. He would study and write about the black slums of Philadelphia, to which he and Nina moved after being married.

Black studies. The resulting book, *The Philadelphia Negro* (1897), was the first attempt to analyze black conditions from an academic or scholarly point of view, that is, as a subject fit for university study. After finishing the project, Du Bois went to Atlanta University, where he continued his academic work on African Americans until 1910. Soon he developed a program for promoting such studies. He suggested that black scholars join him in analyzing various aspects of black life, such as health, housing, education, and jobs, for each decade for a century. These early projects pioneered the now popular academic field of black studies.

Participation: The NAACP and *The Crisis*

Growing activism. As he became more involved in black studies, Du Bois returned to his earlier belief that blacks needed to take a more active role in politics. He also continued to support academic training for blacks, envisioning a "talented tenth" of intellectuals who would provide leadership for the black community (Hamilton, p. 64). His ideas about political involvement opposed those of Booker T. Washington, widely recognized as the spokesperson for American blacks (see **Booker T. Washington**). Washington, founder of the successful Tuskegee Institute, thought that blacks would do best to stay out of politics. He believed in promoting practical, job-related skills for blacks rather than the study of academic fields, such as literature or history. Du Bois's 1903 book *The Souls of Black Folk* argued against Washington's position. Perhaps the best known of Du Bois's works, it established him as Washington's leading critic and his strongest rival for leadership of American blacks.

Niagara Movement. The force and persuasiveness of Du Bois's opposition to Washington brought him growing political influence in the early 1900s. In 1905 Du Bois and supporters such as Monroe Trotter, another Washington critic, met at Niagara Falls. They elected Du Bois as their head and called themselves the Niagara movement, declaring their opposition to Washington's policy of compromise on white practices such as segregation. Instead, the twenty-nine leaders who met at Niagara demanded total and immediate equality for blacks, with no compromises. Soon the Niagara movement was putting its ideas into practice by supporting blacks who challenged the South's Jim Crow laws in court.

NAACP. The movement ran into financial trouble, however, because its all-black members lacked the money to keep paying legal fees and other expenses. Rich, conservative whites had lent their support to Washington because he seemed to stand for black improvement without threatening whites' sense of superiority. Yet liberal whites like Oswald Garrison Villard, grandson of abolitionist William Lloyd Garrison, had begun to question Washington's leadership. In 1909 most of the Niagara movement's members joined with leading white civil rights activists to form the National Negro Committee.

The committee's name was soon changed to the National Association for the Advancement of Colored People (NAACP). Its headquarters was in New York City. Trotter and Ida B. Wells-Barnett, two of Washington's strongest opponents, refused to join the NAACP (see **Ida B. Wells-Barnett**). They opposed white participation in the organization, pointing out that nearly all of the association's officers were white. Du Bois, the only black officer, had been selected as the director of publications and research.

On Booker T. Washington

"Mr. Washington distinctly asks that black people give up, at least for the present, three things,—

First, political power,

Second, insistence on civil rights,

Third, higher education of Negro youth,—

and concentrate all their energies on industrial education, the accumulation of wealth, and the conciliation of the South.... As a result.... There have occurred:

1. The disfranchisement [loss of voting rights] of the Negro.

2. The legal creation of a distinct status of civil inferiority for the Negro.

3. The steady withdrawal of aid from institutions for the higher training of the Negro." (Du Bois, pp. 398-99)

The Crisis. In 1910 Du Bois gave up his job at Atlanta Uni-

145

▲ An early NAACP office

versity. Funds for his research had become hard to find. Du Bois suspected that the Tuskegee Machine, as he called Washington's powerful network of political supporters, was responsible. He and Nina and their ten-year-old daughter Yolande moved to New York so he could devote most of his time to the NAACP. He had published a monthly magazine called *Horizon* for the Niagara Movement and decided now that the NAACP should have a similar magazine. He founded *The Crisis* to publicize the NAACP's work as well as to express his own views on racial matters. Under Du Bois's leadership, the magazine's circulation grew from 1,000 a month in the first year to 30,000 by 1913.

Changing times. At the same time, a great change was taking place among American blacks. From the rural South, they began moving north by the thousands, as the cotton industry went bust and northern factories boomed. Between 1910 and 1920, more than one million rural blacks crowded into cities like New York and

Philadelphia. They lived in ghettos, where a new black culture began to evolve.

In 1915 Booker T. Washington died. His voice had been of a different era, and his ideas applied to a more rural and simpler black society. But urban life brought more complicated problems than had existed in the old days. New black leaders grew more united in demanding equality and integration instead of unequal segregation. (Segregation refers both to laws and customs that prevent the races from mixing, or from mixing as equals.) The NAACP now became the most powerful integrationist voice in America.

Wartime battles. The onset of World War I created new factory jobs in the North, speeding up the changes and bringing its own difficulties. Du Bois and *The Crisis* rose to the challenge. In the pages of *The Crisis,* Du Bois spoke out against new Jim Crow laws proposed by Congress, including laws against blacks marrying whites or immigrating from other countries. Most of the proposed legislation never passed into law, but President Woodrow Wilson did segregate black federal employees from whites, giving them separate workplaces, toilets and cafeterias.

Post-war racism. Black soldiers returned from the war with a new sense of dignity and pride. They had fought as courageously as white soldiers. Yet in spite of such advances—or perhaps in reaction to them—blacks faced a backlash of white hostility following the war. Since the Civil War, lynching (the hanging of blacks supposedly guilty of some offense) had been a way for some whites to control blacks who resisted discrimination. Now lynching and other acts of racial violence increased. Blacks were pulled from streetcars and beaten, and racist organizations like the Ku Klux Klan flourished not only in the white South but also in the rural North.

> ### Du Bois On Racism after World War I
>
> "We return from the slavery of uniform which the world's madness demanded us to don to the freedom of civil garb. We stand again to look America squarely in the face and call a spade a spade. We sing: This country of ours, despite all its better souls have done and dreamed, is yet a shameful land.
>
> It lynches....
>
> It disfranchises its own citizens.... It *steals* from us. It insults us....
>
> This is the country to which we Soldiers of Democracy return.
>
> We *return.*
>
> We *return from fighting.*
>
> We *return fighting."* (Hamilton, p. 124.)

At the same time, following the 1917 communist revolution in Russia, a Red scare swept the country. The government cracked down on suspected communists, socialists, labor leaders, and others it considered dangerous radicals, arresting thousands in more than thirty cities. Black activists also came under suspicion as potential radicals.

Du Bois, as a black and a socialist, was considered a double threat. Federal officers interrogated him at *The Crisis*'s offices, asking what exactly were his purposes and activities. "We are seeking," he answered, "to have the Constitution of the United States thoroughly and completely enforced" (Hamilton, p. 123).

Influential ideas. By 1920 Du Bois was fifty-two years old, now one of the older generation of black leaders. In many ways, he was the opposite of a man like Booker T. Washington. Du Bois led with his ideas, not his personality, which often seemed rather cold and arrogant. He was not especially popular and did not attract a large number of followers. Yet his writings had deeply and widely influenced both blacks and whites, and most blacks knew him as the voice of the NAACP, now the leading black organization.

Other writings. Aside from his work for *The Crisis,* Du Bois continued with other projects. He wrote five books while editing the magazine: *The Quest of the Silver Fleece* (1911); *The Negro* (1915); *Darkwater: Voices From Within the Veil* (1920); *The Gift of Black Folk: Negroes in the Making of America* (1924); and *Dark Princess: A Romance* (1928). The works included novels and short stories as well as black studies.

Pan-African Movement. Beginning in 1900, Du Bois had also been involved in the movement known as Pan-Africanism, which called for African independence from white colonial nations like Germany, Belgium, and France. He had gone to London in 1900 for the first Pan-African conference, and from 1918 to 1923 he organized several Pan-African Congresses with the approval of the NAACP. The congresses met in European cities, bringing black Americans together with blacks from Africa and the West Indies. Although Du Bois supported independence for Africans, he opposed leaders like Marcus Garvey, a Jamaican black who wanted all blacks to return to Africa. Garvey and his back-to-Africa movement attracted a large black following in the early 1920s, until Garvey was imprisoned for mail fraud in 1925.

Harlem Renaissance. If Du Bois lacked a following among the general black population, younger intellectuals and artists viewed him with respect and affection. A flowering of urban black culture had been born out of the great migration of the war period. Known as the Harlem Renaissance, it was named for the famous black neighborhood in New York City where the new culture flourished. It included jazz musicians, artists, writers, playwrights, and poets, many of whom saw Du Bois as a hero who had helped lay the groundwork for their own contributions. In 1928 Du Bois's daughter, Yolande, married Countee Cullen, one of the younger generation of writers. The wedding was a major social event in Harlem, and ushers included the famous poet Langston Hughes.

Resignation. The prosperity of the 1920s ended with the stockmarket crash of 1929 and the Great Depression that followed. Suddenly people could no longer afford luxuries, and *The Crisis*'s subscription list shrunk dramatically. Though *The Crisis* had always been independent from the NAACP, now Du Bois needed money from the organization to keep publishing. It meant giving up his independence and giving the NAACP final approval over whatever he printed. Yet as soon as he accepted NAACP control, he fell into a dispute with the association.

In *The Crisis,* Du Bois had called for economic cooperation among blacks in the form of a planned, separate black economy. But such a program would involve deliberate segregation of blacks from whites. Walter White, the head of the NAACP, objected, saying that the association would never support any kind of segregation. The association's directors then voted that "no salaried officer of the Association shall criticize the policy, work or officers of the Association in the pages of *The Crisis* (Hamilton, p. 146). In protest, Du Bois resigned in 1934, at the age of sixty-six.

Aftermath

"Spiritual disciples." The directors accepted his resignation reluctantly. They had not meant to offend him with their statement but only to promote unity within the association. The NAACP issued a tribute to the achievements of his work in *The Crisis* and elsewhere:

> He created what never existed before, a Negro intelligentsia [an educated and politically active class], and many who have never read a word of his writings are his spiritual disciples and descendants. Without him the Association would never have been what it was and is. (Hamilton, p. 146)

Continued activism. Du Bois returned to Atlanta University, where he again took up his research on American blacks. He also kept on writing, starting a magazine called *Phylon* and publishing his major historical book, *Black Reconstruction,* in 1934. The book told the story of blacks who participated in state and local governments in the period following the Civil War, before Jim Crow laws ended the experiment in Southern democracy. He also gave lectures at universities throughout the United States. In his lectures and articles, he continued to call for social change.

Travels. In 1936 Du Bois spent six months traveling around the world. He was in Berlin, Germany, when black athlete Jesse Owens won his gold medal at the 1936 Olympic games, shocking German leader Adolph Hitler and his Nazi Party, who believed their white athletes superior. Du Bois was horrified at the Nazis' open racism, calling their anti-Semitism, or anti-Jewish sentiments, "an attack on civilization" (Marable, p. 155). He also visited the Soviet Union, where he enjoyed the chance to see Marxism in action.

Growing isolation. When a new university rule forced him to retire in 1944, Du Bois returned briefly to the NAACP. But the association wanted him to act only as a figurehead, without taking an active role. At seventy-six, Du Bois still had the energy of a much younger man and ran into conflicts with the NAACP leadership.

During the next decade, his isolation from other civil rights workers increased as the cold war brought another Red scare in the 1950s. He objected to government persecution of Communists and then came under suspicion himself. In 1951 the government took away his passport because of his involvement with the Peace Information Center, which officials wrongly thought was controlled by the Soviet Union. Black organizations, including the NAACP, now refused to have anything to do with him. Du Bois, however, won a court struggle over the issue. When his passport was given back, he traveled to China, the Soviet Union, and Africa.

Move to Africa. After decades of ill health, Nina Du Bois had died in 1950. Lonely, with many of his friends also dead, Du Bois had turned to the companionship of a former student, Shirley Graham, who had been assisting him for some time. The two were married in 1951. Shirley Graham Du Bois had fought by her husband's side during his struggles with the government in the 1950s. In 1961, on the invitation of its president, Kwame Nkrumah, the Du Boises moved to the new African nation of Ghana. There Du Bois planned to work on a project he had been considering for years, an encyclopedia of black culture. Before leaving, he joined the American Communist party, and once in Ghana gave up his U.S. citizenship and became a Ghanaian citizen.

Age and illness had finally slowed him down, however, and work on *Encyclopedia Africana* went slowly. He died in Ghana before completing it, on August 27, 1963, at the age of ninety-five.

For More Information

Du Bois, W. E. B. *Writings.* (Collection includes *The Suppression of the African Slave-Trade, The Souls of Black Folk, Dusk of Dawn,* and essays and articles.) New York: Library Classics of the United States, 1986.

Hamilton, Virginia. *W. E. B. Du Bois: A Biography.* New York: HarperCollins, 1972.

Marable, Manning. *W. E. B. Du Bois: Black Radical Democrat.* Boston: G.K. Hall and Co., 1986.

Realism in American Literature

1860s
▼
Writing stories about the Far West, Bret Harte meets Samuel Clemens, better known as **Mark Twain.**

1865
▼
Twain writes his first popular story, "The Celebrated Jumping Frog of Calavares County," which is set in the West.

1880
▼
Joel Chandler Harris's collection of African American folk tales, told by the character Uncle Remus, is published.

1875
▼
William Dean Howells publishes in the *Atlantic Magazine* "Old Memories," a series of tales by Twain.

1873
▼
Twain co-authors *The Gilded Age,* a novel about society in the post–Civil War period.

1881
▼
Helen Hunt Jackson publishes *A Century of Dishonor,* about the government's mistreatment of native Americans.

1884
▼
Jackson writes the novel *Ramona* to change attitudes in society about native Americans.

1885
▼
Twain publishes *The Adventures of Huckleberry Finn.*

1887
▼
Dawes Act attempts to break up Indian reservations.

1898-1899
▼
Crane reports and writes stories on the Spanish-American War.

1895
▼
Crane's Civil War novel, *The Red Badge of Courage,* is published.

1893
▼
Stephen Crane publishes his first novel, *Maggie,* a grim tale of life in the inner city.

REALISM IN AMERICAN LITERATURE

Realism is a term used to describe stories that present life in an objective and a realistic way, not in idealized or romantic fashion. The end of the Civil War marked the beginning of this trend in American literature. For the most part, the reality of the brutal war had changed peoples' outlook on life. Soldiers wrote vivid, unromantic accounts of their war experience while photographers presented glaring images of actual battles and their aftermath. The war destroyed plantation life with its genteel ways and encouraged the growth of industries and cities. Slavery, an accepted institution for more than 200 years, had been questioned and toppled. Beginning the scientific study of social problems, the government organized commissions for special purposes. Americans seemed ready to take a closer look at themselves and their changing country. Realism offered them a serious study of their lives through story. Many realistic novels dealt with raw emotions such as fear, greed, and hate, at times with humor. Many also portrayed evils such as poverty, grim city life, the struggles of the working class, and political corruption. Readers recognized their own problems in the new type of literature.

Heightening the realistic effect, fiction writers focused on regional differences. Before the late 1800s, most writing centered around the East Coast. Then the railroad and telegraph tied various regions together, people became increasingly aware of their differences, and writers began working to capture a region's flavor. Through dialect, dress, landscape, and other details, their stories brought the flavor of different regions to readers around the country.

In the late 1800s and early 1900s, stories with regional flavor were created by a number of writers—including William Dean Howells, **Mark Twain,** Bret Harte, Henry James, **Stephen Crane,** Theodore Dreiser, Edith Wharton, and Frank Norris. Interestingly, many of them began their careers as journalists; it seems that reporting on actual events gave writers a solid foundation for creating realistic fiction.

Howells, who spearheaded the American realism movement, was editor of the highly regarded *Atlantic Magazine.* In his most famous novel, *The Rise of Silas Lapham,* Howells created one of the first businessmen in American fiction. Howells went on to write many other novels but is remembered most as a critic who strongly influenced other writers of his day. In 1875 he published a series of stories by Samuel Langhorne Clemens, better known as Mark Twain. Twain had gained fame ten years earlier by writing a humorous short story about a contest involving a jumping frog. He was living in the West at the time, where he met Bret Harte, who wrote vivid tales of life in gold-mining country. Several years later, Twain co-authored *The Gilded Age,* a novel about the false glitter of life after the Civil War. (The book's title caught on as the name for the post–Civil War period.)

Howells, who shared a lifelong friendship with Twain, called him the Abraham Lincoln of American literature. Considered the greatest of the realists, Twain used dialect, regional color, and a down-home, folksy approach to tell stories that were American to the core. On one level, his stories roll along at a pleasant pace, are funny, and have a lighthearted feeling; on another level, however, a vein of sharp social criticism runs through them. His most enduring books— *The Adventures of Tom Sawyer* and *The Adventures of Huckleberry Finn*—are about life along the Mississippi River before the Civil War. *Huckleberry Finn* broke ground in many

THE

GILDED AGE

A TALE OF TO-DAY

BY

MARK TWAIN

(SAMUEL L. CLEMENS)

AUTHOR OF "INNOCENTS ABROAD," "ROUGHING IT," ETC.

AND

CHARLES DUDLEY WARNER

AUTHOR OF "MY SUMMER IN A GARDEN," "BACK LOG STUDIES," ETC.

FULLY ILLUSTRATED FROM NEW DESIGNS

BY HOPPIN, STEPHENS, WILLIAMS, WHITE, ETC., ETC.

SOLD BY SUBSCRIPTION ONLY.

*

HARTFORD:

AMERICAN PUBLISHING COMPANY.

W. E. BLISS & CO., TOLEDO, OHIO.

1874.

▲ Title page from Mark Twain and Charles Dudley Warner's novel of greed and corruption ways, particularly in Twain's use of dialect, the everyday speech of an area. Also using dialect, Joel Chandler Harris produced a collection of Southern black folk tales as told by the character Uncle Remus. Twain, writing several years later, wove several dialects into a single novel.

Some novels of realism dealt with city life. Stephen Crane's treatment of realistic themes is harsher and more immediate than Twain's and not so regional. As a New York reporter in the 1890s, Crane saw and experienced a great deal of the underbelly of city life. He reported on happenings in the slums, along Skid Row, and among the prostitutes and petty thieves of the city. On occasion, Crane made a point of actually living a lifestyle to learn what it felt like. One cold winter, he dressed like a bum and roamed the streets wearing only rags; during the same period, he spent several days living the life of the rich on the Upper East Side.

For his most famous novel, Crane could not do this kind of real-life research. *The Red Badge of Courage* takes place during the Civil War, which ended about six years before the author was born. Yet Crane's realistic, emotional, and vivid account of war through the eyes, mind, and heart of a young soldier made many readers feel sure he had served in the war. Crane later did witness the events of the Spanish-American War, an experience that inspired more wartime stories.

Helen Hunt Jackson, unlike other writers of her time, did not produce novels of realism. In the tradition of Harriet Beecher Stowe, she did, however, write about social issues of the day. Through her writing, Jackson hoped to alter people's attitudes and bring about social change. For the last few years of her life, she devoted herself to the cause of the native Americans. After becoming aware of the brutal injustices committed against them, Jackson wrote books that addressed the issue. In her nonfiction work *A Century of Dishonor,* she outlined the long history of the government's broken treaties with various tribes. Three years later, in 1884, Jackson published *Ramona,* a romantic novel loosely based on the true and tragic story of a young Indian man married to a woman of Spanish ancestry. Readers responded more to the romance than the real problems behind the story. In the end, Jackson's writing helped change U.S. policy, but the changes again proved harmful to the Indians. Toward the end of the nineteenth century, associations were organized on behalf of Indian rights and Congress passed the Dawes Act, which set out to break up the reservations and blend the Indians into mainstream society. Seen as beneficial by many at the time, the act threatened to destroy tribal identity and brought to the Indians disastrous new problems.

Mark Twain

1835-1910

Personal Background

Family. Halley's comet blazed through the night sky when Samuel Langhorne Clemens was born in Florida, Missouri, on November 30, 1835. He was the sixth of seven children, four of whom survived to adulthood. Although his parents, John and Jane, had come from slaveholding, landowning Southern families, the Clemenses were poor and struggling. John, who was a distant and stern father, tried his hand at many trades, from lawyer to country judge to farmer to storekeeper. Always hoping to make a fortune, John invested his money and his dreams in a number of business ventures but always came out a loser. Sam and his brother Orion seemed to inherit this combined trait of poor business sense and an interest in moneymaking schemes; as adults, they both lost money in numerous ventures.

Unlike her quiet, serious husband, Jane Lampton Clemens was playful, warm, and good-humored; she loved playing cards, gossiping, watching parades, and dancing. The auburn-haired beauty claimed to have married her husband in a moment of spite aimed toward the man she really loved, who was too shy to come forth with his feelings. Jane had a soft spot for animals, and the Clemens house was often filled with stray cats that she had taken in. Sam took after his mother in many ways, from his own auburn hair to his quick sense of humor to his love for cats.

▲ **Mark Twain**

Event: Realism in American literature.
Role: As humorist, author, and lecturer, Mark Twain (pen name of Samuel Langhorne Clemens) was one of the most influential and popular voices of the late nineteenth century. His comments on American society, his vivid descriptions of life on the Mississippi, and his witty remarks remain fresh and revealing a century later.

When Sam was four, the family moved to Hannibal, Missouri, a port along the Mississippi River. His home town as a child, Hannibal, along with the adventures he experienced there and the people he knew, figured into much of the author's later writing, especially *The Adventures of Tom Sawyer.* He called Hannibal "a boy's paradise."

Growing up in Hannibal. Sam was born two months prematurely, and during the first few years of his life, he was small and sickly, living, he later joked, mainly on cod-liver oil. He grew into a healthy though slight boy, full of mischief and energy. Much in his early years revolved around the Mississippi River, which he described as "the majestic, the magnificent Mississippi, rolling its mile-wide tide along, shining in the sun" (Lauber, p. 20). In, on, and around the river, he and his friends swam, played, picnicked, fished, skated, and sailed (usually in boats "borrowed" from unsuspecting, absent owners). When someone sounded the call of "Steamboat a-coming," townspeople left what they were doing and hurried to the riverbank to watch the long, slim vessel sail past.

Sam nearly drowned in the river a number of times before he finally learned to swim. He was also famous for the trouble he got into, such as prying loose an enormous boulder that rolled down a hill and almost crushed a passing slave, jumping from rooftops onto the street below, and stowing away at age nine on a steamboat. Also at age nine, Sam started smoking, a habit he continued for the rest of his life. About his childhood tendency of getting into trouble, he later wrote:

> My mother had a good deal of trouble with me but I think she enjoyed it. She had none at all with my brother Henry ... and I think that unbroken monotony of his goodness and truthfulness and obedience would have been a burden to her but for the relief and variety which I furnished in the other direction. I was a tonic. (Sanborn, p. 46)

Apprentice. Sam's father died of pneumonia in 1847, and soon after, the boy quit school to take up a trade and help contribute to the family income. Finding work as an apprentice for the publisher of the Hannibal *Courier,* Sam learned all aspects of the printing trade. A fellow worker remembered the teenaged Sam, dressed like a dandy, puffing away at huge cigars and repeatedly singing a line from a comic drunkard's song: "If I ever get up again, I'll stay up—if I kin" (Sanborn, p. 67). Although his duties included most of the drudge work around the shop—cleaning the floors, tending the fire, and delivering the paper—it was here that Sam's true education began. At the time, printing shops were thought of as the "poor boy's college" because they exposed apprentices to a steady stream of essays and poems, as well as to ideas, information, and news of world events.

Sam, who had been a reluctant and somewhat lazy student in school, learned the printing trade quickly and, at the same time, developed a strong interest in literature. He learned to differentiate between good and bad writing. "One isn't a printer ten years," he said in 1909, "without setting up acres of good and bad literature, and learning ... to discriminate between the two ... and meanwhile he is consciously acquiring what is called a 'style'" (Kaplan, p. 28).

During his decade in the printing business, Sam published his first writing and also began to travel a bit. For a couple of years, he worked for his brother Orion, who had started his own newspaper. He wrote some news pieces for it and, later, some humorous columns, including an advice page (for example: How to prevent dogs from going mad in August—Cut off their heads in July). He occasionally pulled pranks on the readers. Once he printed a headline announcing a terrible accident that had killed 500 but wrote that the article would have to be continued because it had not yet happened. As was the custom for humor writers of the day, Sam signed his articles with various pen names, including W. Epaminondas Adrastus Blabb, Grumbler, John Snooks, and Peter Pencilcase's Son.

When Orion's paper failed, Sam ventured out into the world, living for a while in New York, Philadelphia, and St. Louis, and supporting himself by working in printing. He continued to write and also began keeping a journal, which he would do throughout his life. By his early twenties, however, Sam had become bored with publishing. He left the trade to pursue a childhood dream—working as a steamboat pilot on the Mississippi River.

River pilot. In 1857, under the guidance of pilot Horace Bixby, whom he agreed to pay $100 up front and an additional $400 from his earnings, Clemens learned one of the most respected and well-paid professions of his time. River pilots earned about $250 a month, a salary then equal to that of the vice president and to a Supreme Court justice. Furthermore, river pilots answered to no one, dressed like gentlemen, and felt the pride of having mastered the country's largest and most traveled river. As Clemens later described it, a pilot was "the only unfettered and entirely independent human being that lived in the earth" (Kaplan, p. 31).

Clemens quickly became a skilled pilot, with the ability to "read" the water and to steer a steamboat in the dark of night because he knew the turns and shape of the river so well. One steamboat captain remembered him as someone who was always joking yet never smiled. Clemens took great pride in his skill, saying, "I loved the profession far better than any I have followed since" (Kaplan, p. 31). However, the outbreak of the Civil War cut short his career. After four years on the river, Clemens quit his piloting job and headed west.

Mining for riches. Clemens traveled west with Orion and his wife, Mollie, after Orion was appointed secretary of the Nevada Territory. Taking the $800 he had saved, Clemens planned to make his fortune in the rough and unsettled West, where gold, silver, and timber were making a few other adventurers rich. He tried his luck in the timber business but gave that up when he accidentally set fire to a large stretch of forest near Lake Tahoe. Then he went to various mining sites hoping to find silver or gold. However, his luck and his money eventually ran out. For a time, he worked as a laborer in a quartz mill but was saved from this dull job when an offer came to work as an editor at the *Territorial Enterprise,* a Virginia City, Nevada, newspaper. In late September 1862, Clemens packed up his gear and, according to his own recollection, walked the 130 miles from the mining camp to the newspaper office.

Participation: Realism in American Literature

The birth of Mark Twain. After his first article appeared in print—an invented story of Indians attacking a wagon train—Clemens took to writing in earnest. He felt he had found his true occupation at last. Now in his late twenties, Clemens fit right into the freewheeling, spirited atmosphere at the *Enterprise.* He smoked cigars and pipes, drank beer while he ate Limburger cheese, and frequented saloons with his fellow newsmen, telling stories and

▲ Twain in his study

singing songs. His coworkers liked to arouse his anger by playing pranks on him so that they could listen and laugh as he let loose a steady stream of rich, inspired, and colorful cursing.

Within a few months of starting at the *Enterprise,* Clemens had begun to sign his articles with a new pen name, one that he would use and best be remembered by throughout his life. "Mark Twain" was a term he remembered from his piloting days; it meant two fathoms, or twelve feet, and was used to signify that a steamboat was in safe water.

Voice of the West. After about a year and a half on the *Enterprise,* Mark Twain left Virginia City for San Francisco, where he worked as a reporter and became an increasingly familiar voice to the reading public. He had developed a strong and recognizable style with an appealingly humorous bent. Although he acknowledged his talent for writing humor, he did not seem to regard it highly. In a letter to Orion in 1865, he confessed: "I have had a 'call' to literature, of a low order—i.e., humorous. It is nothing to be proud of, but it is my strongest suit" (Kaplan, p. 60).

Twain's sketches of western life—including a somewhat humorous account of the San Francisco earthquake of 1865—began to appear in various West Coast papers. When one of his stories, "Jim Smiley and His Jumping Frog" (later called "The Celebrated Jumping Frog of Calaveras County"), was published in the November 18, 1865, issue of the *Saturday Press,* a New York weekly, Twain's fame spread to a national level.

Lecturer. Feeling restless and bored in San Francisco, Twain took a trip to the Sandwich Islands (now Hawaii) and wrote articles for the Sacramento *Union* about life on the islands. In the summer of 1866, he landed a spectacular scoop when a raft carrying fifteen shipwrecked men washed ashore on a Hawaiian beach. After their ship, the *Hornet,* had burned at sea, the sailors were stranded in the ocean for forty-three days with only ten days' worth of provisions. Twain interviewed the survivors and captured their story of heroism and suffering in a sensational front-page article.

When he returned to the states, Twain gave lectures on his experiences on the islands and soon became a popular draw on the American lecture circuit. The combination of his slow southern drawl, his deadpan delivery, and his colorful anecdotes won over audiences across the nation. After this, lecturing became an added sidelight to Twain's writing career.

The Innocents Abroad. Twain went back east, living in New York for a time and also returning to Missouri to visit his family. Then he heard that Reverend Henry Ward Beecher's church had organized an ocean cruise which would sail to Europe and stop at various sites around the Mediterranean, including the Holy Land. Twain convinced the publishers of the *Alta California* to send him as a correspondent. The passengers aboard the steamboat *Quaker City* were mostly wealthy, distinguished, devoutly religious, and much older than the thirty-one-year-old Twain. On this pleasure cruise across the Atlantic, the religious passengers frowned on smoking, dancing, and drinking, and the songs they sang were mostly hymns. Nonetheless, they were drawn to and amused by the cigar-smoking eccentric writer and lecturer. One woman wrote to her husband: "There is one table from which is sure to come a peal of laughter, and all eyes are turned toward Mark Twain, whose face is perfectly mirth-provoking" (Lauber, p. 197).

Twain's account of the trip is entertaining, detailed, and often funny. On seeing the cancan, a racy dance of the time, Twain wrote: "I placed my hand before my face for very shame. But I looked through my fingers" (Kaplan, p. 77). Sometimes he poked fun at his fellow travelers, describing tourists in the Holy Land as a "fantastic mob of green-spectacled Yanks … flapping elbows and bobbing umbrellas" (Kaplan, p. 78). By the end of the voyage, however, his tone had taken on a sharper edge. Life aboard the *Quaker City,* he said, consisted of solemn company, dinner, dominoes, prayers, and slander and was like a funeral excursion without the corpse.

By the end of the voyage, Twain had sent a series of some sixty letters to the *Alta California* and other publications. His correspondences made him even more famous and led to a book offer. *The Innocents Abroad* became a best-seller and firmly established Twain as one of America's most popular writers.

Marriage to Olivia Langdon. Meanwhile, aboard the *Quaker City,* Twain fell in love—with a photograph. When a friend on board, Charles Langdon, showed Twain a miniature portrait of his twenty-two-year-old sister, Twain was enthralled. Forty years later, he wrote, "From that day to this, she has never been out of my mind" (Meltzer, p. 55).

Back in the States, Twain found a receptive admirer in Olivia (Livy) Langdon; she agreed to marry him within two months of their meeting. Her wealthy and religious parents, however, were

THE ADVENTURES

OF

TOM SAWYER

BY

MARK TWAIN.

THE AMERICAN PUBLISHING COMPANY,
HARTFORD, CONN.; CHICAGO, ILL.; CINCINNATI, OHIO.
A. ROMAN & CO., SAN FRANCISCO, CAL.
1876.

▲ Frontispiece by True Williams and title page of first American edition of
The Adventures of Tom Sawyer

not so anxious to have their daughter marry the somewhat wild writer. It took months for Twain to convince Olivia's father, Jervis Langdon, that he was worthy of marrying Olivia. When Langdon finally did give his consent, however, he accepted his future son-in-law wholeheartedly. The couple married in February 1870 and moved into a fine home that Langdon had purchased for them. He also loaned Twain a substantial sum to buy a one-third interest in a local newspaper.

Eventually, the Clemenses settled in Hartford, Connecticut, one of the most prosperous American cities of the day. They had four children: Langdon, born 1871, who died in infancy; Susy, Twain's favorite, born 1872; Clara, born 1874; and Jean, born 1880. Clara was the only member of the family who would outlive her father.

The Adventures of Tom Sawyer. Meanwhile, Twain continued writing. In 1872 he published *Roughing It,* a description of his adventures in the West between 1861 and 1866. The next year he published *The Gilded Age,* a novel about the post–Civil War years that he wrote in collaboration with Charles Dudley Warner. Three years later, in 1876, he published *The Adventures of Tom Sawyer,* a story that had been taking form in his mind for years.

Much of the story revolved around Twain's early life in Hannibal. Although he called the town St. Petersburg, many of the experiences he described in *Tom Sawyer* were his own, and the characters were people he had known while growing up. The story centers around a boy named Tom Sawyer, who lives with his Aunt Polly and continually tries her patience with his antics. Tom falls in love with Becky Thatcher, a pretty blonde girl, and befriends Huckleberry Finn, the son of the town drunk. The book follows Tom and his friends through various adventures, including witnessing a murder and then exposing the killer and getting lost in a cave.

After reading *Tom Sawyer,* Twain's good friend and fellow writer William Dean Howells enthusiastically congratulated him on the book: "Altogether the best boy's story I ever read. It will be an immense success" (Kaplan, p. 106). Although sales started out slowly, *The Adventures of Tom Sawyer* was a huge success with children and adults alike. During Twain's lifetime, the book sold more than two million copies, and it remains today his most popular novel. It has been reprinted in many editions and languages and has been portrayed on film and television.

The Adventures of Huckleberry Finn. Soon after finishing *Tom Sawyer,* Twain began work on a book to follow it, based on the character of Huckleberry Finn. However, he wrote the novel in spurts, and it was nine years before he finally published the book in 1885. In both books, but especially the second, Twain showed his gift for writing dialects. He included an explanatory note about the different

A Description of Huckleberry Finn

"Huckleberry was cordially hated and dreaded by all the mothers of the town, because he was idle, and lawless, and vulgar and bad—and because all their children admired him so, and delighted in his forbidden society, and wished they dared to be like him. Tom was like the rest of the respectable boys, in that he envied Huckleberry his gaudy outcast condition, and was under strict orders not to play with him. So he played with him every time he got a chance." (Twain, *The Unabridged Mark Twain,* p. 464)

ON THE RAFT.

▲ Huckleberry Finn and Jim on the raft, from an early edition of
The Adventures of Huckleberry Finn

dialects he used in *Huckleberry Finn*—"the Missouri negro dialect,
the extremest form of the backwoods South-Western dialect; the
ordinary 'Pike County' dialect; and four modified varieties of this

last"—so that readers would not "suppose that all these characters were trying to talk alike and not succeeding" (Kaplan, p. 134).

Unlike *Tom Sawyer,* which is told in third person by Twain, the story *Huckleberry Finn* is told in first person by Huck himself. After running away from a life of abuse and confinement, Huck meets up with a slave named Jim who is running away to find freedom. Together they sail down the river toward Cairo, from where they plan to escape northward. The pair encounter danger throughout the journey but enjoy moments of peace, too, as Huck describes below:

> Sometimes we'd have that whole river all to ourselves for the longest time. Yonder was the banks and the islands, across the water; and maybe a spark— which was a candle in a cabin window; and sometimes on the water you could see a spark or two—on a raft or a scow, you know; and maybe you could hear a fiddle or a song coming over from one of them crafts. It's lovely to live on a raft. (Meltzer, p. 87)

In *Huckleberry Finn,* Twain master-fully blends Huck's youthful voice with the author's own critical insights into such evils of his youth as conformity and slavery. He captures even the confusion of a character like Huck, who, raised in the South, at first views the runaway slave mainly as a lawbreaker. Huck's attitude changes over the course of the novel. *Huckleberry Finn* is considered Twain's masterpiece; decades later, Ernest Hemingway would say that all modern American literature was influenced by this one book. At the time of its release, however, reviews ranged from luke-warm to negative. Critics and readers found the book coarse and vulgar and some libraries banned it. Louisa May Alcott, author of *Little Women,* had some critical advice: "If Mr. Clemens cannot think of something better to tell our pure-minded lads and lasses, he had best stop writing for them" (Kaplan, p. 139).

Mark Twain's Views toward Blacks

During the course of his lifetime, Twain slowly became less fixed in terms of his views toward black people. The Clemenses owned one or two slaves, and, as a boy, Twain accepted the prejudices of his fellow Southerners toward blacks. As he grew older, however, he recognized the unfair-ness of these attitudes and worked to change them. In writings such as *Huckle-berry Finn,* he brought attention to the injus-tices that blacks suffered at the hands of whites. In his public life, he helped to finance the education of a black artist in Paris and a black student at Yale, sup-ported the actions of the black leader Fred-erick Douglass, and read and lectured in black churches.

Aftermath

Personal life. By his mid-forties, Twain possessed "every-thing a man could have"—a beautiful wife and family, wealth, fame, and success (Kaplan, p. 123). The Clemenses were very close and loving. They owned several houses and entertained often and lavishly. However, personal problems and financial woes dampened their domestic happiness.

Although Twain continued to publish and his books sold well, money troubles plagued him. He had made a series of bad investments, including losing ventures in the Paige typesetting machine, a food substance called Plasmon that promised to wipe out hunger, and other get-rich-quick schemes. The publishing house that he owned with his nephew also failed. Eventually, by 1894, Twain had no choice but to declare bankruptcy. To avoid the upkeep on their house, he and Livy and the children lived in Europe for most of the 1890s. By the time he returned to the States in November 1900, Twain had managed to pay off all his debts.

In 1896 Clemens's eldest daughter, Susy, died of meningitis. When she was thirteen, Susy had written a biography of her famous father, and Twain had always admired her intelligence and spirit. The loss devastated him, as well as his wife. The Clemenses went through an extended period of mourning, but when they finally returned to America four years later, it was with renewed vigor and hope.

By now, Mark Twain had become a living legend. He was granted honorary degrees from Oxford University, Yale, and the University of Missouri. Proud of the honors, he joked, "If I am not called at least 'Doc' from now on, there will be a decided coolness" (Meltzer, p. 102). He spent most of his remaining years in New York City, attending luncheons and dinners in his honor, giving speeches and lectures, receiving visitors, and finding little time to write. Friends and reporters sought his opinion on world events, and he gladly gave it. "It always puzzled me," his daughter Clara recalled, "how Mark Twain could manage to have an opinion on every incident, accident, invention, or disease in the world" (Kaplan, p. 185). Dressed in the white suits he had taken to wearing, Twain attracted attention and interest wherever he went.

In 1904, after thirty-four years of a happy but challenging marriage, Livy died following a long illness. Five years later, Jean, the youngest daughter, drowned in the bathtub during an epileptic seizure. Saddened and lonely, Twain spent his final few years in Redding, Connecticut, and began work on his autobiography. In the early months of 1910, Halley's comet again blazed through the night sky for the first time in seventy-six years. Twain had once predicted that since he had come in with the comet, he would go out with it too. His prediction came true. On April 21, 1910, Clemens died. His writings and ideas would live on for generations of readers worldwide.

For More Information

Kaplan, Justin. *Mark Twain and His World.* New York: Simon and Schuster, 1974.

Lauber, John. *The Making of Mark Twain: A Biography.* New York: Houghton Mifflin Co., 1985.

Meltzer, Milton. *Mark Twain: A Writer's Life.* New York: Franklin Watts, 1985.

Sanborn, Margaret. *Mark Twain: The Bachelor Years.* New York: Doubleday Co., 1990.

Twain, Mark. *Mark Twain's Own Autobiography.* Madison: The University of Wisconsin Press, 1990.

Twain, Mark. *The Unabridged Mark Twain.* Edited by Lawrence Teacher. Philadelphia: Running Press, 1976.

Stephen Crane

1871-1900

Personal Background

Family and early years. Stephen Crane was born on November 1, 1871, in Newark, New Jersey, the youngest of fourteen children. His parents were Dr. Jonathan Townley Crane and Mary Helen Peck Crane. They named Stephen after an ancestor who had served at the Continental Congress during the Revolutionary War and who would have signed the Declaration of Independence had he not been called away on duty. Crane was proud of his lineage, and when he became famous, he described his forebears as "pretty hot people" (Cady, p. 23). His more immediate relatives were highly religious. Both his father and maternal grandfather were prominent Methodist preachers. Dr. Crane, a well-educated and respected man, held to a strict moral code that frowned on dancing, drinking, and smoking.

Crane's mother was forty-five when he was born and had suffered through the deaths of the four babies who had been born before him. Mary Helen was a fierce promoter for the temperance movement and spent much of Stephen's boyhood away from home attending meetings and giving lectures along the New Jersey Coast and in cities as far off as Boston, Nashville, and Chicago. She also wrote articles for Methodist journals, and some of Crane's earliest literary attempts were writing these articles when his mother was

▲ Stephen Crane

Event: Realism in American literature.
Role: Using a vividly realistic style, Stephen Crane wrote stories and novels about social and historical events in America. His tales brought to life the horrors of war and the grimness of slum life. Also a reporter, Crane served as a news correspondent in the Spanish-American War.

too busy lecturing. Because Mary Helen was so preoccupied, much of the responsibility for Stephen's care fell to his older sister Agnes. A quiet and serious young women fifteen years his senior, Agnes read a great deal and had some hopes of being a writer. She kept a diary and directed much of Stephen's early reading.

Surprisingly little is known of Crane's early years. What is certain is that he was a somewhat sickly child who suffered from respiratory problems. He did not begin school until he was eight, which was also the year his father died. His family moved often during his youth, from Newark to Paterson and then to Port Jervis, New York, and back to New Jersey, in Asbury Park. The death of his father marked just the first of several dramatic childhood losses. Agnes died of meningitis when he was thirteen, and a year later, his mother suffered a mental breakdown, from which she eventually recovered. Not long after, his brother Luther died tragically, crushed to death by two freight cars. Crane's reactions to these crises, as well as other details of his childhood, remain a mystery, and he probably would have preferred it that way. "I go through the world unexplained," he later wrote (Benfey, p. 42).

Education. As a teenager, Crane attended several schools. First, he enrolled at the Pennington Seminary, a school at which his father had served as principal for a decade and which prepared boys for the ministry. Crane had no interest in becoming a minister, however, so in 1888, he transferred to a military academy in upstate New York, fulfilling his childhood dream of becoming a soldier. He described his two years at Claverack College and Hudson River Institute as the happiest period of his life. After graduating, he enrolled at Lafayette College in Pennsylvania, where he spent one semester devoting more time to baseball than studying. Finally, he transferred to Syracuse University, where he got a full, if brief, taste of college life.

Here again, Crane devoted much of his time and energy to baseball, a sport he loved and excelled at. He was a prized shortstop and catcher for the school's varsity baseball team. Standing about five feet seven inches tall and weighing 125 pounds, Crane was fast, agile, and a steady batter. Rated the best infielder of his time, he received offers to play professional ball. He later wrote, "I am more proud of my baseball ability than of some other things" (Stallman, p. 29).

Crane also contributed to the school paper and, by this time, had decided to become a writer. In spite of his success and popularity at Syracuse, he completed only one class and dropped out at the end of the school year. Later, he explained his short academic career:

> I did little work at school, but confined my abilities, such as they were, to the diamond. Not that I disliked books, but the cut-and-dried curriculum of the college did not appeal to me. Humanity was a much more interesting study. When I ought to have been at recitations I was studying faces on the streets. (Benfey, pp. 49-51)

Participation: Realism in American Literature

New York. After spending the summer in Asbury Park working as a reporter for his brother Townley's news agency, Crane moved to New York City. Barely twenty, he now began his life as a writer in earnest. Working as a freelance reporter, Crane was often broke and frequently hungry. His life-style revolved around writing, looking for work, and spending time with friends, most of whom were painters, sculptors, writers, and actors. Though he found many friends among other artists, Crane was not popular with his fellow journalists; they considered him aloof, stuck up, and spoiled, and, in his own words, called him "that terrible, young rascal" (Stallman, p. 87).

During his years in New York, Crane lived in various apartments, generally sharing a room or two with several other struggling young artists. A friend described Crane's living quarters after a visit to his apartment:

> Steve was in bed although it was near noon—a topsy-turvy place, three cots side by side, bed clothes all awry as if they were never made up. Papers strewed the floor, tables covered with sheets of paper, writings, and cartoons" (Linson, pp. 58-59).

One of his closest friends in New York, a painter named Corwin Knapp Linson, wrote an account of their friendship during Crane's years in New York, between 1891 and 1896. Linson remembered Crane visiting him often at his art studio. There, while Linson painted, Crane would sit for hours on the couch, sometimes lost in thoughtful daydream, but more often writing.

While in New York, Crane took every opportunity to observe human nature—to "study faces"—especially of the less fortunate people in society. Unlike many writers, he did not isolate himself to produce his work but rather wrapped himself in the pulsing drama of city life. Much of his time was spent on skid row, or at prisons and courthouses, studying with fascination people who lived on the fringes of society, such as prostitutes and the homeless. He wrote his observations and experiences in essays known as the "New York City Sketches" and went so far as to dress like a bum and wander the streets in winter to learn what it felt like to be one.

Before long, Crane had achieved quite a name for himself in New York. Some regarded him as a rebellious, arrogant upstart, while others recognized him as a genius. Although he was caught up in a busy and active life, he continued to work doggedly at his craft.

Developing a style. Crane's writing voice and style emerged clear and strong at a young age. In many ways, he wrote as if he were a painter, brushing crisp, broad, and vibrant impressions of life onto the printed page. Above all, Crane sought to express himself in a simple, clear way that would make a story real and true for the reader. He claimed that his "chiefest desire was to write plainly and unmistakably, so that all men (and some women) might read and understand" (Stallman, p. 33).

The Sullivan County Sketches. In his boyhood and early adulthood, Crane had spent much time in the woods around Port Jervis. The summer after he quit Syracuse, he and several friends lived for weeks in these woods, fishing, hunting, and camping out. This rustic vacation would become a yearly ritual. Meanwhile, Crane drew upon the experience to write tales that he regularly contributed to the Sunday supplement of the _New York Tribune_ from the fall of 1891 to the following spring. The stories in _The Sullivan County Sketches_ include the titles "Four Men in a Cave," "Killing His Bear," and "The Cry of Huckleberry Pudding." With images of color and light and an emphasis on lifelike experiences, the tales reveal the author's emerging voice. Crane had a low opinion of these stories, calling them "little grotesque tales of the woods"; he later regretted that he did not burn them (Benfey, p. 56).

Maggie: A Girl of the Streets. At the same time that he was writing these sketches of country life, Crane also was at work on his first novel, a dark tale of life in the inner-city. The story focuses on Maggie, an innocent girl who grows up in the slums of Manhattan. Slowly, and inescapably it seems, she falls into a career as a prostitute after being seduced by a smooth-talking bartender named Pete. Maggie's life becomes increasingly wretched and finally ends in suicide.

Crane wrote *Maggie* under the pseudonym of Johnston Smith and published it at his own expense in 1893. He was disappointed when the public did not rush out to buy the daring work. Apparently, readers were not ready for a novel that was so realistic, and critics, calling it "brutal, coarse, cruel" wondered why Crane bothered to write about such people at all (Linson, p. 21).

The Red Badge of Courage. Published in 1895, when he was only twenty-three, *The Red Badge of Courage* is clearly Crane's greatest work. It tells the story of a young farm boy caught in the bloody turmoil of the Civil War. The novel is so realistic that when it came out many readers thought Crane himself had fought in the war; however, the war ended six years before he was born. According to Crane's friend Corwin Knapp Linson, Crane spent hours in Linson's art studio intently reading magazines about the Civil War. Apparently he was frustrated by the lack of feeling the writers expressed in these accounts. Linson remembers Crane exclaiming, "I wonder that *some* of these fellows don't tell how they *felt* in those scraps! They spout eternally about what they *did,* but they are as emotionless as rocks!" (Linson, p. 37).

Crane set about to write a story that would capture the soldiers' feelings about war. In *The Red Badge of Courage,* he allows readers to enter the mind and experience every gripping emotion of the central character, Henry Fleming. The youth (as Crane continually calls him, reminding the reader that this could be any young soldier) enlists as a soldier, filled with romantic visions of war and dreams of heroism. But when he confronts the reality of

▲ First page of the final manuscript of *The Red Badge of Courage* hand-to-hand combat in war-torn woods during his first battle, he runs away, deserting his company. Ashamed at his cowardice, the youth wanders aimlessly through the woods, the sounds of war raging around him. He sees wounded and dying soldiers, overhears generals discussing strategy at a safe distance from the front lines, and eventually makes his way back to his comrades. In a subsequent battle, he displays courage equal to his earlier cowardice, running directly into the face of battle and seizing the enemy flag.

Crane's novel captures the horror of war in grim, vivid, and emotion-filled detail. Although Henry Fleming is a Union soldier, the sides hardly matter. Crane does not focus on politics or on right or wrong but on the reality of war—of staring into the eyes of the enemy, seeing friends drop to their death, and facing constant danger and the threat of death. Crane painted a vivid and realistic picture of the horrors on the battlefield:

[Enemy soldiers] were so near that he could see their features. There was a recognition as he looked at the types of faces.... The two bodies of troops exchanged blows in the manner of a pair of boxers. The fast and angry firings went back and forth.... But the blows of the antagonist began to grow more weak. Fewer bullets ripped the air, and finally.... The men saw a ground vacant of fighters. It would have been an empty stage if it were not for a few corpses that lay thrown and twisted into fantastic shapes upon the sward. (Crane, pp. 156-58)

Scandal. In September 1896, Crane became involved in a scandal that caused hard feelings between him and New York's police department and estranged him from most of his fellow journalists. By now famous due to the publication of *The Red Badge of Courage,* Crane had agreed to write a series of articles for the *New York Journal.* The articles would focus on activities that took place

The Black Riders

Although Stephen Crane is not widely remembered for his poetry, he claimed that his favorite work was his collection of poems, which he called "lines." Compiled into a book called *The Black Riders,* the poems were originally printed in all-capital letters. The one printed below is about writing.

"MANY RED DEVILS RAN FROM MY HEART
AND OUT UPON THE PAGE.
THEY WERE SO TINY
THE PEN COULD MASH THEM.
AND MANY STRUGGLED IN THE INK.
IT WAS STRANGE
TO WRITE IN THIS RED MUCK
OF THINGS FROM MY HEART."

(Benfey, p. 135)

in the Jefferson Market Courthouse, located in an area known as Satan's Circus. On September 14, after attending several sessions at the courthouse, Crane decided to dig deeper and "study the police court victims in their haunts" (Benfey, p. 174). After a late-night meeting in the neighborhood with three chorus girls, Crane escorted one to a cable car. When he returned to rejoin the other two women, he found them being arrested for prostitution.

Against the advice of colleagues in the press, Crane decided to testify on behalf of one of the girls, Dora Clark. Later, she pressed charges against the arresting officer, perhaps urged on by Crane. During the sensational trial, suggestions of opium use and living with a woman who was not his wife marred Crane's reputation. Eventually, the officer was acquitted (though he later was executed for murder), but the stain left by the scandal remained, and the case had made Crane an enemy of the New York police.

Shipwrecked. Soon after this incident, Crane almost died in a shipwreck. Commissioned to report as a correspondent on the uprising in Cuba, Crane traveled to Jacksonville, Florida, to find a ship bound for Cuba. Before embarking on the *Commodore,* Crane must have had some foreboding, for he wrote out his last will and testament. The *Commodore,* which was smuggling a cargo of ammunition and guns to Cuba, set out on New Year's Eve, 1896. Two days later, on January 2, 1897, the ship sank, and in the wreckage, seven men drowned. Although Crane managed to survive, several American papers prematurely published his death notice.

Love and "marriage." By the time he was twenty-five, Crane had been romantically involved with several women. In 1896 he carried on a correspondence with a woman named Nellie Crouse, whom he had met only once at a party the year before. The letters were intimate and revealing, yet Crane's and Crouse's romance never got past the letter-writing stage. Later, he dated and may have lived with a widowed drama critic named Amy Leslie, who was some ten years older than he. After they broke up, Leslie sued Crane for $800, which she claimed to have loaned him.

While still involved with Amy Leslie, Crane met the woman who would become his common-law wife. Cora Howorth Stewart, under the name Cora Taylor, operated a nightclub called the Hotel de Dream. Though not an actual brothel, the club brought interested men into contact with prostitutes. Cora was six years Crane's senior and came from a respectable Boston family, which she had left to pursue a wilder life-style. Because little remains of their correspondence, not much is known of their early romance, but after their initial meeting, Crane and Cora became inseparable. Cora was not free to marry Crane because she was already married to a man who refused to divorce her; however, the two lived together as man and wife until Crane's death.

True war. After the wreck of the *Commodore,* Crane traveled to Greece to cover the Greco-Turkish war as a correspondent for the *New York Journal.* Some of his enemies in the press joked about the fiction writer covering a real war and poked fun in writing at his reports. Cora accompanied Crane, signing on as the *Journal*'s first female war correspondent. As Crane followed the action of the war, he struggled with a weakening illness. When the short-lived war ended, he and Cora traveled to England.

Thirteen months after leaving the United States, Crane returned to sign up for duty in the Spanish-American War. Turned away by the military, he instead traveled to Cuba as a newspaper reporter for publisher Joseph Pulitzer's *New York World.* Crane refused to take his job seriously. He objected to the widespread practice of yellow journalism, in which reporters wrote exaggerated accounts of the war. The heat was relentless; soldiers sweated in wool winter uniforms, ate out of cans, and fought with old-fashioned rifles. Crane accompanied them, showing almost reckless courage on the battlefront.

> **A News Report by Stephen Crane**
>
> Crane complained in "Captured Mausers" that the location of American troops was known to the enemy by the smoke of every rifle shot, whereas the Spanish used smokeless Mauser rifles: "We cannot without cruel injustice send men using black powder into action against men who use a fair grade of smokeless." (Stallman, p. 402)

Crane reported also on the actions of Colonel Theodore Roosevelt's Rough Riders. Although Crane admired the colonel, Roosevelt did not return the feeling but rather ignored the author. He was aware of Crane's poor reputation and seemed to dislike him.

Besides news reports, Crane wrote memorable stories from

▲ Crane was a reporter during the Spanish-American War

his days in Cuba, such as "The Majestic Lie," about an American spy in Havana, and "Second Generation," about a Senator's son on the San Juan battlefield. He worked for a time as a reporter in Puerto Rico and Cuba for the Hearst newspapers, and then, in weakened health, returned to England in 1899.

Aftermath

England. When Crane had moved to England in the late spring of 1897, he was already a famous writer with an international reputation. He and Cora chose to live there, feeling that the English would be more accepting of their common-law marriage.

The Cranes lived handsomely in the English countryside, first at an estate called Ravensbrook and later at a mansion called Brede Manor. They entertained such writers as Joseph Conrad, H. G. Wells, and Henry James. To meet the expenses of their lavish life-style, Crane continued to write at a constant and almost feverish pace. He mostly wrote short stories for American magazines, sometimes counting the words as he worked to make sure he met his quota. Still, he was often broke, and as throughout his young life, money was a constant worry.

Meanwhile, Crane was growing increasingly ill with tuberculosis. At the beginning of the final year of his life, he held an extravagant New Year's party to bring in the new century. On the invitations, he asked guests, including his literary friends, to contribute to a play called "The Ghost," which would be staged at the party. Beginning on December 27 and lasting several days, the party featured music, drinking, dancing, feasting, and endless poker games. Soon after it was over, Crane suffered a hemorrhage in his lungs from which he never completely recovered. He spent most of the next six months in bed, finally dying on June 5, 1900, at the young age of twenty-eight.

For More Information

Benfey, Christopher. *The Double Life of Stephen Crane: A Biography.* New York: Alfred A. Knopf, 1992.

Cady, Edwin. *Stephen Crane.* New York: Twayne Publishers, 1962.

Crane, Stephen. *Great Stories of Heroism and Adventure.* New York: Platt and Munk, 1967.

Linson, Corwin Knapp. *My Stephen Crane.* Syracuse: Syracuse University Press, 1958.

Stallman, R. W. *Stephen Crane: A Biography.* New York: George Braziller, 1968.

Helen Hunt Jackson

1830-1885

Personal Background

Childhood in Amherst. Helen Maria Fiske was born on October 15, 1830, in Amherst, Massachusetts, an academic community in the western part of the state. Her father, Nathan, had graduated from theology school and was an ordained Congregational clergyman; he taught literature and philosophy at Amherst College. Her mother, Deborah, who had benefited from a well-rounded New England upbringing and education, enjoyed the social life in Amherst.

From Helen's earliest years, Deborah noticed a marked difference between Helen and her younger sister, Ann. "I cannot play with Helen so well as with Ann," Deborah wrote. "Helen is so wild—jumping rope, dressing up in odd things, jumping out behind doors.... They are as unlike, as Papa often says, 'as if they belonged to different nations'" (May, p. 4).

Helen's independent spirit showed itself early. At age six, she ventured into the woods beyond Amherst with a playmate and ended up four miles away in another town. Her parents and other townspeople went out looking for the girls; two Amherst professors finally found them and loaded them into a carriage for the ride home. But Helen jumped out from the carriage on the way. She did not return home until ten o'clock that evening and was sternly punished for her misbehavior.

▲ Helen Hunt Jackson

Event: Realism in American literature.

Role: An accomplished poet, essayist, and novelist, Helen Hunt Jackson spoke out for and wrote about the plight of native Americans in her later years. She hoped she could bring about a change in attitudes and stimulate reform by making the public aware of the injustices done to the Indians by the government.

With the college town of Amherst as her home, Helen grew up in a social, lively, and intellectually stimulating atmosphere. She was a bright student who caught on quickly and asked many questions. Her mother described her abilities: "Helen learns very well...she is quite inclined to question everything; the Bible, she says, does not feel as if it were true" (May, p. 7).

Coincidentally, Helen grew up down the street from one of America's greatest poets, Emily Dickinson. Just two months apart in age, the two became lifelong friends, though they were as different as two people could be. While Helen was outspoken and boisterous, Emily was small, shy, and frail. Yet, the two shared a love for secrets, ghost stories, and make-believe, and they attended Amherst Academy together.

Orphaned. When Helen was just twelve, her mother died of tuberculosis, and the family was torn apart. Helen and her sister were separated, with Ann going off to live with relatives and Helen being sent off to school. About three years later, Nathan died of the same disease as his wife.

By sixteen, Helen had become used to a rootless life, attending different schools and living with relatives during breaks. She was very social, charming, and at ease in most situations. She loved parties. Her engaging, talkative manner, and lively green eyes captivated people. A friend described her as "not exactly beautiful," but "gracious and vivacious" (May, p. 8).

Helen graduated with honors from Abbott Institute, a distinguished boarding school in New York. The institute, run by family friends, offered Helen a teaching post upon graduation, which she happily accepted. "Teaching I enjoy most highly," she wrote, "so much that I can truly say, I was never so happy in my life as at this time" (May, p. 9). However, Helen spent only a year in this satisfying position.

Marriage. After teaching for a term, Helen, now nearly twenty, traveled to Albany to spend the summer at the home of other family friends, the Reverend Ray Palmer and his wife and children. Expecting a rather dull vacation, Helen was surprised to find her summer considerably brightened by her acquaintance with a man named Lieutenant Edward Hunt. Ten years her senior, Hunt was a brilliant student of physics who worked for the government and was later considered one of America's most promising scientists. Within a year after meeting, Edward proposed to Helen, and they married on October 28, 1852. Immediately after the wedding, the couple moved to Washington, D.C., where Edward was stationed.

Children. Life in the nation's capital was busy and exciting; Helen found herself entertaining often and attending various social functions. Meanwhile, she became pregnant with her first child, Murray, who was born the following September. Within a year, however, Murray died of a brain tumor. Helen was deeply grieved by the loss, and when she became pregnant again, worried about facing such a loss again. "I almost dread to find my whole soul so utterly bound up in one little frail life," she wrote to a friend. "You know me well enough to know that I can't love after any *half way* fashion" (May, p. 18).

Meanwhile, Edward had been transferred to Newport, Rhode Island, where, on December 11, 1855, Helen gave birth to a second son, Warren. Helen was devoted to the boy, whom she called Rennie. A friend later wrote that mother and son were "intimate friends when he was little more than a baby" (May, p. 18).

The Hunts moved often during these years, as the Navy stationed Edward at various posts, some as far away as California. Sometimes Helen and Rennie accompanied Edward, but more often they stayed behind, and the responsibility and authority of the household fell to Helen.

Tragic losses. In her early thirties, Helen lost her entire family. Edward died in October 1863, following a botched experiment with one of his inventions, a sea-miner, or submarine gun similar to a modern-day torpedo. Poisonous gas fumes in the hull of the vessel overtook him, and he fell and suffered a concussion. The exposure to the fumes killed him a few days later. A year and a half after Edward's death, Rennie died of diphtheria. On his deathbed, the nine-year-old, knowing that his death would crush his mother, told her, "Promise me, Mama, that you won't kill yourself" (May, p. 21).

Helen did not kill herself, but rather spent several months in isolation, away from family and friends. When she finally appeared, she refused to show her pain, struggling to maintain at least an outward appearance of graciousness and charm. Inwardly, however, she continued to grieve; throughout her life, she could not speak of Rennie without crying. Also, she dabbled a bit in spiritualism, hoping to establish contact with her son from beyond the grave.

She eventually realized that she had to get on with her life and began to think about what she would do. In the months after Rennie died, she had dealt with her sorrow by writing poetry. She decided to work at getting these poems published and to devote the rest of her life to writing.

Participation: Realism in American Literature

Poetry. At thirty-five, Helen began writing poetry, which she published under the name "Marah," and later as "H.H." She moved back to Newport, Rhode Island, where many authors lived. In the wealthy seaside community, she stayed at a boarding house on Broad Street. Another boarder, an old friend of the Hunts, was Colonel Thomas Wentworth Higginson, a liberal clergyman and skilled essay writer. Higginson was Helen's literary mentor; he edited and guided her work and helped her contact publishers. A deep bond developed between them, which might have led to marriage had Higginson not been married already to a frail, unhappy, and sickly woman named Mary.

Although Helen was still depressed when she first arrived in Newport, Higginson described her as a woman "whose very temperament seemed mingled of sunshine and fire" (May, p. 24). Of her efforts to develop her writing, he wrote:

> She entered with the enthusiasm of a child upon her new work. She distrusted herself, was at first fearful of each new undertaking, yet was eager to try everything, and the moment each new plunge was taken lost all fear. (May, p. 26)

In spite of her newness to the literary world, Helen showed a confident business sense in dealing with publishers. When a poem was accepted by the distinguished *Atlantic Monthly,* she appreciated her good luck but at the same time, demanded—and received—a fee that was high for a new poet like herself. "I don't write for money," she later wrote, "I write for love—I *print* for money" (May, p. 27).

During the next four or five years, Helen continued writing and publishing her poetry, and "H.H." become quite popular with American readers. Transcendental poet and scholar Ralph Waldo Emerson, who considered "H.H." one of the best poets in the country, was said to have clipped her poems from newspapers and carried them in his pocket for easy reference.

While Helen continued to write, she also traveled a great deal, giving in to the wanderlust that she had had since her teenage years. As during her marriage, in later life she never really had a permanent home. She did, however, have a broad base of friends, including Emily Dickinson, with whom she continued to maintain a steady correspondence.

Fiction. By 1870 Helen had begun writing fiction under the name "Saxe Holm." Her fifteen novellas, which appeared in various popular magazines from 1871 to 1884, seem to have been inspired by her frustrated feelings toward Higginson. Several center around characters involved in unhappy marriages who cannot honor their true feelings of love because of their marriage vows. Titles include "Whose Wife Is She Anyway?," "Ester Wynn's Love Letters," and "How One Woman Kept Her Husband."

Few suspected the true authorship of the stories, and Helen was amused and sometimes angered by the various impostors who stepped forward claiming to have written the tales. In spite of this, she never admitted to being the author of the Saxe Holm stories, and only on her deathbed did she leave instructions to let the public know of the author's true identity.

At the same time, she published a second series of fiction stories, again anonymously. Called the "No Name" series, it included stories by various authors "of great unknown." The publication of the anonymous works was something of a publicity stunt; readers had fun guessing who the authors might be. The aura of mystery that surrounded the work made the books highly successful.

Meanwhile, Helen continued writing poetry and also regularly contributed essays and articles to magazines, including a series about travels through Europe called "Bits of Travel."

Out West. In 1872 Helen took her first trip to the West. Traveling by train with a friend, she made her way to northern California, where she visited San Francisco, Santa Cruz, Lake Tahoe, and other areas. Her favorite spot was Yosemite, which she called by its Indian name, Ah-Wah-Ne Falls. Helen was awed by the wondrous glacier-carved valley, with its rushing waterfalls, lush meadows, and magnificent trees.

After returning from the two-month trip, Helen stayed on the East Coast for only a few months before once again heading west. This time, in November 1872, she went for medical reasons—her doctor recommended the air and climate of Colorado for her weakened health. In Colorado Springs, Helen registered at a boarding house, where she met William Jackson, a thirty-eight-year-old bachelor who was the vice president of a railroad company and founder and president of a local bank.

The two began seeing each other and, after a long courtship, they married on October 22, 1875. Now known as Helen Hunt Jackson, the new bride moved into the house Will had bought for her. She immediately began decorating and remodeling with a flourish. Although it was the first real home she had had in years, it was not long before wanderlust again overtook her.

Struggle for native American rights. In 1879 Jackson visited Boston to attend the seventieth birthday party of U.S. Supreme Court Justice Oliver Wendell Holmes. At the event, which included a reading of her poetry, two Ponca Indians spoke on the injustices their people suffered because of greedy whites. The government had forced them off their rightful lands in the dead of winter and made them live on barren stretches of Nebraska hills. The people, who could not grow any food to feed themselves, were slowly starving to death. Now Ponca representatives had traveled to the East Coast to make whites aware of the injustices they had suffered and to try to win back their rights.

One of the Indians was a woman named Bright Eyes, and her story touched Jackson deeply. Jackson, who had always looked with scorn at "cause women" (women who devoted themselves to fighting for the vote or other causes), now found herself deeply committed to a cause of her own. She wrote: "I have done now the last of the things I had said I would never do; I have become what I have said a thousand times was the most odious thing in life, 'a woman with a hobby'" (May, p. 61).

But for Jackson, fighting for native American rights was not an idle pastime. She wrapped herself in the cause, writing passionate letters to editors around the country, publishing articles on the topic, and helping to raise money for the Ponca lawsuit against the federal government. She helped form the Boston Indian Citizenship Association. When her efforts seemed to have little effect, however, Jackson decided to write a book that would put the injustices in print for all the world to see.

A Century of Dishonor. In the book, which she published in 1881 under her own name, Jackson listed a record of the government's broken treaties with various tribes and its unjust practices. The tribes she wrote about included the Cheyenne, Nez Percé, Ponca, and Cherokee Indians. Jackson did not claim to have written a complete history of the conflicts between whites and Indians, but rather, a sketch.

> I give an outline of the experiences of a tribe—broken treaties, removals, etc.—telling the history of each tribe straight through by itself.... I have been through all the law authorities in the Astor library on these points.... All the heart and soul I possess have gone into it. (Jackson, *A Century of Dishonor*, p. xiii-xiv)

From *A Century of Dishonor*

"There is not among these three hundred bands of Indians one which has not suffered cruelly at the hands either of the Government or of white settlers. The poorer, the more insignificant, the more helpless the band, the more certain the cruelty and outrage to which they have been subjected.

"It makes little difference, however, where one opens the record of the history of the Indians; every page and every year has its dark stain. The story of one tribe is the story of all, varied only by differences in the main facts. Colorado is as greedy and unjust in 1880 as was Georgia in 1830, and Ohio in 1795; and the United States Government breaks promises now as deftly as then, and with an added ingenuity from long practice." (Jackson, pp. 336-37)

A Century of Dishonor shocked the public. For the first time in American history, the plight of the native Americans and the many injustices that had been inflicted upon them were clearly spelled out and described. Although at first the book seemed to have little impact, in the years following its publication, many reforms were put into effect and new laws were passed intending to benefit Indians.

Within a year after the book was printed, the powerful Indian Rights Association was established.

Some critics accused Jackson of being sentimental and of oversimplifying and overstating the problem. In Colorado, where settlers were involved in conflicts with area tribes, Jackson became widely unpopular and the focus of much anger.

Ramona. After this, Jackson spent most of her remaining years traveling, often away from her home state and her husband. No one knows of the strain that this must have put on her marriage, but as the years passed, she and Will seemed to live very separate lives. Nonetheless, they continued a steady correspondence and saw each other when they could.

Between 1881 and 1883, Jackson took two extended trips to southern California, staying as long as six months at a time. She traveled through the area, visited missions, met local Indians and learned about their problems, and spoke out for their cause. During one of these visits, after hearing a tragic story from a young Indian woman named Ramona, Jackson was ready to write another book, this time a novel. Her aim was to write a story that would do for native Americans what Harriet Beecher Stowe's *Uncle Tom's Cabin* had done for African Americans.

Oddly, Jackson returned east to write the work. From a hotel in New York, surrounded by Indian baskets, rugs, and embroideries and with her photograph of Rennie at her desk, Jackson began writing at lightning speed. The story that she had been burning to tell poured out of her. As the icy cold and stormy New York weather pressed at her window, she wrote of the pastel sunsets, orange groves, and desert landscape of southern California. She told the true story of Ramona in fictional terms, adding her own variations and sometimes using as characters people she had met in her travels. "I didn't write *Ramona;* it was written through me," she explained. "My lifeblood went into all I had thought, felt, and suffered for five years on the Indian question" (May, p. 135).

The novel, published in 1884, tells of life in southern California among the Californios (descendants of the Spanish), Indians, and white settlers, or Anglos. In rich detail, Jackson describes life on a

▲ **Illustrations by Henry Sandham for an edition of *Ramona***

busy ranch, activities in the Indian villages, and people who occupy
the area. The tale revolves around an Indian man named Alessandro who marries a Californio woman, Ramona. The couple faces
prejudice because of their mixed marriage. White settlers push
them off their land, until they move to a lonely mountaintop to live.
One day, in a state of confusion, Alessandro mistakenly walks off
with a white man's horse thinking it is his own. The angry settler
finds Alessandro at his home and brutally kills him in front of
Ramona and the baby.

Aftermath

After *Ramona*. The romantic novel did not bring about quite the reaction Jackson had hoped for. Critics and readers responded more to the romantic tale of the colorful, far-off land, than to the story of injustice done to Indians. There was, however, angry reaction among some of the white settlers in southern California. The book grew increasingly popular throughout the country and was reprinted in numerous editions.

Attracted by Jackson's descriptions of southern California, readers from the eastern parts of the country flocked to the area, which flourished with the increased income they brought. Residents pointed the tourists to the church where Alessandro and Ramona married (seventy-two Catholic churches claimed the honor). Various towns advertised themselves as Ramona's birthplace, and bold Indian women claimed to be the heroine herself. Years later, Hollywood continued *Ramona*'s popularity, producing three films of the romance.

In addition to its popularity as a romance, Jackson's novel did bring about some changes in society and government. Within a few years, Indian rights associations had formed in every major U.S. city. At the same time, largely as a result of *Ramona,* the Dawes Act was passed in 1887, allotting sixty acres of land to each head of an Indian household.

Final days. Writing *Ramona* had taken its toll on the author's weakening health. After completing the novel, Jackson returned to Colorado for a rest. But while she was recuperating, she tripped and fell headlong down a staircase, shattering one leg, which further weakened her. The leg never fully healed. At this point, she returned to California, hoping to recover her strength and health in the warm climate. But cancer was racking her body, and she grew progressively sick.

From a room in San Francisco with a beautiful view of the bay, Jackson put her accounts in order. She wrote Will, telling him how deeply she loved him but admitting that she had always felt like she was not the right wife for him. She urged him to remarry after her death, which he did, to her niece and namesake, Helen Banfield.

She also wrote to President Grover Cleveland asking him to read *A Century of Dishonor* and urging him to right the wrongs committed against the Indian race.

During these final days, Jackson even planned a trip to her beloved Yosemite with the famous naturalist John Muir. She grew too sick to take the trip, however, and died on August 12, 1885. Upon her death, Emily Dickinson sent a note to Will commemorating her friend:

> Helen of Troy will die,
> Helen of Colorado, never.
> 'Dear friend, can you walk?'
> were the last words I wrote her—
> 'Dear friend, I can fly.'
> —her immortal reply.
>
> (Dickinson in May, p. 133)

For More Information

Jackson, Helen Hunt. *A Century of Dishonor: The Early Crusade for Indian Reform.* New York: Harper and Row, 1881, 1965.

Jackson, Helen Hunt. *Ramona.* New York: Grosset and Dunlap, 1969 (originally published 1884).

May, Antoinette. *Helen Hunt Jackson: A Lonely Voice of Conscience.* San Francisco: Chronicle Books, 1987.

Women and Social Reform

1868
▼
Fourteenth Amendment guarantees the right to vote to males.

1869
▼
Elizabeth Cady Stanton helps form National American Woman's Suffrage Association to gain vote for females.

1884
▼
First Working Girls Club is formed. **Josephine Shaw Lowell** writes *Public Relief and Private Charity.*

1879
▼
Willard becomes WCTU president.

1874
▼
Frances Willard joins the Women's Christian Temperance Union (WCTU).

1870
▼
Fifteenth Amendment prohibits discrimination in voting due to race or color but says nothing about sex.

1887
▼
Willard joins the Knights of Labor.

1890
▼
New York Consumers League is founded. Lowell serves as president.

1891
▼
Willard becomes worldwide WCTU president.

1895
▼
Stanton writes *The Women's Bible.*

1933
▼
Eighteenth Amendment is repealed.

1920
▼
Nineteenth Amendment guarantees the vote to women.

1917
▼
Eighteenth Amendment passes prohibiting the manufacture and sale of alcohol.

1903
▼
National Women's Trade Union League is established for working-class women.

1899
▼
National Consumers League is founded.

WOMEN AND SOCIAL REFORM

Of concern to some men and an increasing number of women in post–Civil War America were the nation's mounting social problems: the flood of immigrants to rapidly growing cities, unclean neighborhoods, abusive labor practices, alcoholism, and the struggle for material wealth. While the rapid spread of industry catapulted a few Americans from rags to riches, it also plunged thousands into slums and poverty.

Pre-Civil War reformers, such as **Elizabeth Cady Stanton,** transferred their energies to the postwar issues and were joined by a new group of reformers. They prescribed social remedies for society's ills and used scientific data to support their proposals. One of the first remedies for the state of society was suggested by Henry George. Author of *Progress and Poverty*, George pointed out that wherever individuals amassed the richest fortunes, society was plagued by the deepest poverty; he recommended a special tax on landlords. Believing that people could change social conditions, he won over others to this position. George's book became a best seller—two million copies were purchased in twenty-six years.

Other reformers organized groups to deal with the ills of the times. Stanton sought the right to vote for women. During the war, she had put aside her cause to collect nearly 400,000

▲ **Women protesting the actions of a sewing-machine dealer to the Working-Women's Protective Union**

signatures on a petition to Congress for the Thirteenth Amendment, which abolished slavery. The Fourteenth and Fifteenth Amendments followed, guaranteeing citizenship and the vote to blacks but not to women. Outraged, Stanton broke away from the Equal Rights Association for whose goals she had worked. Feeling betrayed by the men in the group, she and Susan B. Anthony formed the National American Woman's Suffrage Association. Another organization, the American Woman Suffrage Association, was also formed in 1869 to try to gain the vote for women. Both groups would continue to operate separately for twenty years, differing on tactics. The second association believed the vote could be gained only by avoiding issues that would upset powerful men in the community, such as divorce or a union for working women. By contrast, Stanton and Anthony's organization considered other issues, though voting rights remained its primary cause. In her seventies, Stanton lost the leadership of the National American Woman's Suffrage Association to younger women. She had argued that women were entitled to the vote because they were republican citizens, but the new leaders shifted to more practical reasons why women should vote, saying they needed to pass laws against rape, unsafe working conditions, unjust child labor, and so forth. Stanton nevertheless continued to argue on moral grounds, writing the *Woman's Bible,* which attacked Biblical arguments that were used to keep women from gaining equality.

Frances Willard, one of the most remarkable leaders of the nineteenth century, molded the Women's Christian Temperance Union (WCTU) into the largest women's organization in the country. At first, its purpose was just to prevent the use of alcohol in the United States, but Willard broadened its goals when she became president of the WCTU in 1879. She led women gradually to understand that they could not safeguard their homes and families from liquor and harmful influences unless they had the vote. Willard submitted a petition in Illinois that demanded women be able to vote on the local issue of the sale and manufacture of alcohol. Gathering 110,000 names of women and men on the petition, she helped inspire a desire for the vote in women and impressed the legislature with their potential power. Willard, who served as president of the organization for nineteen years, also turned the WCTU into a multipurpose, do-everything organization, organizing departments to work with prisoners, prostitutes, and the ill. Believing that social hardships were at the root of drunkenness, she acted to combat them.

Founded in 1890, another organization, the New York Consumers League, won the support of middle and upper class women. **Josephine Shaw Lowell** served as its president

▲ **Women lobbying at the White House**

until 1896, struggling to alert the buying public to the ghastly working conditions that prevailed among women in sales and the garment industry—two-dollar-a-week salaries, sixteen-hour workdays, no seats behind sales counters, and no vacations. The Consumers League also investigated sweatshops where clothes were manufactured and factories in which foods were processed. Its members worked for state legislation to improve conditions, feeling government should regulate industry. Lowell had personal experience with government involvement in social problems, having been appointed early in her career to

New York's State Board of Charities. She was the first woman to ever hold a government position on reform.

In 1903 working women formed the National Women's Trade Union League. The league supported women on strike, publicizing their grievances, raising money, and passing out relief supplies. The league experienced most success with New York garment workers. In fact, working women in New York had already begun to organize several years earlier. In 1884 twelve factory workers formed the first Working Girls Club in New York with the help of Grace Dodge, member of a wealthy copper mining family. The women's club movement grew, forming a general federation that lobbied in Congress for factory inspection, criminal reform, honesty in politics, and more. Begun with the help of Ida Wells-Barnett, the first national black women's club appeared during this period too. A primary purpose of the organization was to combat the false notion that black women of the time had little intelligence and few morals.

Meanwhile, men founded organizations such as the Populist party to curb the growth of big business and combat excessive railroad fees. The ills of the period, however, had moved women to participate in society in greater numbers than ever before. Frances Willard once described government as housekeeping on the largest scale. There was a feeling that men had handled the job poorly; the woman's touch was needed.

Elizabeth Cady Stanton

1815-1902

Personal Background

Elizabeth Cady Stanton was born on November 12, 1815, in Johnstown, New York, to Margaret Livingston Cady and Daniel Cady. Elizabeth's father, a local judge, was elected to Congress the same year as her birth. The Cadys were strict Puritans and raised their six children comfortably in the rural setting of the Mohawk Valley in upstate New York.

Sister's birth. Among Elizabeth's first memories was the birth of her sister Margaret. When friends who had come to visit the infant said, "What a pity it is she's a girl," Elizabeth was shocked and felt compassion for the small baby (Stanton, p. 3). Thus at the early age of four, Elizabeth first became aware of the ill regard for women by nineteenth-century American society. The compassion she felt for her sister—and all women—would last a lifetime.

Why "no"? Along with her brothers and sisters, Elizabeth attended public school at the Johnstown Academy and went to church services regularly. A curious and energetic girl, Elizabeth continually questioned why there were so many "nos" in religious doctrine. One day she asked her nurse, "Why [is it] that everything we like to do is a sin, and everything we dislike is commanded by God or someone on earth. I am so tired of the everlasting no! no! no!" (Stanton, p. 9). Elizabeth's nurse, like her parents, was upset by

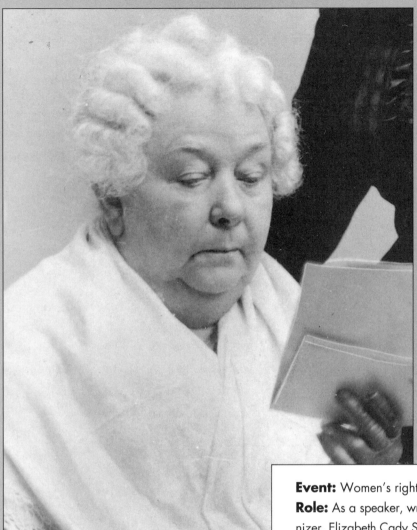

▲ **Elizabeth Cady Stanton**

Event: Women's rights movement.
Role: As a speaker, writer, and organizer, Elizabeth Cady Stanton led the women's rights movement in the United States and the world and was the first to lobby for women's right to vote. Together with Lucretia Mott, Stanton organized the first women's rights convention in Seneca Falls, New York, in 1848, and with Susan B. Anthony founded the National American Woman's Suffrage Association in 1869.

her rebellious tone and urged Elizabeth to cultivate the virtues of obedience and humility. However, Elizabeth's quick and curious mind would not rest, and she continued to question authority throughout her childhood. In fact, she would make it her life's work to challenge the status quo.

Reverend Simon Hosack. At about age ten, Elizabeth met a man who had a profound influence on her life. Because her father was often away or busy with legal affairs, Elizabeth looked to Reverend Simon Hosack for daily guidance. She would assist the elderly pastor by driving his horse-drawn carriage and he, in turn, would teach her rhetoric, or the art of speaking, and Greek and read her the classics. Unlike Elizabeth's father, Hosack had a deep appreciation of women and of Elizabeth's capabilities in particular. He thoroughly encouraged her in her studies and urged her to prove to her father—and the world—that a girl's mental capacity equaled that of a boy's.

When Elizabeth's only brother, Eleazer, died in 1826, Cady was crushed. Elizabeth hoped that she could fill Eleazer's place in her father's broken heart. But, to her disappointment, he only remarked that he wished she had been born a boy. He thought her not capable of filling her brother's shoes. Elizabeth did not give up, however. With Hosack's help, she vowed then and there to be at the head of her classes and thus fill her father with joy. Hoping to impress him, she learned to ride a horse, moved to the top of her class in school, and even won a prize for her mastery of Greek. Trophy in hand, she rushed to her father's office thinking that now he would be satisfied with her and hoping that he would say a girl was, in fact, as good as a boy. But no such words came from Cady. Instead, he uttered his usual, "You should have been a boy!" and, in Elizabeth's own words, "turned her joy to ashes" (Stanton, p. 25).

Soon after, Hosack died. He willed his books to Elizabeth, who cherished them along with her fond memories of the kind pastor. She felt she had truly been blessed by having such a friend and teacher and said she knew his spirit was with her during all of life's subsequent struggles.

Education. As a teenager, Elizabeth divided her time between school and her father's law office, which was usually filled with young law students. Elizabeth thoroughly enjoyed debating with and learning from them. One day, a student explained through an anecdote how unfair the property laws were for women. Elizabeth was wearing a coral necklace and bracelet, and the young man said:

> Now, if in due time you should be my wife, those ornaments would be mine. I could take them and lock them up, and you could never wear them except with my permission. I could even exchange them for a cigar, and you could watch them evaporate in smoke. (Stanton, p. 34)

From this exchange, Elizabeth learned about English common law, in effect in America at the time, which basically stripped married women of their property rights as well as of their rights to guardianship of their children. Elizabeth also met many women who were victims of this unjust law at her father's office. She became more and more convinced that it was necessary to take active measures against these unjust practices. Cady offered her advice that she took to heart:

> When you are grown up, and able to prepare a speech, you must go down to Albany and talk to the legislators; tell them all you have seen in this office—the sufferings of these women, robbed of their inheritance and left dependent on their unworthy sons—and, if you can persuade them to pass new laws, the old ones will be a dead letter. (Stanton, p. 35)

Little did Cady realize that is exactly what Elizabeth would later do.

Boarding school. At fifteen, Elizabeth graduated from the Johnstown Academy and, because young women were not allowed to attend college, was sent to a female boarding school called Mrs. Willard's Academy in Troy, New York. There, though frustrated at being segregated from boys, Elizabeth learned a great deal. She studied with young women from throughout Europe and Canada and was privileged to have a very brilliant teacher in Emma Willard. Willard taught the young women French and, as a very proficient homeopathic physician herself, taught them much about physiology, anatomy, and homeopathic medicine. Elizabeth later relied heavily upon this knowledge while raising her seven children.

Gerrit Smith. Elizabeth's cousin, the brilliant abolitionist Gerrit Smith, lived in nearby Petersboro, New York, and the Cadys visited him yearly. Smith's house was not only a stop for the Underground Railroad but was also a meeting place for reformers from throughout New England. There, Elizabeth encountered famous abolitionists such as Frederick Douglass, Abby Kelly, William Lloyd Garrison, and Lucretia Mott and became interested in the antislavery and temperance movements. She considered the abolition movement to be the best school the American people ever had in which to learn republican principles and ethics.

A second benefit from visiting Smith's home was meeting Henry B. Stanton, an antislavery speaker whose passionate words impressed Elizabeth tremendously. The two met in 1839, when she was twenty-four and he was thirty-four. The couple were wed (omitting the "to obey" lines from the bride's vows) the following year on May 10, 1840. Soon after, Elizabeth Cady Stanton's life as a reformer began.

Participation: Women's Rights Movement

For their honeymoon, the couple traveled to London for the World's Antislavery Convention. To Stanton's outrage, women, some of whom had traveled all the way from America to present their lectures, were denied the right to address the assembly. Stanton noted:

> It struck me as very remarkable that abolitionists, who felt so keenly the wrongs of the slave, should be so oblivious to the equal wrongs of their own mothers, wives, and sisters, when, according to common law, both classes occupied a similar legal status. (Stanton, p. 75)

Convention discussed. Another who shared these views was Lucretia Mott, who had planned to speak at the convention. When she and Stanton, along with the other women in attendance, were placed in a dark corner of the convention hall and denied public speech, they began to discuss their predicament. They decided it was time they made some demand for new freedoms for women. Stanton and Mott resolved to hold a convention as soon as they returned home and to form a new society dedicated to winning rights for women.

Inspired by meeting, for the first time, a group of women who believed, as she did, in the equality of the sexes, Stanton returned to America determined to work for women's rights. However, the demands of her young and growing family, which she and Henry were starting, would postpone the plan of holding a women's rights convention for eight years.

Motherhood. Considering motherhood the most important of all the professions, Stanton felt the same drive to excel at home-making as at school in the different branches of learning. From 1840 to 1848, she devoted the bulk of her time and attention to domestic work and to raising her five boys and two girls. During this time, the family moved from their first home in Boston to Seneca Falls, New York.

But when the family moved to that remote, rural town, Stanton, though she enjoyed many aspects of domestic life, began to feel a mental hunger. She craved outside intellectual stimulation. In Boston she had lived near William Lloyd Garrison

> ## Steps Toward Progress
>
> Responding to critics of the early suffrage movement, Stanton at age eighty wrote that each of her efforts when first tried were referred to by many as "grave mistakes" but were later referred to as "grand steps in progress." Stanton urged that all people be willing to take these "steps" toward progress and disregard those who label them as "mistakes." (Stanton, p. 352)

and other equally famous reformers and had been active in the abolitionist cause herself. In Seneca Falls, however, she lived miles from her nearest neighbor and felt completely cut off from political and social events. For the first time in her life, Stanton fully understood the practical problems most women had to face in the isolated household. She became more certain than ever that women, in addition to being mothers, needed a life outside the home.

At the highest point of her frustration, Stanton became reacquainted with Mott. Over dinner on July 13, 1848, Stanton poured out her long-accumulating discontent. She and Mott decided to finally hold a women's rights convention. Without further hesitation, they wrote the announcement that evening for the first women's rights convention to be held in Seneca Falls on the 19th of July—just six days away.

Seneca Falls Convention. In spite of the short notice, the convention was a thorough success. More than 100 men and women attended the event, at which eleven resolutions were passed. Stanton's resolution proved to be the most controversial and was the only one not passed unanimously. It read: "Resolved, that it is the duty of the women of this country to secure to themselves their sacred right to the elective franchise" (Stanton, p. 146).

With that announcement, Stanton became the first woman to publicly call for women's right to vote and, from that point on, she dedicated her life to making women's voting rights become a reality.

Controversy. The Seneca Falls Convention was hailed by supporters as a momentous event, the first organized protest against the injustice practiced for ages on one-half of the human race. Detractors abounded, however. They considered Stanton and the other feminists in attendance as thoroughly unfeminine revolutionaries who were out of their "sphere." The criticism became so strong that many women who had signed the resolutions at Seneca Falls soon withdrew their names and support for the movement. But Stanton and a few others would not be deterred. Instead of backing down, they planned and held women's rights conventions throughout New England each year for more than twenty years.

Meets Anthony. After 1848 Stanton divided her time between her family and writing and lecturing for women's rights, specifically calling for the right to vote above all others. It was during these busy years that she met the woman who would become like her other half.

After an antislavery rally in Seneca Falls in 1851, newspaper publisher Amelia Bloomer introduced Stanton to Susan B. Anthony, who also wrote and lectured in support of women's rights. Sharing nearly the same beliefs, the two women took an immediate liking to one another and began collaborating at once. The two combined their talents very effectively, with Stanton writing lectures and Anthony delivering them. Or, as Stanton put it, "I forged the thunderbolts and she fired them" (Stanton, p. 154). They organized conventions, wrote columns for Bloomer's paper, *The Lily,* and other reform newspapers, wrote and delivered lectures, and held nightly meetings at the Stanton household. As Stanton later wrote of her lifelong friend, "In thought and sympathy we were one, and in the division of labor we exactly complemented each other" (Stanton, p. 155). Anthony described their early years together as a long, happy struggle:

> When the whole world was against us ... we had to stand the closer to each other ... I would go to her home and help with the children and the housekeeping through the day and then we would sit up far into the night preparing our ammunition and getting ready to move on the enemy. The years since ... have brought no enjoyment like that. (Oakley, p. 138)

Father comes around. In 1854 Stanton was granted the opportunity to address the New York Legislature on the subject of women's property rights. The legislature was considering a bill that would extend rights to married women, and Stanton was to speak in its favor. When her father learned of her pending government address, he summoned her home to hear the speech before it was to be delivered. As she read it to him, describing the horrors suffered by widows who were left paupers after being denied their rightful inheritance—scenes she had witnessed in her father's office as a young girl—he started to cry. Suddenly, the man whom Stanton had worked a lifetime to impress was moved beyond words. He at last saw through her eyes the injustice women suffered under the laws. He lauded his daughter's efforts and offered her his help, saying he thought he could find her even crueler laws than the ones she had quoted. His acknowledgment of her talent and support of her efforts seemed to elate his daughter as much as the legislature's speaking invitation and its subsequent passage of the married women's property rights bill in 1860.

Divorce and the church. In her later years, in addition to working for the vote and property rights for women, Stanton dedicated a great deal of her time to advancing liberal divorce laws and getting women admitted as church leaders. At this time, only the Quaker church allowed women as leaders, and divorce laws were very strict.

> ## Other People's Problems
> "They who have sympathy and imagination to make the sorrows of others their own can readily learn all the hard lessons of life from the experience of others." (Stanton, p. 161)

In one of many editorials Stanton wrote concerning marriage and divorce, she insisted that the contract of marriage was by no means equal. Stanton called for major reforms, including requiring women to be older than the then-legal age of twelve before being allowed to marry. She was convinced of a woman's right not only to separation but to absolute divorce.

On the issue of women in the church, Stanton was again one of the first to call for female inclusion in leadership roles. She also wrote a book in 1895, *The Woman's Bible,* in which she attacked inequality within the church and challenged long-standing Biblical arguments that had been used for centuries to keep women in a lower position than men in society. She wrote: "From the inauguration of the movement for women's emancipation, the Bible has been used to hold her in the 'divinely ordained sphere' prescribed in the Old and New Testaments" (Oakley, p. 130). Stanton argued that a true reading of the Bible did not advocate such treatment of women but rather illustrated that "God created man in his own image, *male and female.* Thus Scripture, as well as science and philosophy, declares the eternity and equality of sex" (Oakley, p. 130).

Stanton's controversial stands, especially on women and religion, did not win her a lot of support at first. But many of the reforms she advocated were eventually implemented, and she had a profound impact on their adoption.

Aftermath

Until the end of her life, Stanton continued to fight for women's rights on all fronts. In 1869 she and Anthony founded the National American Woman's Suffrage Association and subsequently published a newspaper, the *Revolution,* with Stanton as editor and Anthony as publisher. The two also wrote the *History of Women's Suffrage,* Volumes I and II, and lectured extensively throughout the country and throughout Europe, with Stanton giving a memorable speech in Glasgow, Scotland, after women had been granted the right to vote in Great Britain.

By the 1890s, Stanton's eyesight had begun to fail her, but she continued to write letters and speeches in support of women's rights. In a letter to President Theodore Roosevelt, written just one day before her death, she urged him to bring about the "complete emancipation of 36 million women" (Oakley, p. 137). The following afternoon, October 26, 1902, she died in her home at age eighty-seven.

Few women have worked so diligently for social reform in America. Though Stanton did not live to see women achieve voting rights in 1920, she was instrumental in gaining support for the women's rights movement. Through her painstaking efforts to record the history of women's suffrage as well as through her life's work, Stanton provided a strong foundation on which women could build the future. As Mary Lowe Dickinson said on Stanton's eightieth birthday, "No woman ... could fail to be impressed with what we owe to the women of the past, and especially to this one woman" (Stanton, p. 350).

> ### Stanton on Happiness
> "I put my soul into everything, and hence enjoyed it." (Stanton, p. 135)

For More Information

Banner, Lois. *Elizabeth Cady Stanton: A Radical for Women's Rights.* Boston: Little, Brown and Co., 1980.

Oakley, Mary Ann B. *Elizabeth Cady Stanton.* New York: Feminist Press, 1972.

Stanton, Theodore. *Elizabeth Cady Stanton: As Revealed in Her Letters, Diary and Reminiscences.* New York: Harper and Brothers Publishers, 1922.

Josephine Shaw Lowell

1843-1905

Family Background

Josephine Shaw Lowell was born December 16, 1843, in West Roxbury, Massachusetts, to Francis George Shaw and Sarah Blake Sturgis Shaw. The third daughter and fourth of five children, Josephine was born into an intensely patriotic and liberal-minded family, whose members firmly backed the abolitionist movement and were highly involved in the politics of the day. Her parents came from prominent Boston-area merchant families; they counted radical reformists William Lloyd Garrison and Margaret Fuller among their friends and contributed both time and money to the social causes they supported.

Travel abroad. In 1851, when Josephine was seven, her family began a Grand Tour of Europe. During their nearly five years abroad, Josephine attended school in Paris, spent a winter in a convent in Rome, and learned to speak French, German, and Italian so well that by the time she was ten her mother pronounced her "the genius of the family" (James, p. 437).

New York. In 1855, after returning to the United States, the Shaws moved to West New Brighton, on Staten Island in New York. Shortly thereafter, Josephine's older sister Anna married the well-known editor and reformer George William Curtis. The newlyweds moved into the Shaw home. Curtis brought with him his

▲ **Josephine Shaw Lowell**

Event: Social reform movement.
Role: Josephine Shaw Lowell dedicated her life to reforming the welfare and charity systems in New York because she believed that the best way to help the impoverished and working poor was to provide the means of making a decent living. She also helped change school curriculums to include exercise and industrial training, and she worked to curb political corruption and make government more responsible to the people it was elected to serve.

library and zest for politics—each of which had a significant impact on Josephine, who was nearly thirteen. Curtis encouraged Josephine in her reading, especially of Emerson, and invited home (and introduced her to) such literary greats as English novelist William Makepeace Thackeray. Josephine not only became an avid reader, a habit which lasted her entire lifetime, but took Emerson's words to heart and adopted his view that "he who gives me something does me a low benefit; he who teaches me to do something for myself does me a high benefit" (Stewart, p. 195).

First charity work. The Shaws lived comfortably in Staten Island, but while growing up, Josephine saw that there were many less fortunate families all around her. Specifically, there was a settlement of poor Irish families near her home. Josephine decided to help. Seeing that they lacked food and that the children rarely enjoyed any extravagant treats, she took it upon herself to have lawn parties for the children, and she routinely invited the families to her house for ice cream and cake. Though this early effort was slight, it sparked an interest in Josephine for charity work that she would never relinquish.

Civil War. While Josephine was finishing school, first in New York and then in Boston, the Civil War broke out. Her brother Robert Gould Shaw was among the first to volunteer for military service, which made her very proud but also envious that she could not participate and help her country.

Desperately wanting to do her part to save the Union, Josephine joined the Central Association for Relief for the Army and Navy of the United States at age seventeen, when her education was complete. There she worked full days packing supplies and writing letters to Union soldiers. During this time, Josephine met Colonel Charles Russell Lowell, a comrade-in-arms of her brother. Charles and Josephine saw each other approximately nine times from 1861 to 1863, when Charles had leave from fighting in the war. Though they had not spent a great deal of time together, it was enough for Charles to ask Josephine to marry him, which she did on October 31, 1863.

Marriage and death. Just shortly before Josephine's marriage, her brother was killed in action. His death was difficult for her, but she had her charity work and husband as an outlet for her grief. She moved with Charles to his military headquarters in Vienna, Virginia, and spent the winter with him, helping injured soldiers and continuing to support the war effort in any way she could. Before they could celebrate their first anniversary together, however, Charles was shot and killed. Their daughter, Carlotta Russell, was born a month after that, on November 30, 1864.

Distraught over the loss of her brother and her husband, but blessed with the birth of her daughter, Josephine returned to her parents' home on Staten Island, where she turned to her charity work and began to rebuild her life.

Participation: Social Reform Movement

A widow at age twenty, Lowell first took up her father's cause and began working with him at the Freedman's Association, helping to educate newly freed slaves. She continued this work through 1870, when she left the States briefly to take her daughter to Europe. Upon her return, Lowell decided that Carlotta should attend school in New York City, and the two moved into a house that her father bought for them at 120 East 30th Street. The move did more than just provide a better education for Carlotta. Lowell became involved in a drastic reformation in New York City charities and soon helped engineer the city's—as well as the nation's—welfare system.

Charities Aid Association. After the Civil War and the signing of the Emancipation Proclamation, the nation's attention turned from abolition to other areas of social reform. The Central Relief Association, for whom Lowell had worked during the war, evolved into the New York State Charities Aid Association (NYSCAA). Lowell became active in this organization and was appointed a member of one of its visiting committees, which toured poorhouses, prisons, and other reformatories around the state. They then reported to the main body and made recommendations as to the treatment and living conditions of the inmates.

To her horror, Lowell found atrocious living conditions during her many visits to these institutions. Furthermore, there was widespread corruption in the system, with no efforts being made to rehabilitate the inmates. Lowell issued a scathing report for the fourth annual NYSCAA meeting, listing the numerous abuses she had witnessed. Though she was unable to attend the meeting and read the report herself, it captured the attention of all in attendance, including New York governor Samuel Tilden. Charging that "as usual, in our unhappy State, 'politics' is at the bottom of these evils as of most others," Lowell's paper called for drastic changes in the system (Stewart, p. 80). As the well-respected attorney Joseph H. Choate read Lowell's report, he praised the committee's work. He singled out Lowell's efforts as superior, saying that "here the curiosity of women, that unfailing power and strength, came in. They proposed to find out the facts, and in the masterly report ... signed by Mrs. Lowell, you have the whole subject" (Waugh, p. 293).

State Board of Charities. Tilden, impressed by Lowell's report, requested that she become the first female member of the State Board of Charities and begin to implement some of her proposed reform measures. The year was 1876, and Lowell, with her usual humility, told her friend, "If the Governor and the State wish to appoint me, I will gladly serve ... I know what the work of the Board is. I shall try to do it" (Waugh, p. 296).

> ## Josephine Shaw Lowell Describes Her Work Habits
>
> "Usually I allow no business on Sunday, keeping the day for friendly letters, but I have been at it all day. At 10 to 11:30 visit and talk with an agent of the COS; at 11:30 to 1 to talk about Woman's Suffrage and a little speech I'm giving next Thursday; at 3 the president of the COS came to talk business and then til 6 I wrote COS "things," so I have not read nor written any letters until now, 8:45." (Stewart, p. 136)

Lowell did more than try. She succeeded in drastically changing the way charities operated in New York State and, later, in the United States. Being a widow made Lowell acceptable as a public figure and her forthright but always polite speaking style added to her popularity. The president of the Charity Organization Society of New York, Robert de Forest, described her as having "the strength and courage of a man...[she] never hesitated to strike, and strike hard when duty called to strike, but her woman's gentle touch bound up the wounds and the blow left no sting behind" (Waugh, p. 297). Always dressed simply and in black out of respect for her deceased husband, Lowell's feminine power of persuasion not only appealed to her allies but won over many enemies.

Given the radical restructuring proposals she made, it was understandable that she had enemies. Lowell immediately sought to take control of charities away from local politicians, who were paid for each vagrant they put into poorhouses. Instead, a civil service would run the charities, earning rewards if it lowered the number of vagrants. Next, she lobbied to discourage "tramping" by putting able-bodied vagrants to work and committing criminals and the mentally ill to prisons and asylums.

Among the reform measures Lowell succeeded in passing while working with the State Board of Charities and the Charity Organization Society were: a measure ensuring cooperation between charities, with Lowell serving as the chairman overseeing the policy's administration (Stewart, p. 125); a law that removed the mentally ill from prisons and poorhouses and placed them in state asylums where they could be properly cared for (Stewart, p. 236); and two resolutions that removed women and children from poorhouses and placed them in either reformatories or with responsible family members (Stewart, p. 244-45).

Women's reformatories. Next, Lowell focused on the resolutions concerning women and children. In her tours of state facilities, she had found that women and children lived in the same poorhouses and reformatories as men. Also, like the men, they were not in any way being rehabilitated or given any training or education that might turn them into self-sufficient individuals. She reported to the board in 1877, "one of the most important and most dangerous causes of the increase in crime, pauperism and insanity is unrestrained liberty allowed to vagrant and degraded women" (Stewart, p. 92).

Lowell proposed a reformatory for women, managed under the same principles as those of the State Reformatory at Elmira. Rather than simply jailing the women, however, the reformatory would rehabilitate and re-educate women so they could support themselves and gain self-respect. She argued: "In neither jail, poorhouse nor penitentiary, will they find anything to help them turn back; on the contrary, all the surroundings will force them lower" (Stewart, p. 98). Further, she insisted:

> The unhappy beings we are speaking of need, first of all, to be taught to be women; they must be induced to love that which is good and pure, and wish to resemble it ... they must be cured,

both body **and** soul, before they can be safely trusted to face the world again. (Stewart, pp. 99-100)

By 1881 Lowell succeeded in gaining support for her women's reformatories and, in 1887, the first Women's House of Refuge opened in Hudson, New York.

The concept of saving the body and soul was a radical one in the late nineteenth century. Before Lowell's ideas gained popularity, vagrants and criminals were simply locked up without ascertaining the root of the problem. This led the inmates, once released, to either commit their crimes again or continue to live as vagrants because they still did not have the skills or self-confidence to support themselves. Lowell proposed not only to discover the causes of criminal behavior and vagrancy but to use that information in order to rehabilitate those under public care.

> ### Motto of the Charity Organization Society
>
> "Charity organization is not a work to which any man should put his hand unless he is prepared to give it some measure of devotion." (Stewart, p. 142)

Public charity over private. In addition to pushing for a new type of reform system, Lowell also worked to consolidate the seventy-one charities in New York State and turn them all public. In this way, all charities could be operated under one umbrella and monitored for corruption and duplication of services. Lowell proposed that "the chronically homeless and unemployed ... be dealt with almost entirely by a system of public relief ... to provide home and work and education and religious teaching for them" (Stewart, p. 178). She further insisted that the three things necessary for true rehabilitation were knowledge, adequate relief for the body, and moral oversight for the soul. She maintained: "In New York City it seems to me that we have the means of supplying all three, if only we would use them" (Stewart, p. 180).

Rehabilitation, not relief. Lowell's views on the subject of public charity were complex. Simply put, she felt that helping others to help themselves should be the goal of philanthropy. She did not believe in outright charity because:

> Relief is an evil always. Even when it is necessary, I believe it is still an evil ... because energy, independence, industry, and self-reliance are undermined by it.

1. SCENE IN A "SWEATER'S" FACTORY. 2. THE END. 3. SCENE AT THE GRAND STREET FERRY.
THE FEMALE SLAVES OF NEW YORK.—"SWEATERS" AND THEIR VICTIMS.
FROM SKETCHES BY A STAFF ARTIST.—SEE PAGE 191.

▲ An 1888 newspaper photostory on poor working and living conditions
in New York

But do not misunderstand me. I am talking of relief. We must help people ... but we often do not know how to help, and there are many ways in which we can hurt people even when we mean to help them. (Stewart, pp. 212-13)

Lowell believed that the best service that could be done for people was to give them the tools and training to make a decent living. This was best not only for the recipient but for the whole of the community, which would no longer have to pay for public assistance.

Aftermath

To that end, Lowell's work evolved from helping the homeless to fighting for the working poor, of which there were many. She lobbied for fair wages—what she called a "living wage" as opposed to a "dying wage"—and formed a women's Consumers League in 1886 that supported fair employers and boycotted the products of unfair employers.

Lowell also used her power and authority to change school curriculums to include industrial training and outdoor activity, both of which, she felt, would help raise strong and capable adults and reduce the amount of people needing public assistance. In 1884 Lowell wrote a widely read book, *Public Relief and Private Charity,* which made her even more well known and recognized as the leading expert on philanthropy of her day.

Lowell remained close to her family her entire life. After Lowell's father died, her mother moved into an apartment next door to Lowell and Carlotta. The three generations of Shaw women worked and lived together until Lowell's mother died in 1902.

Lowell continued to live and work with her daughter in New York City, championing the causes of social rehabilitation, government accountability, and workers' rights until her death by cancer on October 12, 1905, just two months shy of her sixty-second birthday.

Thousands mourned her death, and at least five poems were written in her honor, hailing her as the "Saint of New York." Lowell had not only had a huge impact on New York, but her views helped change the welfare system in the United States from that of blind philanthropy to the "preventive social work of the Progressive era" (James, p. 439). Poet John Finley wrote this verse in tribute to Lowell:

> There's an old Icelandic rune,
> Chanted to a mournful tune,
> Of the service-tree, that grows,
> O'er the sepulchres of those,
> Who for others' sins have died,—
> Others' hatred, greed, or pride,—
> Living monuments that stand,
> Planted of no human hand
>
> So from her fresh-flowered grave,—
> Hers who all her being gave
> Others lives to beautify,
> Other ways to purify,—
> There shall spring a spirit-tree,
> In her loving memory,
> Till its top shall reach the skies
> Telling of her sacrifice.
> (Finley in Stewart, pp. 541-542; from *Century Magazine,* May 1906)

For More Information

Ginzberg, Lori. *Women and the Work of Benevolence.* New Haven, Conn.: Yale University Press, 1990.

James, Edward T., ed. *Notable American Women.* Cambridge, Mass.: Belknap Press, 1971.

Stewart, William Rhinelander. *The Philanthropic Work of Josephine Shaw Lowell.* New York: Macmillan, 1911.

Waugh, Joan. *Unsentimental Reformer.* Los Angeles: University of California Press, 1992.

Frances Willard

1839-1898

Personal Background

Frances Elizabeth Caroline Willard was born on September 28, 1839, in Churchville, New York, to Mary Hill and Josiah Willard. She joined an older brother, Oliver, and was soon followed by a younger sister, Mary.

Fitting of her later international fame, Frances was named for the English novelist Frances Burney and the American poet Frances Osgood. However, young Frances often went by the nickname "Frank," which was quite appropriate for her tomboy nature.

When Frances was two years old, the family moved to Oberlin, Ohio. There, her parents attended Oberlin College, one of the only coeducational universities in the country. But within five years the Willards were forced to abandon their studies and move the family west, to the country, in order to improve Josiah's health. He was showing signs of tuberculosis, the disease that later killed him.

Wisconsin frontier. From age seven to eighteen, Frances lived on a farm outside of Janesville, Wisconsin. Their "Forest Home," as they called it, was heaven for Frances but torture for her mother. Forced to give up her educational pursuits and live in a remote wilderness, Mary turned her attention to her children, especially Frances. She encouraged the three to grow up as independent

▲ **Frances Willard**

Event: Social reform.
Role: As the most influential female speaker of her day, Frances Willard rallied support for the temperance movement, women's suffrage, public kindergarten, and a host of social reforms that were eventually adopted by American society. During her twenty-year reign as worldwide president of the Women's Christian Temperance Union, Willard became internationally famous, and her yearly presidential address drew nearly as much notoriety as state-of-the-union speeches by contemporary U.S. presidents.

and forceful individuals. As Mary put it, "I had many ambitions but I disappeared from the world that I might reappear at some future day in my children" (Leeman, p. 5).

To further that end, Mary taught her children at home for most of their childhood and encouraged each of them to pursue individual interests. Throughout her childhood, Frances was allowed to do what intrigued her, which was usually whatever Oliver was doing. Unlike Mary, who did the housecleaning and thoroughly enjoyed sewing and cooking, Frances preferred outdoor farm chores and reveled in playing with toy guns and climbing trees with her brother.

Father serves as legislator. Shortly after the move to Janesville, Josiah was elected to the Wisconsin State Legislature. As a legislator, he represented the Free-Soil party, organized to fight the expansion of slavery, and worked for several social causes, including temperance and obtaining state funding for the blind. Though he advocated that "women were to find their sphere in the home," Josiah's dedication to social service and his gift for public speaking soon became evident in Frances; his role as a public leader greatly influenced her development (Bordin, p. 20).

Days of dreams. From an early age, Frances loved to read and write, was very curious, and possessed great ambition. Her mother recalled that in addition to "believing in herself" as a young girl, Frances was often "in an ecstasy of aspiration" (Bordin, p. 20). She would commonly sit in her room, plotting and planning future events, and was also known to organize clubs with her siblings and friends, taking full control over writing the by-laws, and creating constitutions and elective offices. These skills later proved very valuable when she ran for president of the Women's Christian Temperance Organization.

Education and writing. Though Frances received the bulk of her education at home from her mother, she was very well read and had a broad range of knowledge. By age sixteen, she had published poetry in local newspapers and was producing her own small magazine, *The Tyro*. When she was seventeen, she and her sister were sent to public school. First attending the Normal Institute, a teacher training institution, in Milwaukee, founded by Catherine Beecher,

Frances went on to Northwestern Female College in Evanston, Illinois, where she earned a "Laureate of Science" degree in 1860. Frances was named valedictorian of her class but could not read her commencement speech because of a battle with typhoid that kept her in bed all summer. In her speech, Frances had written that "advancement is directly proportional to effort" and had urged her fellow students to "endeavor" to achieve (Bordin, p. 31). She heeded the advice herself. In her journal that summer, Frances wrote, "I am going to earn my own living, fight my own battles, and be a felt force in the world" (Bordin, p. 31). And that is just what she set out to do at age twenty.

Teacher. Tackling the first of her goals, Willard got a job as a schoolteacher in the fall of 1860 and taught in small local schools for the next three years.

In 1861, while teaching in Cook County, Illinois, she became engaged to a friend of her brother's, Reverend Charles Fowler. An educator and Methodist minister, Fowler courted Willard for nine months before she abruptly broke the engagement. Apparently she did not love the man and wrote in her journal, "For a woman to marry a man whom she does not love, is to make one man as good in her sight as another; hence it is prostitution" (Leeman, p. 8).

For the times she lived in, Willard had strong and unconventional views toward marriage, and she refused to compromise her beliefs. Though she and Fowler remained friends for some time, relations finally became strained when the two were forced to work together at Northwestern University years after the broken engagement. Willard entertained the idea of marriage only one other time but never married.

Mary's death. In June 1862, while Willard was away teaching, her only living sister died of tuberculosis. A beautiful, quiet, and extremely feminine young woman, Mary was only nineteen when she died. Her early death devastated the Willard family and prompted Willard to write a book, a memorial to her sister called *Nineteen Beautiful Years,* published in 1863. Though Mary's death crushed Willard, it inspired her to write and gain confidence in her skills. This launched her writing career and, at the same time, made her a public figure.

Reform work begins. By 1866, at age twenty-seven, Willard began working for her first social cause. While still employed as a teacher, she became corresponding secretary for a Methodist church organization that was raising money to build a school house. As she notes, this was her "first introduction to a really public career," and she learned a great deal about organization and fundraising from it (Bordin, p. 43). But more importantly, through this experience Willard made herself known to politicians and reformers. These important contacts would later prove invaluable in aiding her reform efforts.

Travel abroad. From 1868 to 1870, Willard traveled to Europe and the Middle East with friend and fellow teacher, Kate Jackson. Although Willard wrote newspaper articles to help finance the journey, Jackson, who came from a wealthy family, paid most of the expenses.

During her travels, Willard's vague goal of becoming a "felt force in the world" gained a clear direction. As she witnessed the unequal treatment of women in most countries she visited, and the abuse suffered by women at the hands of alcoholic husbands, she began to believe that limiting the sale of alcohol would improve the quality of women's lives. She also saw the clear need for leadership on this front, and by journey's end she decided to "give my little help to it in all possible ways" (Bordin, p. 52).

College president. Firmly believing that woman was placed on earth to do what she can and should be "unfettered by any law or custom so long as our freedom touches on the just rights of no other human soul," Willard returned to the United States ready to dedicate her life to the "woman question" (Bordin, p. 52). She decided that she could best influence women through teaching, so she took a position at her alma mater, Northwestern Female College, outside of Chicago. On February 14, 1871, Willard was chosen to head the college, making her the first woman in U.S. history to serve as a college president.

In her role as president, Frances flourished. She worked doggedly and performed a wide range duties from fundraising to curriculum planning to morality teaching. She felt like an "elder sister of [the] girls" she taught and saw to it that the education her students received was equal to that of the men at adjacent Northwestern University (Bordin, p. 57). Willard instituted a variety of reforms during her two years as college president, including replacing archaic rules of conduct with an honor system in which the women were trusted to act according to "their own individual sense of responsibility" (Bordin, p. 58). One of many innovative ideas Willard promoted, the honor system proved a success and was later adopted by Northwestern University.

But just as Willard thought she had found her niche in life, Northwestern underwent reorganization and incorporated the female college into the university in 1873. She was demoted from president to dean of the women's college, and her ex-fiancé, Charles Fowler, was made university president. Frustrated in her new role—especially at having to answer to Fowler—Willard remained at Northwestern just one more year and tendered her resignation in June 1874.

Participation:
The Temperance Movement

Temperance. Watching the doors close on her university career, Willard decided to take her teaching abilities and reform ideas to the streets. In 1874 temperance had become "the women's issue," and Willard naturally gravitated toward the cause. She joined the Women's Christian Temperance Union (WCTU) and was elected president of the Chicago chapter. However, temperance work did not pay well—if at all—and so Willard was forced to lecture and write in order to support herself and her mother, who now lived with Willard in Evanston, having been widowed in 1868.

Relationship With Elizabeth Cady Stanton

Even though Frances Willard was often in the company of and worked for many of the same causes as Elizabeth Cady Stanton, the two were not friends. It seems that before Stanton had met Willard, she wrote an editorial attacking Willard's honor system policy. Willard was used to attacks from conservative newspapers or angry men but considered Stanton's editorial the "unkindest cut of all" (Bordin, p. 102). The two later met and worked together but Willard did not forgive Stanton for her attack, and the two never became friends.

As the local WCTU president, Willard began lecturing to audiences throughout Illinois, calling for "streams of healing even to those far-off shores" of Europe (Bordin, p. 69). But Willard deviated from speaking strictly on the temperance issue. She not only advocated worldwide prohibition in her lectures but asserted the need for higher education of women, education and shelter for homeless skid row alcoholics, and free public kindergarten for all children. She began calling for what she termed the "home protection ballot," which advocated women's right to vote on laws concerning the sale of alcohol. She also spoke for the need for all Christians, regardless of individual church affiliation, to work together as one unified body.

Willard loved lecturing, or "preaching" as she called it. By 1875 she was working diligently at it—delivering more than forty speeches that summer alone—and was fast developing into one of the great speakers of her day. As one male listener said to Willard: "I do not care for women speakers generally [but] you are one of my magnificent exceptions" (Bordin, p. 86). The Des Moines *Daily Leader* described Willard as possessing "a fluent tongue and vivid imagination.... She is an orator of practical knowledge, and burrows into the heart of her hearers even to the inmost recess" (Leeman, p. 17).

WCTU president. By 1880, after working her way up the local ranks, Willard, now forty, was elected as national WCTU president. In this role, she became the most famous woman in the United States. Under her presidency, the WCTU grew from 27,000 members to 200,000, and its influence widened along with its platform. Incorporating, as always, a whole range of social reforms along with the temperance cause, Willard considered herself a "do everything" reformer and strongly advocated action on all fronts. She saw most social issues as deeply intertwined. For example, in one of her most famous speeches, Willard asserted that the only way to defeat "King Alcohol" was by allowing women to vote against its sale. "Give her, at least, a fair chance to offset by her ballot the machinations which imperil her son," Willard said, insisting that "New England must lead" the way in giving women the right to vote (Leeman, p. 134).

In addition to her lectures and yearly presidential address,

Women's Congress

In one of her early but most important efforts, Willard helped found the Women's Congress in 1873. A group of women writers and journalists, the Congress included such notable members as Sarah Grimke, Lucy Stone, and Elizabeth Cady Stanton. At their first annual meeting on October 15, 1873, the women began an association within the Congress called the Association for the Advancement of Women, much like the NAACP today, which worked to advance women's rights.

which, as one contemporary said, was as popular as the U.S. president's annual state-of-the-union address, Willard wrote columns and books, including the first truly feminist guidebook for women, entitled *How to Win: A Book for Girls.* As part of her "do everything" platform, she advocated dress reform for women; she backed the growing labor movement in the United States; she called for women to be allowed to serve as ordained ministers; and she rallied for WCTU support in the South, where there were few women's organizations.

Aftermath

By 1890, after ten years as WCTU president, Willard had succeeded in getting many regulations passed concerning the sale of alcohol, including the setting of a minimum drinking age. She also pioneered many new techniques, such as the hiring of paid lobbyists and the use of petitions, that resulted in vast political and social change and are standard operating procedure in politics today.

In 1891 Willard was elected worldwide WCTU president. The following year, her mother died, leaving Willard free to travel away from Evanston. She began to split her time between the United States and England, where she had many friends and colleagues. Years of traveling back and forth across the Atlantic took its toll, however. On February 17, 1898, while in New York City awaiting a ship to England, Willard died.

Though she did not live to see prohibition enacted in the United States, she was the driving force behind its later inception. She profoundly influenced social reform on all fronts and dedicated her life to achieving temperance laws, women's rights, equal and accessible public education, the establishment of labor unions, and a host of other social reforms. Through her exhaustive efforts, Willard not only created change in American society but showed succeeding generations how to take action and "do everything."

For More Information

Bordin, Ruth. *Frances Willard: A Biography.* Chapel Hill: University of North Carolina Press, 1986.

Leeman, Richard W. *Do Everything Reform.* New York: Greenwood Press, 1992.

Willard, Frances E. *Glimpses of Fifty Years.* Chicago: H. J. Smith and Co., 1889.

Spanish-American War

1867-1870
Americans entertain the ideas of annexing Cuba and Santo Domingo.

1895-1896
Cubans resume rebellion against Spanish; send agents to New York to raise money and support for their cause.

1898
May: Commodore George Dewey captures Manila Harbor in the Philippines.

1898
April: President **William McKinley** asks Congress to send troops to Cuba. Spain declares war.

1898
February: **William Randolph Hearst** publishes Spanish minister's note, which insults the U.S. president. The *Maine* is mysteriously sunk in Havana Harbor.

1896
Spanish military governor, Valeriano "Butcher" Weyler, arrives to govern Cuba. Cuban peasants are herded into camps.

1898
July: **Theodore Roosevelt** helps Americans win battle of San Juan Hill. The United States annexes Hawaii.

1898
August: American troops occupy the Philippines. First copy of a peace treaty is signed.

1898
December: Final peace treaty is signed. United States gets Guam and Puerto Rico and buys Philippines.

1899
Filipino-American War begins. Roosevelt writes *The Rough Riders.*

1945
Philippines gains full independence.

1903
United States signs treaty with Panama for construction of a canal through the Isthmus of Panama.

1902
Filipino-American War ends with surrender of guerrillas.

1901
McKinley is assassinated. Roosevelt becomes president.

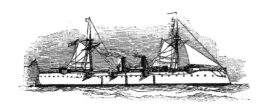

SPANISH-AMERICAN WAR

In 1867 Secretary of State William Seward believed the United States was fated to become the richest country in the Pacific Ocean. With this in mind, he purchased Alaska from Russia for $7.2 million. He also pushed for the United States to annex Cuba and other islands of the West Indies.

Opponents said that such plans were against the American ideals of a people's right to self-government and that native Caribbeans, who were viewed as inferior, would not blend well with the American population.

Ideas of annexing Cuba or nearby Santo Domingo were dropped, but business interest in the Caribbean grew. Americans raised sugar on the islands there and eagerly eyed Latin America and Asia as markets for American goods. Seward and others wanted to build a canal across Panama to promote trade to Asia and the Pacific Islands. The rapid growth in U.S. industry after the Civil War had led to overproduction and a need for foreign buyers for the excess product. There was also a missionary impulse to spread Christian beliefs and America's democratic ideals to nearby countries.

Cubans had been in a state of periodic rebellion against the Spanish for almost twenty-five years before 1898, when U.S. involvement helped bring the conflict to a climax. To

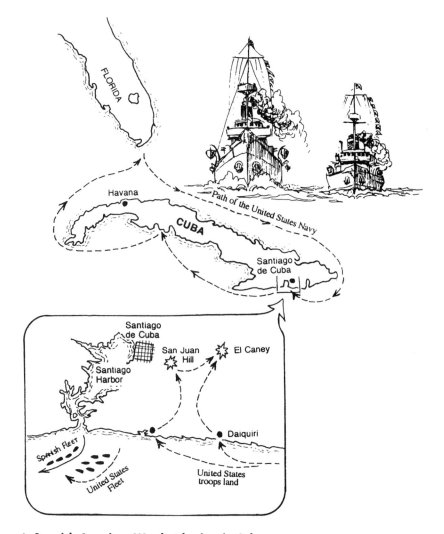

▲ **Spanish-American War battle sites in Cuba**

raise money and sympathy for their cause, the Cubans sent agents to New York City who spread horror stories about the brutal treatment of Cubans at the hands of the Spanish.

Popular pressure for U.S. involvement rose. Businessmen interested in the region were joined by those in sympathy with the Cuban colony's struggle against Spain. Newspaper publishers Joseph Pulitzer and **William Randolph Hearst,** eager for sensational news to boost the circulation of their papers, recorded the Cuban predicament vividly. Their stories stirred sympathy for the rebels, and the general population began to identify with their dogged struggle for freedom. Earlier in the 1890s, President Grover Cleveland had kept the United States out of the conflict, but public sentiment for participation was on the rise. President **William McKinley** began to ask his officials how they would react to American entry in a Cuban war.

Meanwhile, in 1896 Spain sent a brutal Spanish military governor to Cuba. Valeriano "Butcher" Weyler attempted to put down the rebels by imprisoning peasants who supplied them with food. Fenced into pens without decent meals or sanitation, the peasants died by the thousands, adding more fuel to the sensational news accounts of Hearst and his rival Pulitzer. Hearst fanned the flames himself when he secured and published a note written by the Spanish minister in Washington describing McKinley as a weakling. Then came the explosion of the *Maine,* a U.S. battleship stationed in Havana to protect American citizens there. Rumors blamed the Spanish for the explosion, which blew up the ship, killing 260 men. Hearst papers exhorted American readers to remember the *Maine,* and the public cried out for action. After repeated attempts to avoid war, McKinley sent a message to Congress asking for authority to use armed forces in Cuba. Congress authorized the troops and recognized Cuba as independent, an action that led to war with Spain.

> **Some Causes of the
> Spanish-American War**
>
> Sinking of the *Maine*
> Note insulting President McKinley
> Sympathy for Cuban rebels
> Missionary zeal to spread democracy
> Business interests in the Caribbean

McKinley's undersecretary of the navy, **Theodore Roosevelt,** had prepared for this moment by equipping the navy and sending letters to key commanders about what would be expected of them in case of war. McKinley would follow Roosevelt's plans to a great extent in the days to follow.

The U.S. Navy, supported by the army, brought defeat on the enemy in short order. Commodore George Dewey led the U.S. squadron in the Pacific Ocean, crushing Spain's fleet in the Philippines at the Battle of Manila Bay. Meanwhile, the squadron in the Atlantic, under Admiral William Sampson, crushed the Spanish fleet at Santiago, Cuba. They requested ground support for their invasion. Led by General William Shafter, 18,000 troops accompanied by a swarm of news writers landed near Santiago. Some 5,000 Cuban revolutionaries joined them. Amidst great confusion, the armies defeated the Spanish at the battles of San Juan Hill and El Caney. Roosevelt led a regiment of volunteers, the Rough Riders, into battle. His men seized a key hill as black troops protected them from the side, a victory followed by success in the Battle of Santiago, which in effect ended the war. Altogether only 385 Americans were killed by Spanish bullets in the war, but more than 5,000 died due to yellow fever and other tropical diseases. The fighting had lasted about four months. In its final version, the peace treaty recognized Cuban independence, gave Puerto Rico and Guam to the United States, and sold the United States control of the Philippines for $20 million.

Americans Who Protested U.S. Control of the Philippines
Andrew Carnegie
Grover Cleveland
Samuel Gompers
George F. Hoar
Carl Schurz
Mark Twain

There was controversy in the United States over the Philippines. America had supposedly entered the war to help spread democracy. Opponents raised a storm of protest against the Philippine purchase, arguing that it betrayed the Constitution and the Declaration of Independence. To be true to her founding principles, they said, America could not govern a foreign people against their will simply because she thought it would be to their benefit. But the majority of Americans favored U.S. control of the Philippines.

The Filipinos had earlier begun to fight the Spanish for independence. Led by General Emilio Aguinaldo, they now began a four-year guerrilla war against the Americans. Ending with Aguinaldo's defeat in 1901, the Filipino-American War killed 4,300 U.S. soldiers and 18,000 Filipinos. The few protesters in America lamented that U.S. soldiers were killing a people they had supposedly set out to benefit. With the lands gained in the Spanish-American War, the United States

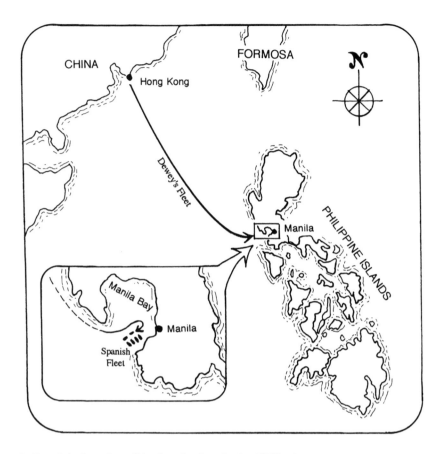

▲ Spanish-American War battle sites in the Philippines

had become a world power, but some of her citizens mourned the change. America, they felt, had betrayed her founding promise.

William McKinley

1843-1901

Personal Background

William McKinley, the son of an iron furnace operator, was born January 29, 1843, in Niles, Ohio. He was educated at the Union Seminary in Poland, Ohio, and in 1860 entered Allegheny College in Meadville, Pennsylvania. Unable to continue his education because of illness and financial problems, he found work as a schoolteacher and later as a postal clerk.

Military service. In 1861 the Civil War erupted, and McKinley enlisted in a unit of Ohio volunteers. He earned a promotion to sergeant due to his action at Fayetteville, then to lieutenant for his role in the Battle of Antietam in 1862. McKinley saw action throughout the war and earned other promotions for his deeds of heroism. By war's end, he had earned the rank of brevet (honorary) major. However, the death, destruction, and brutality of war disgusted him so that he left the military.

Political career. When the war ended, McKinley found work as a law clerk for an Ohio judge and began to study law. In 1867, after a year in law school, he was admitted to the bar and began to practice law in Canton, Ohio. He soon became a prominent trial lawyer. McKinley at the same time began to take an interest in politics, speaking for Republican candidates and causes. As a reward for his campaign services, the Republicans nominated him as their

▲ **William McKinley**

Event: The Spanish-American War.
Role: As president of the United States, William McKinley at first tried to persuade Spain to settle the struggle for Cuban independence peacefully. Prodded by sensational news stories from such publishers as William Randolph Hearst and Joseph Pulitzer, the American people sympathized with the Cuban rebels and demanded United States action. The voices of the people and of Congress pushed McKinley into a war that neither he nor the Spanish leaders wanted.

candidate for prosecuting attorney for Stark County, Ohio, in 1869. Although the county was heavily Democratic, he won.

Marriage. At five feet six inches tall, McKinley was a short man. He wore a serious expression on his face yet was a kindly man with a fine sense of humor. He had conservative habits and refused to drink, dance, gamble or smoke in his early years, though later he became addicted to tobacco.

While serving as prosecuting attorney, McKinley fell in love with Ida Saxon, whom he married in 1871. Ida's father was so impressed with his hard-working son-in-law that he gave the couple a fine house as a wedding present. Ida bore two daughters, one of whom died in infancy in 1873. That same year, Ida lost her grandfather and her mother. These tragic blows unnerved her, and she was never well again. The future First Lady would develop epilepsy and become a near invalid during McKinley's presidency. Yet he would remain devoted to her and to their marriage until his assassination in 1901.

Ups and downs in politics. Defeated for reelection in 1871, McKinley returned to his private law practice but maintained an interest in politics. Five years later, in 1876, he was elected to Congress. After serving one term, he again lost a bid for re-election, only to regain his seat in Congress in 1884. Four years later, McKinley served as a delegate to the Republican National Convention, where he received eight votes for the party's presidential nomination.

In 1890 he again lost his seat in Congress. Ohio Republican leaders, however, persuaded him to run for governor. He was narrowly elected in 1891, and during his two terms as governor, McKinley rose to national prominence. He spoke for the party in neighboring states and began developing presidential ambitions. "McKinley for President" clubs began to form around the country.

Over the years, McKinley developed a friendship with Mark Hanna, an Ohio industrialist and the political boss of Cleveland. Hanna hoped to be a "king maker" and become the power behind the presidency. He provided McKinley with advice on financial and political matters and even traveled to Georgia to gain Southern Republican support for a McKinley candidacy. In 1896, with Hanna as his campaign manager, McKinley ran for the presidency as a candidate of "the people" opposed to the party bosses. At the Republican National Convention in June, he won the nomination on the first ballot.

The next month, the Democratic party nominated William Jennings Bryan of Nebraska as its candidate. Bryan proposed the free coinage of silver to inflate the value of currency. He also called for government regulation of big business. His positions made him popular with farmers and voters in the silver-producing states of the Far West. With the Democrats in solid control in the South and in the majority in the West, Bryan, who also received the Populist party's nomination, seemed a favorite to win the presidency.

Front porch campaign. McKinley began to campaign in earnest. While Hanna raised funds and supervised the campaign, McKinley addressed crowds from his home in Canton in a "front porch" campaign. Republican supporters distributed millions of pamphlets and newspaper ads and arranged for inexpensive fares to Canton so voters could hear and see McKinley in person.

It soon became clear that the Republicans were gaining strength. Bryan did poorly in the big cities and among the workers and small business people of the Midwest. Meanwhile, farm prices rose and the farmers lost interest in free silver. McKinley easily won the 1896 election for president.

Participation: Spanish-American War

Cuban revolution. At his inauguration, McKinley stated that "we want no wars of conquest" and that "peace is preferable to war in almost every contingency" (Blow, p. 79). Even as he spoke, however, a war that eventually would involve the United States was raging in the Spanish colony of Cuba. Spain's harsh and corrupt rule of the colony had sparked a revolution in 1895. Most Cubans resented Spanish rule and desired independence, while most Spaniards considered Cuba to be part of Spain. The war between Spanish overlords and Cubans soon reached a stalemate. While Spaniards held the developed areas of western Cuba and all of the large cities, the rebels controlled much of the countryside, including the mountainous area of the east. Hoping to make Cuba worthless to Spain, the rebels attempted to destroy the farms of the country. Plantations were burned and farm workers terrorized. In the process, American property in Cuba was being destroyed by both sides. Some Cuban-born Americans, in Cuba at the time, were jailed and killed.

Cubans in the United States formed an organization known as the Junta to raise money for the rebels and publicize their cause. They were aided by newspapers such as the *New York Journal* (see **William Randolph Hearst**) and the *New York World,* which found in the Cuban plight a rich source for sensational stories to build up newspaper sales. Supporters in the United States shipped arms to Cuban rebels, though this was in violation of American neutrality laws.

Weyler's brutality. To crush the rebellion, Spain in 1896 sent to Cuba a ruthless professional soldier, General Valeriano Weyler y Nicolau. Weyler began a policy of "reconcentration," forcing Cuban peasants to move from the countryside to fortified towns and camps to prevent their supporting rebel fighters. These centers lacked food, housing, and medical supplies for the large numbers of "reconcentrados." By the end of the Spanish-American War, about 200,000 peasants would die in the camps.

When news of the Cuban camps reached America, Weyler was condemned as a "butcher." He would later defend his policy with the retort, "How do they want me to wage war? With bishop's pastorals and presents of sweets and honey?" (Carr, p. 385). However cruel his measures, the rebels continued to fight. Meanwhile, Americans were shocked by the sensationalized news reports of the plight of the rebels and began to sympathize with their cause. This feeling was reflected in Congress. In May 1897 the Senate passed a resolution recognizing the rights of the Cuban rebels. Public and congressional pressure soon forced presidential action—action that McKinley originally opposed. In May 1897 he requested Congress to provide $50,000 in aid for American citizens in Cuba, and the request was quickly approved.

Growing American concern. In the same month, McKinley sent William J. Calhoun on a fact-finding mission to Cuba. When he returned four months later, Calhoun reported widespread destruction and starvation as well as considerable support for the revolution among Cuban people. He told the president he doubted that Spain could put down the rebellion.

McKinley was now determined to restore peace in Cuba. He sent a message to the Spanish ambassador denouncing Spain's treatment of the Cubans. Then he appointed Stewart L. Woodford as a minister to Spain. Arriving in Madrid in September 1897, Woodford repeated the president's demand that Spain end its "cruel, useless, and horrid warfare" in Cuba and negotiate peace (Offner, pp. 61-62).

For a short time, tensions eased. The Spanish premier had been assassinated in July and was replaced by Praxedes Mateo Sagasta. Sagasta recalled Weyler to Spain and announced a series of reforms in Cuba, including the release of all Americans held by the Spanish and a plan to set up self-government in Cuba. McKinley was only cautiously optimistic about these plans for reform. In December, he called on Spain to continue the reform process and hinted that American patience had its limits. He, however, also called on Congress not to take any action that would endanger the reform process. By the end of the year, this policy of patient pressure on Spain seemed to be paying off. However, a series of dramatic events was about to cause McKinley's Cuban policy to fall apart.

The approach of war. Sagasta's reforms did not appear to satisfy anyone. The rebels rejected self-government under Spain and continued to demand independence. Meanwhile, the Spanish and some Cuban allies resented the reforms and the recall of Weyler.

On January 12, 1898, a mob led by Spanish officers rioted in Havana, attacking newspaper offices. For months, Fitzhugh Lee, a former Confederate general serving as the American counsel in Cuba, had urged the government to send a warship to Havana. On January 24, McKinley, concerned for the safety of American lives and property, ordered the battleship *Maine,* which was off the coast of Florida, to sail to Havana. Although Spanish officials protested the presence of the *Maine* in the Havana harbor, it was officially taken as a "friendly" visit, and arrangements were quickly made for a Spanish warship to visit New York. Meanwhile, Spain was taking a harder line in Cuba. Some rebels were being won over, and the Spanish were objecting to America's criticism of Spain's military policies. Clearly, Spain intended to continue its war with the Cuban rebels.

A few days into February 1898, Spanish-American relations were further strained when William Randolph Hearst's *New York*

Journal published a private letter from Spain's minister to the United States, Enrique Dupuy de Lome, to a Spanish official in Cuba. Cuban rebels had intercepted the letter and sent it to the *Journal*. In it, Dupuy had called the president "weak" and a "would-be politician" (Offner, p. 115). Publication of the letter further angered the American public and strained relations between the two governments. Spain, however, offered an apology, which McKinley accepted.

Just as the de Lome affair began to quiet down, Spanish-American relations received an even greater jolt. During the evening of February 15, the *Maine* exploded and sank in Havana harbor, taking the lives of 260 American officers and men. The public, much of the press, and Congress reacted with outrage to the disaster. They blamed it on the Spanish. McKinley, however, remained calm. He was determined to find the cause of the explosion and then take appropriate action.

With sensational newspaper lines such as "Remember the *Maine*/To Hell with Spain" stirring up Americans and a naval court of inquiry investigating the disaster, McKinley continued his efforts to settle the Cuba issue. He considered the possibility of purchasing Cuba from Spain and granting it self-government under American protection, but neither the Spanish nor the Cuban rebels were interested. At the same time, he stepped up preparations for a possible war. In early March, when he learned that Spain was attempting to buy two Brazilian warships, McKinley asked Congress for an additional $50 million for national defense. Within two days, Congress unanimously approved the request. The United States promptly bought the Brazilian ships. In addition, the president ordered the battleship *Oregon* to sail from California to the Atlantic Ocean.

In late March, the naval court of inquiry released its report on the *Maine*. The court concluded that an explosion from outside the ship had destroyed it. The Spanish had also investigated the sinking and concluded that it had been caused by an explosion *inside* the ship. The American press and Congress paid no attention to the Spanish investigation. (Years later, in 1976, another naval investigation concluded that the *Maine* had, indeed, been destroyed by an internal explosion, probably caused by a spontaneous fire in a coal bunker that ignited ammunition stored nearby.)

McKinley continued to press for peace. Spain was willing to make some concessions, but these were unacceptable. The president threatened to annex Cuba, hoping to force the rebels to accept an armistice proposed by Spain. This, too, was refused. The president delayed his speech on the subject to Congress to allow for the movement of Americans out of Cuba.

Just before he was to give his speech, the Spaniards yielded on several points, making some last-minute concessions. They stopped reconcentrating peasants, agreed to arbitrate (meet to settle) the *Maine* explosion, and declared a suspension of fighting with the rebels. American political leaders urged the president not to ask for time for the cease-fire to work. In their opinion, Spain was offering too little, too late. Their distrust proved correct. Spain was using the concessions to hide its efforts to find allies among European powers. It now appeared that the death and destruction in Cuba would go on indefinitely.

War. McKinley had been left with no choice when he finally made his speech to Congress on April 11. He called on Congress to give the president power to take military action to "secure a full and final termination of hostilities between the government of Spain and the people of Cuba" (O'Toole, p. 169). Congress carried the matter one step further, wording approval of his request in what amounted to a declaration of war. Spain immediately broke relations with the United States and, on April 25, McKinley asked Congress for a formal declaration of war to be effective April 21.

McKinley's undersecretary of the navy, Theodore Roosevelt, had been quietly getting ready for this moment (see **Theodore Roosevelt**). In fact, he wished it had come earlier and criticized McKinley, saying he had no more backbone than a chocolate éclair. Meanwhile, Roosevelt armed and prepared instructions for naval ships. The president ordered the navy to blockade Cuba, and on April 24, the secretary of the navy ordered the American fleet near Asia, which was commanded by Commodore George Dewey, to attack the Spanish fleet at Manila Bay in the Philippines. On May 1, Dewey's ships destroyed the Spanish fleet at Manila without losing a ship or a man.

The army, however, was unprepared for war. Consisting of only 25,000 soldiers, it was short on ammunition and supplies.

McKinley called for 125,000 volunteers; in the end, about 200,000 enlisted. He used the volunteer force to improve the relations between North and South that had been strained by the Civil War. He appointed some ex-Confederate officers to key U.S. Army positions. Fitzhugh Lee was made a major general, and "Fighting Joe" Wheeler led a cavalry regiment.

McKinley's staff set up a War Room in the White House with telegraph connections to army and navy units. Maps and charts filled the walls of the War Room, which never closed as staff members plotted troop and ship movements.

In May, the administration learned that the Spanish fleet had arrived at Santiago de Cuba on the southern coast of the island. McKinley decided to send ground troops to besiege the town while the navy blockaded the harbor. The ground troops finally arrived near Santiago on June 22. By early July, American troops and Cuban rebels had Santiago under siege. On July 4, the American fleet destroyed the Spanish fleet as it attempted to escape. Shortly afterward, Santiago surrendered. Meanwhile, American forces had taken the Pacific Island of Guam and were overrunning Puerto Rico.

Spain was now ready to sue for peace. On July 30, the United States demanded that Spain give up its claims to Cuba, Puerto Rico, and other islands in a peace agreement. The Philippines were another matter. The president's cabinet was divided on what to do with this collection of islands. They considered returning the Philippines to Spain or granting Philippine independence. McKinley decided to annex the Philippines, and the United States finally agreed to pay Spain $20 million for this territory.

World power. On December 10, the United States and Spain signed the Treaty of Paris, formally ending the Spanish-American War. The United States had lost fewer than 400 men in combat, although thousands died from disease. It now possessed Puerto Rico, Guam, and the Philippines. Cuba received its independence, although it would remain under American military occupation until 1902.

While he was directing the war with Spain, McKinley was also lobbying Congress for a resolution that would allow the United States to annex Hawaii. Some congressmen opposed this move.

▲ The U.S. Navy destroys the Spanish fleet off Santiago, Cuba

Speaker of the House of Representatives Thomas B. Reed blocked House action on the resolution for three weeks. McKinley invited congressmen to the White House to discuss with them why he considered Hawaii to be important to the United States. He issued press releases outlining his position and even leaked to the press information suggesting that he might simply use his power as commander in chief of the armed forces to occupy the islands. Reed finally allowed debate on the issue to begin. The resolution passed in July, and Hawaii became a United States territory.

From Cuba to Hawaii, the United States had become a colonial power with global interests. McKinley had taken a direct hand in conducting the war; his office had coordinated the movements of the War and Navy Departments. At first he had entered it to free Cuba from Spain, but during the course of the war, McKinley had adopted another goal—acquiring new U.S. territory. Later he pursued this goal, developing the nation into a world power, a role that would bring problems as well as new responsibilities.

Aftermath

In the Philippines, American troops were soon fighting Filipinos who wanted independence. The Philippine insurrection, which lasted from 1899 to 1902, would cost more lives than the Spanish-American War. In 1901 American troops began fighting the Moros, Moslems living in the southern Philippines. The Moro War, which ended in 1917, would be America's longest war.

After the Spanish-American War, the McKinley government began negotiating a treaty with Great Britain that would allow the United States to build a canal through Central America. The treaty was finally approved after the president's death in 1901. American work on the Panama Canal began in 1904.

The United States also became involved in China. In 1899 McKinley's administration called on Japan and the European colonial powers to respect each other's trade rights in China as well as to recognize China as an independent nation. This was the beginning of what would become known as the Open Door Policy.

Then, in 1900, rebels known as Boxers led a revolt in China and laid siege to foreign diplomatic offices in Peking. McKinley sent 2,500 troops along with naval units to China to join an international force that fought its way into Peking and rescued the diplomats. Following the rebellion, Secretary of State John Hay again called on the great powers to respect China. Lacking sufficient military force in the area, the United States was unable to enforce its Open Door Policy, but until World War II the country would insist that nations respect the trading rights of other countries with China.

In 1900 the Republicans renominated McKinley for a second term. He faced Bryan in a rematch and won more easily than he had in 1896. Hanna again managed his campaign. In September 1901, as

McKinley greeted visitors at a fair in Buffalo, New York, Leon Czolgosz, an anarchist (a person against all forms of government), shot McKinley in the stomach with a pistol he had hidden in a bandaged hand. Aides moved in to capture the assassin while the president ordered, "Don't let them hurt him." His next thoughts were of his wife: "My wife—be careful, [Private Secretary] Cortelyou, how you tell her—oh, be careful!" (Boller, p.190). McKinley's doctors were unable to remove the bullet, and the president soon developed gangrene. His wife was with him when he died September 13, 1901.

Ida McKinley returned to Canton, Ohio, to live with her sister and was continuously depressed after the assassination. She died May 26, 1907.

For More Information

Blow, Michael. *A Ship to Remember: The "Maine" and the Spanish-American War.* New York: William Morrow and Co., 1992.

Boller, Paul F., Jr. *Presidential Wives.* New York: Oxford University Press, 1988.

Carr, Raymond. *Spain 1808-1939.* London: Oxford University Press, 1966.

Offner, John L. *An Unwanted War: The Diplomacy of the United States and Spain Over Cuba, 1895–1898.* Chapel Hill: University of North Carolina, 1963.

O'Toole, G. J. A. *The Spanish War: An American Epic.* New York: W. W. Norton and Co., 1984.

William Randolph Hearst

1863-1951

Personal Background

Parents. William's father, George Hearst, was a rough-and-tumble man who cussed and chewed tobacco constantly. In his younger years, he had worked in mines, where he learned about minerals and mining. With the knowledge he gained and some luck, George staked successful silver claims in Nevada and then went on to own prosperous mines throughout the Southwest and in Mexico. Apparently, despite his rough language and coarse habits, he was charming and exciting. These traits attracted Phoebe Apperson, nearly two decades younger than he was. They married and settled in San Francisco, where their only child, William Randolph Hearst, was born on April 29, 1863. George would go on to become a U.S. senator.

Early life. George's mining ventures required him to spend most of his time away from home. Phoebe, therefore, spent much of her time caring for her son. She was determined that he have the best of everything, including a sound education. Even as a young boy, William loved the theater. He and his mother spent many hours seeing the best shows in San Francisco.

Phoebe was determined that William attend the finest American university, which in her mind was Harvard. She hired a tutor to prepare him. William also attended school, but his schooling was

▲ **William Randolph Hearst**

Event: The battle for Santiago in the Spanish-American War.
Role: William Randolph Hearst, owner of the *New York Journal* and a string of other newspapers, assigned himself to cover the war in Cuba as a war correspondent. Taking with him photographers, authors, and reporters, along with his own printing press, he became so closely involved in the battles he was observing that he is credited with taking more than twenty prisoners of war.

often interrupted by trips across the country or to Europe. Besides, the energetic boy did not do well in classrooms, where he was fond of disturbing the class by arguing with the teacher. Still, at age sixteen, William entered a school that would prepare him for Harvard. In 1879 he was packed off to attend St. Paul's, a private preparatory school in Concord, New Hampshire. The young man hated the formality of St. Paul's and the requirement that he attend church services three times a week. He was soon up to his old ways, arguing with the teachers and playing pranks on his fellow students. During his second year, William was asked to leave St. Paul's. He returned home to his private tutors and to the free and lively way of living he enjoyed in San Francisco.

Harvard. At the age of nineteen, Hearst was admitted to Harvard University. A story circulated that he received a fist-sized gold nugget from his father's mines each month he was there. It was at Harvard that Hearst showed an interest in journalism in all its aspects. He took charge of the school's fading newspaper, the *Lampoon.* Hearst edited the *Lampoon,* wrote many of the articles for it, sold advertising, and solicited subscriptions from the Harvard students. He revived the old journal and made it profitable. His work on the *Lampoon* was his major achievement at Harvard. Meanwhile, he continued playing pranks, one of which resulted in his being banished from the university in 1885, during his junior year.

The *Examiner*. Meanwhile, his father had become interested in politics. He supported the Democratic party candidates and the newspaper that took up their cause, the *San Francisco Examiner.* In the past, he had loaned money to keep the paper afloat and, in 1880, took over the paper because the money could not be repaid. This suited him, for he wanted a vehicle he could control to serve as a strong voice for the Democrats. That the paper did not make money was of no concern to him; he continued to earn millions of dollars through his mines, which included the Anaconda copper mine and a successful silver mine in Silver City, New Mexico.

Journalist. Even before he was thrown out of Harvard, William had asked his father to give him the newspaper. He was sure that his ideas would make it profitable. His father, however, had talked with newsmen, asking how much the owner of such a newspaper could hope to earn in a year. When the best estimates were that even a successful *Examiner* might bring in only $100,000 a year, he refused to give the paper to William. That annual earning was, he thought, not a large enough ambition for his son. But William was committed to journalism. He took a job as a reporter for the *New York World.*

In 1886 George was appointed to complete the term left by the death of U.S. senator John Miller. When George was, to everyone's surprise, elected for a six-year term of his own, he finally relented and presented his son with the ownership of the *Examiner.* By this time, George had lost $250,000 on the paper. He was willing to lose a little more to see if William could really manage the paper.

Publisher. William plunged into his new venture with his usual abundance of energy. He hired the best writers and reporters, among them, Ambrose Bierce. He wanted the *Examiner* to be the first newspaper to report any event and to report the event more sensationally than any other newspaper. His idea was that the newspaper should be exciting to read. Hearst personally took charge of a front-page column. The staff of the *Examiner* searched for sensational news items and wrote the news articles as lively and recklessly as possible. The newspaper was soon accused of practicing "yellow journalism," that is, of exaggerating and playing up violence and scandal stories to increase sales.

At first, the paper continued to lose money. After a year or two, Hearst found himself in such debt that he needed $50,000 quickly to fend off creditors. By then, his father had grown weary of supporting the venture and refused to help. Hearst managed to get the money from his father by deceit. A friend asked George for $100,000 to support Democrats in an election, a cause that the senator did not question. Only half the money reached the Democratic party—the other half went to Hearst. It would, however, still benefit the Democratic party. In return for his share of the money, Hearst agreed to direct the *Examiner* to support Democratic candidates. Afterward, Hearst never had to look for more money for the paper; it soon became the most successful on the West Coast.

Champion of the people. Supporting Democratic candidates was no problem for Hearst, who thought of himself as a champion of the cause of the average people. The Democratic party, he felt, represented the masses and deserved his support. Hearst used the *Examiner* and, later, other papers, to champion Democratic candidates and smear their opponents.

So successful were his methods that the *Examiner* began to prosper, and Hearst thought of starting a similar paper in the East. In 1895 he acquired the *New York Morning Journal* and a year later added the *New York Evening Journal*. Moving to New York, he devoted much of his time to these newspapers. Hearst was writing and editing the *Journal* when difficulties with Spain began in 1898.

The Hearst Newspaper Empire Spreads Across America

San Francisco Examiner
Atlanta Georgian
New York Evening Journal
Atlanta Sunday American
New York Morning Journal
Boston Record
New York American
Albany Times
New York Mirror
Syracuse Journal
Los Angeles Examiner
Baltimore News-Post
Los Angeles Herald Express
Pittsburgh Sun-Telegraph
Chicago Herald and Examiner
Detroit Times
Seattle Post-Intelligencer
Chicago American
Oakland Post-Intelligencer
San Antonio Light

Participation: The Battle for Control of Santiago

Spanish Cuba. For nearly a century, the American lands controlled by Spain had one by one withdrawn from its empire and formed their own governments. Mexico, Puerto Rico, and some South American states had separated from Spain, often under the protection of the United States. Perhaps partly to appease Spain, Cuba had been preserved as a Spanish territory. and that relationship was respected by the United States. Still, the idea of a European base so near to the United States was unsettling, and American officials began to think about ways to separate Cuba from Spain.

In 1868 the Cuban people started a revolution to do just that. The United States took little part in the affair except to offer to help peacefully settle the issues. However, by 1875, the American government was trying to get an idea of the world's reaction to U.S. military involvement in Cuban affairs. Conditions grew increasingly tense until, in 1895, Cubans again rebelled. Under presidents Grover Cleveland and

William McKinley, the United States tried once more to act as a peaceful go-between. The situation grew so impossible that by 1897 the young undersecretary of the navy, Theodore Roosevelt, began to prepare for war with Spain. Meanwhile, Hearst started to campaign for war through his newspapers, printing horror stories told by Cuban mothers and even engineering a daring rescue of a Cuban girl held in prison by the Spanish.

Evangelina Cosio y Cisneros, a Cuban beauty, was imprisoned for resisting the advances of Spanish officers. When Hearst heard about her, he immediately saw the potential to stir readers and sentiment for American involvement in the war. Though she was sentenced to life in prison, he was determined to help free her. There was to be a jailbreak, and Hearst had petitions started in America to champion her cause. He in time would enlist the aid of the nurse Clara Barton, by then in her seventies, who also served in the war; McKinley's mother; and even the queen of Spain.

At the same time, a war for newspaper sales was being waged in New York between the *Journal* and Joseph Pulitzer's *New York World.* Now the *World* fought back, investigating and discovering that Cisneros was well treated in prison and an admitted rebel. It tried to correct the "false and stupid impression" of her plight "which has been created by some newspapers" (Blow, p. 65). But little attention was given to its sober report. Readers instead anxiously followed the campaign to free Cisneros in the *Journal.* A Hearst reporter daringly rescued her from prison, and she arrived in New York to a heroine's welcome.

War with Spain. The final stimulus to war came in 1898 when a United States vessel, the U.S.S. *Maine,* anchored in Havana Harbor, was sunk in a mysterious explosion. Investigators thought the explosion came from outside the battleship, perhaps from a mine or bomb set off by the Spanish. Of the 350 men on board, 260 were killed. With the cry "Remember the *Maine*" resounding through American newspapers, especially the Hearst papers, McKinley called for the Spanish to leave Cuba. Spain responded by declaring war on the United States. All the while, Hearst papers created sensational articles—with sensational headlines—out of the activities in Cuba and encouraged war with Spain to liberate the downtrodden Cubans:

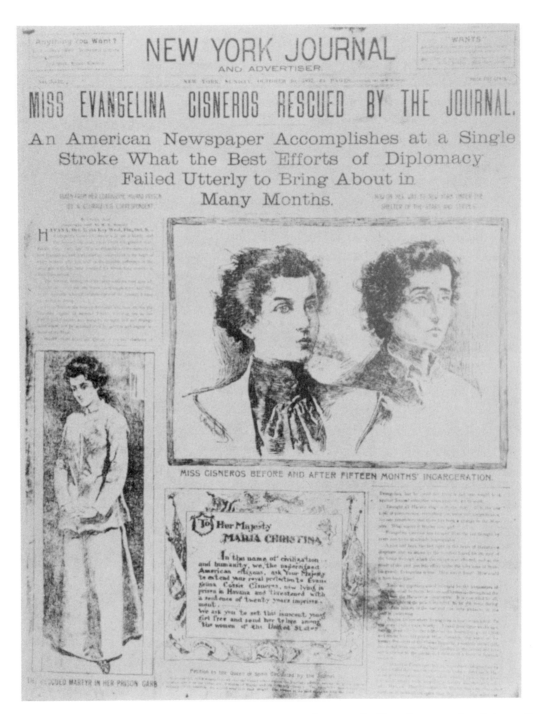

▲ Front page of Hearst's *New York Journal* telling the sensational story of Evangelina Cisneros—and criticizing the government

THE WARSHIP MAINE WAS SPLIT IN TWO BY AN ENEMY'S
SECRET INFERNAL MACHINE

HOW THE MAINE ACTUALLY LOOKS AS IT LIES, WRECKED
BY SPANISH TREACHERY, IN HAVANA BAY

To further excite public opinion, the *Journal* offered a $50,000 reward to solve the mystery of who exploded the ship (Swanberg, p. 164).

Naval campaigns. The U.S. Navy was well prepared for the war, which took place mostly at sea. Some American ships patrolled the Caribbean Sea, and others entered the Philippine harbor at Manila to meet and conquer the older Spanish fleet. But ports and a land base in Cuba became important. Some distance from Spanish-controlled Havana were Guantanamo Bay and the Cuban city of Santiago. To trap the Spanish fleet, the navy would need the help of a land force. Volunteers joined regular army troops in an effort to capture Santiago. The major force of about 17,000 soldiers advanced on a path that took them through the small but fortified town of El Chaney.

"We must be first." Hearst was determined that his *New York Journal* reporters would be first to publish accounts of the battles. Assigning himself as the key reporter, he gathered a small force of the best reporters, artists, and writers. He leased a ship, equipped it with a printing press, and sailed for the war. The ship, *Sylvia,* landed at Siboney only to find that nearly 100 reporters from other papers were already on hand. However, one of Hearst's employees, Colonel Honoré Laine, was a member of the Cuban rebels. Through him, the *Journal-Examiner* team was able to stay close to the front lines of battle, so close that they were accused of drawing enemy artillery fire on troops near the town of El Pozo. When the U.S. force began to close in on the fortified castle at El Chaney, the Hearst group came so near the action that leading reporter James Creelman was wounded. Hearst's reaction was typical of his attitude toward the war. To him it was a grand adventure. Now as he knelt beside his wounded reporter, he supposedly comforted him with, "I'm sorry you're hurt, but wasn't it a splendid fight? We must beat every paper in the world" (Swamberg, p. 156). Creelman apologized that the wound had left him unable to write

255

but offered to dictate the story if Hearst would do the writing. Hearst did, and then hurried off to the *Sylvia* to send the story.

Brutality in Cuba. As the Americans were closing in on Santiago, aided by a valiant but reckless strike up San Juan Hill by Colonel Theodore Roosevelt's Rough Riders (see **Theodore Roosevelt**), Hearst again caught up with Laine. The account of this meeting reveals the bias with which Hearst recorded the news. Laine recounted how the rebels had cut off the heads of forty captured Spanish soldiers given to their care by American forces. In his report, Hearst excused the action as a natural outcome of Spanish oppression and described Laine as being "tender and gentle. One seldom finds a man of more generous and gracious impulses than this same Laine. His hour has come and he is lost in the almost savage enjoyment of it" (Swanberg, p. 156). Despite such bias, other newspapers took care to credit the courage and skill of a millionaire newspaper owner who would risk his own life to be the first to report the news.

Taking prisoners. As the battle for Santiago neared an end, word came that some of the Spanish fleet had been spotted nearby. Hearst hurried to the *Sylvia* and joined American warships in pursuit. The Hearst ship arrived in time to survey the wreckage as one by one the older and slower Spanish ships were tracked down and sunk. Cruising along the Cuban coast, the men on the *Sylvia* spied a group of Spaniards on shore. Hearst hastily put a launch into the water and headed for the Spaniards, who had escaped from a burning ship the day before. He found the Spanish ready to surrender rather than risk meeting Cubans on shore. The twenty-nine prisoners of war were the only ones taken by a newspaper team. They were fed and taught to give three cheers at the naming of George Washington and President William McKinley. On the Fourth of July, the prisoners were transferred to the battleship *St. Louis,* for which Hearst demanded and received a receipt.

The short war of 1898 with Spain was nearly over. When Spain asked for peace, Hearst and his crew returned to the United States. Hearst's mementos from the experience were the receipt for the prisoners he captured, a tattered Cuban flag, and a lump of silver from a Spanish ship that he kept as a paper weight.

▲ Scenes from the Spanish-American War

Aftermath

Building a news empire. When his father died, Hearst inherited the rich mine interests. The Spanish-American War had meanwhile greatly increased his influence in the publishing industry. The *New York Journal* had grown to a circulation of more than a million. Hearst used these vast resources to build a publishing empire. The empire grew to include two dozen newspapers and a dozen magazines, including *Cosmopolitan, Good Housekeeping, Harper's Bazaar,* and *Motor Magazine.*

Politics. Even this empire was not enough for Hearst's boundless energy, however. In 1903 he was elected to the House of Representatives, where he served for four years. During this time he ran unsuccessfully for mayor of New York, losing the election by just 6,000 votes. He was suggested as a Democratic candidate for president of the United States. However, Hearst's long love affair with the Democratic party faded, and in 1906 he formed his own party, the Independence League. As a candidate for this party, he ran an unsuccessful campaign for governor of New York.

Throughout his life, Hearst used his news empire to back political candidates, mostly Democrats, and to smear those he did not like. He attacked presidential candidates Alfred Smith and Charles Evans Hughes, campaigned half-heartedly for Woodrow Wilson in 1912 then turned against him in World War I, considering him too partial to England. Hearst next befriended Franklin D. Roosevelt, then turned against his policies.

In turn, other newspapers were fond of quoting Hearst's political enemies. Theodore Roosevelt blasted Hearst when he ran for governor of New York. In other instances, Hearst was accused of being a capitalist who pretended friendship for labor, a tax-evader, a reporter thriving on the sensational and promoting hatred, and a weak congressman who was absent during 160 of 185 votes in the House. His sensationalized reporting was blamed for McKinley's assassination (even though the assassin had not read his papers).

By 1908 Hearst had given up his ambition to become president and contented himself with supporting another candidate, Thomas Hisgen. Hisgen ran against Republican William Howard Taft and Democrat William Jennings Bryan in an election won by Taft. The defeat ended Hearst's Independence Party.

Family. On April 28, 1903, just before his fortieth birthday, Hearst married Millicent Willson, an actress. At the wedding, Hearst revealed a different side of his personality. While he had spent his life searching for news and seemed to care little for the privacy of those he reported on, he insisted on total privacy at his own wedding. He refused to let reporters and photographers into Grace Church to view the ceremony. The marriage found its way only to page nine of the *American,* which reported that the bride was twenty-one years old. The couple went on to have five sons, some of whom became publishers of Hearst newspapers in later years. The two youngest were twins born in 1915.

Marion Davies. In 1917 Hearst met a Ziegfield Follies chorus girl, Marion Davies, and fell in love with her. He tried to divorce his wife to marry Davies, but his wife refused. They instead arranged a friendly separation—Millicent would remain his wife and would sometimes join him in public appearances, but he would live with Davies. All parties seemed to be happy with the unusual arrangement. Hearst built a great castle overlooking the Pacific Ocean for Davies while his wife stayed in her plush New York hotel suite. Later in her life, Millicent would tell reporters that her husband was a great man.

World War I. When World War I broke out, Hearst once again sought to become governor of New York. He had already gained a reputation for opposing the war, and his opponents capitalized on his unpopular stand. The *New York Tribune* portrayed him as a snake— "Hears-s-s-s-t." He was accused of being pro-German and of sowing distrust among the allies. Hearst responded by taking ads in other newspapers titled "What the Hearst Papers Have Done to Help Win the War." He had, in fact, announced his goal to keep America out of the war and had without objection printed articles by his chief editorial writer slanted in favor of Germany. However, in 1917, when the United States was about to join the Allies, Hearst saw that his position would lose subscribers and probably help an enemy gain public office. He forbid his newspapers to publish anything that seemed pro-German. Yet, the feeling that Hearst was pro-German spread even to England, where officials censored news dispatches from his International News Service. Although Hearst was opposed to America entering the war, he seemed more concerned by the possibility of losing subscribers than by working against the Allied forces. Once America had entered the war, he advocated an early peace, but even that was taken to be a pro-German stance.

World War II. Decades later, as World War II loomed in the early 1940s, Hearst again objected to American involvement. He wrote that rulers would have their names written large in history, while bereaved mothers would be given gold stars to mend their broken hearts. When it seemed most likely that the United States would indeed become involved, Hearst campaigned for preparedness. He predicted that the United States would be at war with Japan as well as Germany, Italy, and perhaps Russia. The Japanese navy, he argued, was growing stronger and the United States Navy weaker, and Japan might even provoke a war. When Pearl Harbor was attacked, the Hearst newspapers abandoned their argument against involvement and campaigned for an all-out effort to win against the Japanese.

His actions before the war, however, had damaged his reputation beyond repair. He had invited Father Charles E. Coughlin, an avowed fascist, to be his house guest in 1932. Then in 1934, on a visit to Germany, he had been invited to meet with Adolph Hitler. He had advised the German Nazi leader that he would win more world approval if he gave up persecuting the Jews. Hitler assured him that he favored democracy and promised to stop the attacks on Jews, which he did for a few days. The news that reached America, however, came in the form of a photograph that showed a jovial Hearst and Hitler leaving the meeting. Hearst was again accused of being pro-German.

Miserable or misunderstood? In fact, William Randolph Hearst remains difficult to define. He favored peace but pushed for the Spanish-American War. He was hated by many but revered by his own employees. He was accused of yellow journalism but used his publishing empire to champion causes of the poor. He fought for fair treatment of laborers but did nothing to ease the grueling ten-hour-a-day, six-day work week of the workers in his mother's Homestead Mine. He loved and respected his family but lived apart from them with another woman. Perhaps the only thing that can be said with certainty about William Randolph Hearst was that he was consumed with passion for reporting the news and for writing it so that the average person would want to read about world affairs.

> ## Hearst about Hearst
>
> Perhaps the public prefers to consider me as an 'austere' person—which God forbid that I should be—instead of the 'human' person I earnestly strive to be. (Coblentz, p. ix)

Hearst died August 14, 1951, at his home in Beverly Hills, California. By that time, his newspaper empire had become a corporation headed by another man, Richard Berlin.

Hearst had led the flood of journalists who played up the war in Cuba before and after the United States got involved. His critics argued that it was an unnecessary war to fight, but Cubans such as

Evangelina Cisneros countered that they never would have become independent without American aid. "My country and I owe everything to Mr. Hearst and the American people," she said (Blow, p. 451).

For More Information

Blow, Michael. *A Ship to Remember: The "Maine" and the Spanish-American War.* New York: William Morrow and Co., 1992.

Coblentz, Edmond D. *William Randolph Hearst: A Portrait in His Own Words.* New York: Simon and Schuster, 1952.

Swanberg, W. A. *Citizen Hearst.* New York: Charles Scribner's Sons, 1961.

Theodore Roosevelt

1858-1919

Personal Background

Early life. Theodore Roosevelt was born on October 27, 1858, in New York City, where the Roosevelts were a wealthy and prominent family. He was a scrawny child who suffered from several health problems, including severe asthma.

When he was seven years old, Theodore became interested in biology and geology. He and two cousins started the Roosevelt Museum of Natural History at his home with displays of rocks, bones, and dead mice. Encouraged by his father, the boy also learned hunting and taxidermy, the art of preserving and mounting animal skins. (He continued to collect specimens throughout his life and eventually became a respected authority on zoology.)

His collecting interests were aided by travels with his family. In 1869 they visited Europe, and in 1872 Egypt, Palestine, Syria, and Lebanon, and Europe again. In Giza, Egypt, the determined boy climbed to the tops of the famous pyramids.

Despite his ill health, Theodore was determined to become stronger by following a strict program of physical training. As his health gradually improved, he became involved in sports, including boxing, which he was later forced to give up after suffering an eye injury during a sparring match in the White House.

▲ **Theodore Roosevelt**

Event: The Spanish-American War.
Role: As assistant secretary of the navy, Theodore Roosevelt foresaw the war between the United States and Spain that began in 1898. He was largely responsible for preparing the U.S. Navy for the short and successful war. At the start of actual warfare, Roosevelt resigned his post to accept a commission in the army and led his troops, the Rough Riders, in a successful battle for San Juan Hill overlooking an important road to Santiago, Cuba.

Theodore's aunt oversaw his education, which he supplemented by reading adventure stories in his spare time. He enjoyed learning about American war heroes and later explained, "I had a great admiration for men who were fearless and could hold their own in the world, and I had a great desire to be like them" (Miller, p. 39). He would in fact demonstrate such courage in later years during the Spanish-American War.

College years. Although he had been educated at home, Roosevelt passed the entrance examinations for Harvard University in 1875 and enrolled as a freshman the following year. His studies at Harvard included Greek, Latin, German, mathematics, and science. He achieved honor grades in all subjects except Greek. Meanwhile, during his spare time, he read books about naval tactics and other subjects of warfare. He did not neglect his social life, either. At Harvard, Roosevelt met Alice Lee, whom he would marry in 1880.

Since boyhood, Roosevelt had wanted to be a scientist but found he preferred field work to the laboratory activities required for Harvard biology courses. While still at the university, he also began to develop an interest in politics, which gradually replaced his interest in science. He decided to study law after completing his undergraduate degree. In 1880 Roosevelt graduated from Harvard with honors—21st in a class of 177—and after a summer of hunting in the Midwest, he enrolled in Columbia Law School.

The Naval War of 1812. Roosevelt soon became bored studying law. He spent his time away from classwork researching a book, *The Naval War of 1812,* which he had begun writing during his last year at Harvard. He worked long and hard on the research, reading the literature, learning naval terms, and drawing illustrations. By the time the book was published in 1882, he had dropped out of law school. *The Naval War of 1812* is still considered one of the most honest studies of its subject.

Politics. Meanwhile, Roosevelt's interest in politics continued to grow, even though, at the time, well-to-do young gentlemen such as he normally shunned politics. While at Harvard, he had expressed a desire to "try to do something to help the cause of better government in New York" (Miller, p. 110). He also expressed a desire to become part of the "governing class." He mastered and made a career of politics, as one biographer explained, "because he loved power" (Miller, p. 110).

Roosevelt became a Republican, his family's political party of choice. He joined the Republican Club in New York City and was soon running for State Assembly. During the campaign, he earned an enduring reputation for speaking his mind. After winning the election in November 1882, he became, at age twenty-two, the youngest member of the state legislature.

Although a rookie, Roosevelt soon became a leader among reform-minded legislators. He supported bills that called for the improvement of conditions for industrial workers. He joined other reformers in calling for an investigation of a state supreme court justice on charges of corruption. Although the investigation was blocked by the powerful financier Jay Gould, Roosevelt's involvement in the fight brought him fame.

His determination to root out dishonesty in government surfaced early in his career, as did other personality traits. On the one hand, Roosevelt tended to act on impulse and to be preoccupied with himself. Yet he also displayed tremendous energy and intelligence, bravery, honesty, friendliness, and a practical sense about the need in politics to compromise.

During the presidential campaigns of 1884, he supported Senator George F. Edmunds, an underdog who was backed by reform-minded Republicans. When Edmunds lost the nomination, Roosevelt threw his support behind the winner, James Blaine. This angered the other Republican reformers, who were known as *Mugwumps,* from the Algonquian word meaning "chief." They bolted to the Democrats, and with their help, Grover Cleveland defeated Blaine for the presidency. The defeat would add to Roosevelt's anguish that year. He suffered personal tragedies; shortly after his daughter, Alice, was born, his wife and mother died on the same day.

Cattle ranching. Saddened by the deaths and frustrated by the political developments, Roosevelt decided he needed a change. Leaving his daughter in the care of relatives, he bought a cattle ranch on the Little Missouri River in 1885 and soon lost himself in learning the cattle business and living the rugged life of the territory. He worked with cowboys and in the process, earned their respect. Roosevelt also hunted big game, captured three thieves at gunpoint and brought them to justice, and with his fist felled a drunk who threatened him with a pistol. Meanwhile, he found time to write three books about hunting and ranch life.

Remarriage. Roosevelt periodically returned to New York to see his daughter and to take care of business. On one of these trips, he rekindled his relationship with Edith Carow, a childhood friend and teenage sweetheart. They were soon engaged, and in 1886 they traveled to Europe to be married.

Theodore Roosevelt as an Outdoorsman	
1881	Climbed the Matterhorn in Switzerland
1883-1885	Ranched and hunted buffalo in North Dakota
1909	Hunted big game in Africa
1910	Wrote *African Game Trails*
1912	Explored Brazil

While in Europe, Roosevelt learned that disaster had struck his ranch. A series of blizzards had killed thousands of cattle, including most of his own herd. He decided to sell the ranch and return to New York. In 1887 he, Edith, and Alice moved to an estate he had built, called Sagamore Hill, on Long Island in New York.

That year Roosevelt and Edith had their first son, Theodore, who was followed by three more boys and a girl. Roosevelt spent much of his time writing and had soon completed two biographies. He also began work on a multivolume history of the settlement of the American West, *Winning of the West.*

How Sagamore Hill Got Its Name

According to Roosevelt, the estate took its name from the sagamore Mohannis, a chief who had signed away rights to the land 250 years earlier. *Sagamore* is a term for an ordinary chief among the Algonquian Indians as opposed to a superior or head chief.

Return to politics. In 1888 Roosevelt campaigned for the Republican presidential candidate, Benjamin Harrison. When Harrison won the presidency, a mutual friend, Henry Cabot Lodge, talked the new president into appointing Roosevelt civil service commissioner. As commissioner, Roosevelt immediately launched a crusade against bribe-takers, embezzlers, and other corrupt government officials.

Due to his crusade, a scandal surfaced in Baltimore that damaged Harrison's chances for reelection, and he lost to Grover Cleveland in the 1892 elections. Cleveland asked Roosevelt to stay on as commissioner even though he had campaigned for Harrison before the election. Cleveland ordered all department heads to cooperate with him, and Roosevelt remained civil service commissioner until 1895.

Police Commission. Roosevelt eventually became bored running the Civil Service Commission. In 1895 he accepted an offer from New York City mayor William L. Strong to sit on the city's Police Commission, which oversaw the police department. He was soon the commission's chairman. Again, Roosevelt found himself crusading against corruption. He roamed the streets at night wearing a black cloak and a hat pulled down over his eyes, seeking lazy, drunken, or crooked policemen. Journalists such as Jacob Riis and Lincoln Steffens often accompanied him. Roosevelt forced the police chief to resign by threatening to show newspapers information about bribes the officer had taken.

In 1896, while still on the Police Commission, Roosevelt campaigned for William McKinley, the Republican candidate for president. When McKinley won the election, he offered Roosevelt the post of assistant secretary of the navy, which he accepted.

Participation: The Spanish-American War

Preparing the navy. Having settled into his new position, Roosevelt began making speeches calling for expansion of the navy. He advocated building experimental submarines and showed interest in manned flight. He also called for annexing Hawaii, building a canal through Central America, and expelling Spain from Cuba. Other Latin American areas had withdrawn from Spanish dominion, and the people of Cuba were rebelling against the harsh treatment of the Spaniards. Roosevelt was convinced that the United States must soon become involved and that war with Spain would follow. He drew up plans for a naval war with Spain, which McKinley would later use. Then, when the secretary of the navy went on a trip and left Roosevelt in charge, he began earnestly increasing supplies to the navy ships, equipping them for war. He sent messages to navy commanders such as Commodore George Dewey outlining what would be expected of them in case of war. "The secretary is away," Roosevelt said, "and I am having immense fun running the Navy" (Nash, p. 685).

Somewhat later than Roosevelt, McKinley also became convinced that war with Spain was inescapable. In 1898 an American ship, the *Maine,* anchored in Havana harbor, mysteriously blew up and sank. It was suspected that the explosion had come from outside the ship. Newspapers in the United States carried banners calling for people to "Remember the *Maine.*" McKinley, mindful of the public's view of the events, called on Spain to withdraw from Cuba. Angered by this demand, Spain declared war.

Roosevelt had prepared the navy well. Soon Dewey demolished the Spanish fleet in Manila Harbor and took command of the Philippines. Other U.S. ships were in pursuit of Spanish vessels in the Caribbean Sea. The American fleet gained control of the Spanish on the seas, but it needed support from land forces in Cuba.

Rough Riders. Roosevelt, anxious to be part of the action, resigned from the navy to accept an army commission offered by the secretary of war. He spent his last week in Washington preparing himself, ordering a dozen pairs of steel-rimmed eyeglasses to take with him into action. Some of these glasses he had sewn into his new uniform and hat.

Roosevelt was appointed lieutenant colonel and, along with his superior officer, Colonel Leonard Wood, began organizing the First United States Volunteer Cavalry Regiment. There were about 1,000 recruits—western cowboys, ranchers, miners, and gamblers, as well as eastern college men from Harvard, Yale, and Princeton, some of whom arrived at the camp in San Antonio, Texas, with their golf clubs in tow. The unit shortly became known as Roosevelt's Rough Riders.

The Rough Riders were sent to the front lines in Cuba, without horses because of a shortage of ships. At Las Guasimas, on the southern coast, they came under enemy fire for the first time. Roosevelt remained calm under pressure, though he was nearly hit by a Spanish bullet. After the Rough Riders beat back the attack, Roosevelt was promoted to colonel and given acting command of the regiment.

The Rough Riders soon joined the American assault on the port of Santiago de Cuba. Flanking the road to Santiago were Kettle Hill to the north and San Juan Hill to the south. Both hills were held by the Spaniards.

▲ Roosevelt leading his Rough Riders at San Juan Hill

On July 1, the Americans advanced. While the main body of about 16,000 soldiers moved toward Santiago, Roosevelt led his troops forward through heavy fire in an effort to take command of the hills where the Spanish controlled the road. Mounted on a horse, Roosevelt moved up Kettle Hill but abandoned his horse when he reached barbed-wire entanglements protecting the Spanish position. After taking heavy casualties from the Spaniards, who had fewer numbers but were armed with the most modern Mauser rifles, the Rough Riders and a unit of African American soldiers finally took Kettle Hill. The advance continued over neighboring San Juan Hill. Here, Roosevelt killed a Spanish soldier with a revolver.

Roosevelt regarded the charge as one of the high points of his career, describing it as "the greatest day of my life." He later said, "I would rather have led that charge and earned my colonelcy than served three terms in the United States Senate" (Stefoff, pp. 48-49). Although Roosevelt had led his Rough Riders beyond what his orders commanded and put them at high risk, his brash action had won the Americans access to the main road to Santiago.

The fighting. Roosevelt spoke of the capture of San Juan Hill as a bully (meaning "splendid") fight. Yet he had an awful time trying to get into the fighting and do what was right once in it. All the while he was thinking he was the only man who did not know what to do and where to go next; later he found out everybody else was as much in the dark as he. He complained that the army was incredibly disorganized:

> The mismanagement has been beyond belief.... We are half starved; and our men are sickening daily. The lack of transportation, food, and artillery has brought us to the very brink of disaster; but above all the lack of any leadership. (O'Toole, p. 346)

Perhaps the most frustrating fact was that he and his men couldn't see the enemy. Finally a reporter traveling with them spotted the Spaniards. The Rough Riders commenced fire. For a minute or two, there was no return fire, then:

> the Spaniards suddenly sprang out of the cover through which we had seen their hats, and ran to another spot; and we could now make out a large number of them.

> I [Roosevelt] accordingly got all of my men up in a line and began quick firing. In a very few minutes our bullets began to do damage, for the Spaniards retreated to the left into the jungle, and we lost sight of them. (O'Toole, p. 276)

Roosevelt and his men chased the enemy in a running battle through the jungle. At every chance, they took advantage of cover, sinking down behind any bush or tree trunk that might appear. The chorus of an old fox-hunting song ran through Roosevelt's brain— "Here's to every friend who struggled to the end" (O'Toole, p. 276). Meanwhile, his men dashed from tree to bush, stopping to shoot, then running forward again. American author Stephen Crane, then a news correspondent, reported, "I know nothing about war, but I have been enabled from time to time to see brush fighting, and I want to say here plainly that the behavior of those Rough Riders while marching through the woods shook me with terror" (O'Toole, p. 277). Crane praised Roosevelt:

> Say, this fellow worked for his troopers like a cider press. He tried to feed them. He helped build latrines. He cursed the quartermasters and the—'dogs'—on the transports to get quinine and grub for them. Let him be a politician if he likes. He was a gentleman down there. (Stallman, p. 384)

Santiago soon fell to the Americans, at great cost. Of the 17,000 U.S. soldiers involved, 2,000 were killed or injured in the battles, and at least 5,000 lay ill with a tropical fever. With the port of Santiago in American hands, the fighting now fell almost completely to the navy. American fleets chased Spanish ships, trapping them near Cuba and finally ending the war. The Rough Riders came home from Cuba to cheers of welcome. As a result of his heroism, Roosevelt had become one of the most famous men in America.

Aftermath

Return to politics. Roosevelt jumped back into politics after the war by accepting an offer from the New York Republican party to run for governor. In November 1898, he won by a slim margin. As governor, he championed reform legislation, persuading the legislature to pass laws limiting working hours for women and children, raising teachers' salaries, and imposing tighter regulations in business. He also supported conservation measures and signed a law banning racial segregation in New York schools.

His reform actions put him at odds with the party bosses, however, and they soon found a way to get rid of him. In 1900 New York Republican party boss Thomas C. Platt and Pennsylvania boss Matthew Quay arranged for Roosevelt's nomination for vice president to run with McKinley, who was seeking reelection. Fearing that the vice presidency would be a political dead end, Roosevelt did not particularly want the nomination. But, when the bosses finally secured it for him, he reluctantly accepted.

After McKinley's reelection, Roosevelt was an unhappy vice president. He spent much of his time on hunting trips and began again to study law.

President Roosevelt. In September 1901, McKinley was assassinated. At the time, Roosevelt was climbing Mount Marcy, New York's highest peak. It was twelve hours before he could be located. He returned to take the oath as President of the United States.

During his presidency, Roosevelt again promoted social reform, naval expansion (the navy grew from fifth- to second-largest in the world), and nature conservation (he was called the "great conservationist"). Early in his administration, he sought to curb the power of trusts, or large holding companies, which were often accused of creating monopolies. He soon had his attorney general filing suits against trusts for violating antitrust (antimonopoly) laws. Later, he called for increased government regulation of business, including railroad rates and stock market activities.

In 1902, when Pennsylvania coal miners went on strike and mine owners refused to negotiate, Roosevelt stepped in to settle the matter. Winter approached as a coal shortage threatened. Noting that "great masses of people" faced "misery and death," Roosevelt warned that he would seize the mines and operate them with troops (Miller, p. 374). The owners quickly backed down and reached a settlement with the miners.

Race relations. Roosevelt believed blacks should be given more opportunity to participate in government. Accordingly, he appointed several blacks to responsible positions, often on the recommendation of Booker T. Washington, the influential black educator. However, in 1906, when armed men attacked the town of Brownsville, Texas, residents accused members of a black army unit stationed nearby of conducting the raid. In response, Roosevelt ordered 167 members of the unit, including six Medal of Honor awardees, dishonorably discharged. Black leaders, including Washington, criticized the decision, but Roosevelt refused to back down. In 1972, having reopened the case, the army found no evidence of wrongdoing by the troops and reversed the discharges.

Retirement. After serving as president for two terms, Roosevelt declined to run for a third term as president. However, by 1912, he had had a falling out with President William Taft, the man he had supported as his own successor. He decided to run against Taft for the Republican nomination. When it appeared that Taft would control the

Republican party, Roosevelt formed his own Progressive Party and ran as its nominee. With the Republicans thus divided among two popular candidates, Democrat Woodrow Wilson won the election.

Roosevelt turned to travel, exploring the jungles of Brazil with his son Kermit. Returning to the United States, he began to speak for U.S. involvement in World War I. When the United States did get involved, Roosevelt asked to be allowed to lead a division of volunteers but was refused. In 1918 he even considered running again for the presidency in the 1920 elections. However, his health declined and he became bedridden with inflammatory rheumatism. On January 6, 1919, Roosevelt died in his sleep.

The Spanish-American War remained his proudest moment. The Rough Riders held reunions that were important occasions to Roosevelt. He had memorialized their experience in *The Rough Riders* (1899). Convinced that he himself had acted as a true hero, Roosevelt asked for but never won the nation's highest military award, the Congressional Medal of Honor. His failure to receive it bothered him throughout his lifetime.

For More Information

Miller, Nathan. *Theodore Roosevelt: A Life*. New York: William Morrow and Co., 1992.

Nash, Gary. *The American People: Creating a Nation and a Society*. Vol. 2. New York: Harper and Row, 1990.

O'Toole, G. J. A. *The Spanish War: An American Epic 1898*. New York: W. W. Norton and Co., 1984.

Stallman, R. W. *Stephen Crane: A Biography*. New York: George Braziller, 1968.

Stefoff, Rebecca. *Theodore Roosevelt: Twenty-sixth President of the United States*. Ada, Okla.: Garrett Educational Corporation, 1988.

Theodore Roosevelt as President

- Established 50 wildlife refuges and 15 national monuments
- Reserved 235 million acres of forests as public lands
- Acted as peacemaker in dispute between Russia and Japan, for which he was awarded the Nobel Peace Prize (1905)
- Proposed a solution to the disagreement between Germany and France over Morocco (1906)
- Directed the restoration of Cuba (1906-1909)
- Took control of the Central American Isthmus from Colombia
- Signed treaty with Panama to construct the Panama Canal (1904)
- Created the Department of Commerce and Labor (1903)
- Signed acts for meat inspection and pure food (1906)
- Called a Conservation Conference of state governors (1908)
- Began "Square Deal" program to attack social problems, control big business and railroads, and conserve natural resources

Bibliography

Andrews, Wayne, ed. *The Autobiography of Carl Schurz.* New York, N.Y.: Charles Scribner's Sons, 1961.

Bailyn, Bernard, et al. *The Great Republic: A History of the American People.* Vol. 2. Lexington, Mass.: D. C. Heath and Company, 1992.

Bates, Samuel P. *Our Country and Its People.* Crawford County, Penn.: W. A. Fergusson and Company, 1899.

Beebe, Lucius. *Mr. Pullman's Elegant Palace Car.* Garden City, N.Y.: Doubleday and Co., 1961.

Blum, John Morton. *The Republican Roosevelt.* Cambridge, Mass.: Harvard University Press, 1954.

Bontemps, Arna. *Young Booker: Booker T. Washington's Early Days.* New York, N.Y.: Dodd, Mead and Co., 1972.

Chalmers, Harvey II. *The Last Stand of the Nez Percé: Destruction of a People.* New York, N.Y.: Twayne Publishers, 1962.

Clemens, Susy. *Papa: An Intimate Biography of Mark Twain.* Edited by Charles Neider. Garden City, N.Y.: Doubleday and Co., 1985.

Current, Richard Nelson. *Old Thad Stevens: A Story of Ambition.* Madison: The University of Wisconsin Press, 1942.

Earhart, Mary. *Frances Willard: From Prayers to Politics.* Chicago, Ill.: University of Chicago Press, 1944.

Fetherling, Dale. *Mother Jones, The Miners' Angel: A Portrait.* Carbondale: Southern Illinois Press, 1974.

Fink, Gary, ed. *Biographical Dictionary of American Labor Leaders.* Westport, Conn.: Greenwood Press, 1974.

Fuess, Claude Moore. *Carl Schurz, Reformer.* New York, N.Y.: Dodd, Mead and Company, 1932.

Gould, Lewis L. *The Presidency of William McKinley.* Lawrence: The Regents Press of Kansas, 1980.

Hoyt, Edwin P. *William McKinley.* Chicago, Ill.: Reilly and Lee Co., 1967.

Jackson, Helen Hunt. *Poems By Helen Hunt Jackson.* Boston, Mass.: Roberts Brothers, 1895.

Morris, Edmund. "Theodore Roosevelt, President." *American Heritage,* Vol. 32, No. 4, June/July, 1981, pp. 4-15.

Murray, Ken. *The Golden Days of San Simeon.* Garden City, N.Y.: Doubleday and Co., 1971.

Nash, Gary, et al., eds. *The American People: Creating a Nation and a Society.* Vol. 2. New York, N.Y.: Harper and Row, 1986.

BIBLIOGRAPHY

Odell, Ruth. *Helen Hunt Jackson*. New York, N.Y.: D. Appleton-Century Co., 1939.

Robinson, Judith. *The Hearsts: An American Dynasty*. Newark, Del.: University of Delaware Press, 1981.

Schafer, Joseph, ed. *Intimate Letters of Carl Schurz, 1841-1869*. Madison: State Historical Society of Wisconsin, 1929.

Twain, Mark. *The Unabridged Mark Twain*. Edited by Lawrence Teacher. Philadelphia, Penn.: Running Press, 1976.

Warne, Colston E. *The Pullman Boycott of 1894: The Problem of Federal Intervention*. Boston, Mass.: D. C. Heath and Company, 1955.

Woodley, Thomas Frederick. *Great Leveler: The Life of Thaddeus Stevens*. New York, N.Y.: Stackpole Sons, 1937.

Index

Boldface indicates profiles.